EMPOWERING ADOLESCENT GIRLS IN DEVELOPING COUNTRIES

Adolescence is a pivotal time in a girl's life when girls develop a range of political, economic, familial, psychosocial, physical and educational capabilities enabling them to make their own decisions in life. However, it is also possible that the roles which women and girls are expected to play in their families and communities can prevent them from developing these capabilities fully.

Empowering Adolescent Girls in Developing Countries explores the detrimental impact of discriminatory gender norms on all aspects of adolescent girls' lives and across very different contexts. Grounded in four years of in-depth research across Ethiopia, Nepal, Uganda and Viet Nam, the book adopts a holistic approach to girls' well-being, examining the links between different aspects of girls' lives, while exploring the different forces that can lead to change in gender norms, such as the spread of mobile technology, economic developments, information campaigns, and new laws on early marriage and compulsory education. This book demonstrates how more egalitarian gender norms can enable disadvantaged adolescent girls to change the course of their lives and develop full capabilities in every area.

Accessible and informative, this book is perfect for policymakers, think tanks, NGOs, activists, academics and students of gender and development studies alike.

Caroline Harper is Principal Research Fellow and Head of the Social Development programme at the UK-based Overseas Development Institute (ODI), focusing on gender, age and exclusion.

Nicola Jones is a political scientist and Principal Research Fellow at ODI, as well as Director of the longitudinal Gender and Adolescence: Global Evidence (GAGE) research programme.

Rachel Marcus is a freelance social development researcher focused on gender, childhood, youth and adolescence.

Grace Kyomuhendo Bantebya is Professor in the School of Women and Gender Studies at Makerere University in Uganda.

Anita Ghimire is Director for social science research at the Nepal Institute for Social and Environmental Research (NISER).

EMPOWERING ADOLESCENT GIRLS IN DEVELOPING COUNTRIES

Gender Justice and Norm Change

Edited by Caroline Harper, Nicola Jones, Anita Ghimire, Rachel Marcus and Grace Kyomuhendo Bantebya

Routledge
Taylor & Francis Group

LONDON AND NEW YORK

First published 2018
by Routledge
2 Park Square, Milton Park, Abingdon, Oxon OX14 4RN

and by Routledge
711 Third Avenue, New York, NY 10017

Routledge is an imprint of the Taylor & Francis Group, an informa business

British Library Cataloguing-in-Publication Data
A catalogue record for this book is available from the British Library

Library of Congress Cataloging-in-Publication Data
A catalog record for this book has been requested

ISBN: 978-1-138-74715-9 (hbk)
ISBN: 978-1-138-74716-6 (pbk)
ISBN: 978-1-315-18025-0 (ebk)

Typeset in Bembo
by Apex CoVantage, LLC

MIX
Paper from
responsible sources
FSC   FSC™ C013985
www.fsc.org

Printed in the United Kingdom
by Henry Ling Limited

CONTENTS

List of figures   *viii*
List of tables   *ix*
List of boxes   *x*
List of acronyms and abbreviations   *xii*
Book editor and author introductions   *xiv*
Acknowledgements   *xvii*
Preamble   *xix*

Introduction: the significance of adolescence
in the life course   1
Nicola Jones, Elizabeth Presler-Marshall and Fiona Samuels

1 What can a focus on gender norms contribute
   to girls' empowerment?   22
   Caroline Harper and Rachel Marcus

PART 1
Ethiopia   **41**

2 'Sticky' gendered norms: change and stasis in the
   patterning of child marriage in Amhara, Ethiopia   43
   Nicola Jones, Bekele Tefera, Guday Emirie
   and Elizabeth Presler-Marshall

3   The politics of policy and programme implementation
    to advance adolescent girls' well-being in Ethiopia   62
    Nicola Jones, Elizabeth Presler-Marshall,
    Bekele Tefera and Bethelihem Gebre Alwab

PART 2
Uganda   **81**

4   The paradox of change and continuity in social norms
    and practices affecting adolescent girls' capabilities
    and transitions to adulthood in rural Uganda   83
    Carol Watson, Grace Kyomuhendo Bantebya
    and Florence Kyoheirwe Muhanguzi

5   From national laws and policies to local programmes:
    obstacles and opportunities in communications
    for adolescent girls' empowerment in Uganda   102
    Grace Kyomuhendo Bantebya, Florence
    Kyoheirwe Muhanguzi and Carol Watson

PART 3
Viet Nam   **121**

6   Intersecting inequalities: the impact of gender norms
    on Hmong adolescent girls' education, marriage
    and work in Viet Nam   123
    Nicola Jones, Elizabeth Presler-Marshall and Tran Thi Van Anh

7   Triple invisibility: the neglect of ethnic minority
    adolescent girls in Viet Nam   140
    Nicola Jones, Elizabeth Presler-Marshall and Tran Thi Van Anh

PART 4
Nepal   **159**

8   Small but persistent steps on the road to gender equality:
    marriage patterns in Far West Nepal   161
    Fiona Samuels and Anita Ghimire

9   Continuity and slow change: how embedded programmes
improve the lives of adolescent girls   177
Fiona Samuels, Anita Ghimire and Matthew Maclure

Conclusion: Pushing the boundaries of social order:
adolescent girls and norm change   190
Caroline Harper and Rachel Marcus

Index   *203*

FIGURES

2.1 Amhara research sites   47
4.1 Map of Uganda showing study districts   85
6.1 Ha Giang map   127
6.2 Hmong girls are uniquely situated   128
8.1 Characteristics of good wives and good daughters-in-law   162
8.2 Map of Nepal showing study sites   163
9.1 Map of Nepal showing Kailali district   178
9.2 Girls' reflections on programming   182

TABLES

0.1   Percentage of students who are female by education level
      and country   2
0.2   The Girls' Opportunity Index   4
0.3   Percentage of women aged 20–24 who were married as children   6
0.4   Interview types by country and instrument   13
2.1   Educational statistics   45
5.1   Reported changes at individual, household and community levels   109

BOXES

0.1 Indices for girls and women   4
0.2 The impacts of education and marriage on girls' capabilities   6
0.3 'I have a dream'   10
0.4 Qualitative methodological tools   13
2.1 The Amhara context for girls   45
2.2 Unabated parental control   48
2.3 Informal protection mechanisms for child brides   51
2.4 Girls' work   54
2.5 Migration   56
3.1 Communication programmes aimed at shifting discriminatory
     social norms hindering Amharan adolescent girls'
     capability development   64
3.2 The role of schools in combating child marriage   68
3.3 The fraught transition to secondary school   70
3.4 Local variability in institutional commitment to adolescent girls   72
3.5 New notions for men and boys   74
3.6 The risk of backsliding   75
3.7 Intensive training in small group formats reaps high dividends   76
4.1 Sobering national statistics in Uganda   84
5.1 Case study projects   105
6.1 The Hmong at a glance   124
6.2 The advantages of boarding school   128
6.3 A 'good daughter' listens to her parents   130
6.4 Bride kidnapping   132
6.5 When one's best is not enough   134
7.1 Vietnamese case study examples   141
7.2 The notion of 'social evil'   142

7.3   'One of these things is not like the other'   143
7.4   Helping girls to dream   146
7.5   Data lacunae   149
7.6   Lessons from Meo Vac High School   151
8.1   Support of in-laws and husband in continuing education   165
8.2   Girls have more of a say in their prospective husband: the role
      of peers   168
9.1   Kailali   178
9.2   NGO programming for girls   179

ACRONYMS AND ABBREVIATIONS

ADA	Amhara Development Association
AIDS	Acquired Immune Deficiency Syndrome
ANPPCAN	African Network for the Prevention and Protection Against Child Abuse and Neglect
AWID	Association for Women's Rights in Development
BIAAG	Because I Am a Girl
CBS	Central Bureau of Statistics (Nepal)
CEMA	Committee for Ethnic Minority Affairs
CSA	Central Statistical Agency (Ethiopia)
CSO	Civil Society Organisation
DDC	District Development Committee (Nepal)
DFID	Department for International Development
DHS	Demographic and Health Survey
EPRDF	Ethiopian People's Revolutionary Democratic Front
FGM	Female Genital Mutilation
FGM/C	Female Genital Mutilation/Cutting
GBV	Gender-Based Violence
GDI	Gender Development Index
GDP	Gross Domestic Product
GIGA	German Institute of Global and Area Studies
GII	Gender Inequality Index
GNI	Gross National Income
GREAT	Gender Roles, Equality and Transformations (Uganda)
GSO	General Statistics Office (Viet Nam)
HDI	Human Development Index
HEP	Higher Education Programme
HIV	Human Immunodeficiency Virus
HTP	Harmful Traditional Practice

ICRW	International Center for Research on Women
IFAD	International Fund for Agricultural Development
IFPRI	International Food Policy Research Institute
ILO	International Labour Organization
IPV	Intimate Partner Violence
IRH	Institute for Reproductive Health (Georgetown University)
MDG	Millennium Development Goal
MENA	Middle East and North Africa
MICS	Multiple Indicator Cluster Survey
MRMV	My Rights, My Voice
NDPII	Second National Development Plan (Uganda)
NER	Net Enrolment Rate
NGO	Non-Governmental Organisation
NISER	Nepal Institute for Social and Environmental Research
NORAD	Norwegian Agency for Development Cooperation
NPC	National Planning Commission (Nepal)
ODI	Overseas Development Institute
OECD	Organisation for Economic Co-operation and Development
SDG	Sustainable Development Goal
SGBV	Sexual and Gender-Based Violence
SIGI	Social Institutions and Gender Index
SRGBV	School-Related Gender-Based Violence
SRH	Sexual and Reproductive Health
SRHR	Sexual and Reproductive Health Rights
STF	Straight Talk Foundation (Uganda)
TFR	Total Fertility Rate
TVET	Technical and Vocational Education and Training
UBOS	Uganda Bureau of Statistics
UN	United Nations
UN Women	United Nations Entity for Gender Equality and the Empowerment of Women
UNDP	United Nations Development Programme
UNESCAP	United Nations Economic and Social Commission for Asia and the Pacific
UNESCO	United Nations Educational, Scientific and Cultural Organization
UNFPA	United Nations Population Fund
UNICEF	United Nations Children's Fund
USAID	United States Agency for International Development
VDC	Village Development Committee (Nepal)
VND	Vietnamese Dong (currency)
WDA	Women's Development Army (Ethiopia)

BOOK EDITOR AND AUTHOR INTRODUCTIONS

Dr Caroline Harper is Principal Research Fellow at the Overseas Development Institute (ODI), and Head of the Social Development programme, focusing on gender, age and exclusion. She is an anthropologist with research experience on gender, poverty, childhood, adolescence and life course, and the processes of progressive social change for gender equality. Caroline was the ODI project lead for the four-year, multi-country research programme, Transforming the Lives of Adolescent Girls, funded by the Department for International Development (DFID), and she is Senior Advisor on the Gender and Adolescence: Global Evidence (GAGE) research programme and Director of the Advancing Learning and Innovation on Gender Norms (ALIGN) community of practice.

Dr Nicola Jones is a political scientist and works as Principal Research Fellow at the Overseas Development Institute (ODI). She is also Director of the longitudinal Gender and Adolescence: Global Evidence (GAGE) research programme. Nicola specialises in research and advisory work on gender, childhood and adolescence, social policy and social protection in Africa, Asia and the Middle East and North Africa (MENA). Nicola was the ODI lead for the Ethiopia and Viet Nam research for the DFID-funded Transforming the Lives of Adolescent Girls programme.

Rachel Marcus is a freelance social development researcher focused on gender, childhood, youth and adolescence. She has particular expertise in conducting rigorous evidence reviews and is co-leading the evidence synthesis work for the Gender and Adolescence: Global Evidence (GAGE) research programme. Rachel led the Overseas Development Institute's (ODI) work on communications and gender norm change as part of the DFID-funded Transforming the Lives of Adolescent Girls programme.

Professor Grace Kyomuhendo Bantebya is a social anthropologist, researcher and advocate for gender equality and social transformation. Grace is currently Professor in the School of Women and Gender Studies at Makerere University in Uganda. Grace was the Uganda country lead for the DFID-funded Transforming the Lives of Women and Girls programme which was conducted in Mayuge district.

Dr Anita Ghimire is a researcher focusing on mobility, social norms related to gender and adolescence, and youth. She is Director for social science research at the Nepal Institute for Social and Environmental Research (NISER), based in Kathmandu, Nepal. Anita was the country lead for the DFID-funded Transforming the Lives of Women and Girls research which was conducted in the Far West region of Nepal in the Doti and Kailali districts, and in the district of Ilam in the Eastern region.

Dr Fiona Samuels is a social anthropologist and works as Senior Research Fellow at the Overseas Development Institute (ODI). She has extensive research experience crossing the fields of public health and social development, with a focus on linkages among health, poverty, risk and vulnerability. Fiona also works on gender, adolescence, social protection and psychosocial well-being in Africa, Asia and the Middle East. Fiona was the ODI lead for the Nepal research undertaken as part of the DFID-funded Transforming the Lives of Women and Girls programme.

Carol Watson is a social anthropologist and development specialist with 30 years of experience in the field, including 20 years working with UNICEF. She is currently an independent consultant focusing on policy research, qualitative studies, social protection and gender analysis. Carol was the Overseas Development Institute (ODI) lead for the Uganda research for the DFID-funded Transforming the Lives of Women and Girls programme. She contributed to early conceptual thinking for the project and was also responsible for yearly syntheses of lessons learned from the research across countries.

Dr Florence Kyoheirwe Muhanguzi is a researcher, gender activist and Senior Lecturer in the School of Women and Gender Studies, Makerere University, Uganda. Florence was part of the Ugandan research team for the DFID-funded Transforming the Lives of Women and Girls programme.

Bekele Tefera is a researcher with 20 years of experience in development policy and programming, including 10 years working with the Young Lives programme, an international childhood poverty study. For the DFID-funded Transforming the Lives of Women and Girls programme Bekele was the country lead for Ethiopia, where research was conducted in eight districts in the Amhara Regional State.

Dr Tran Thi Van Anh is a research consultant focusing on issues of women's empowerment and gender equality. While working with the Institute for Family and Gender Studies, at the Vietnam Academy of Social Sciences, she was the country lead for the DFID-funded Transforming the Lives of Women and Girls programme, which was conducted in Ha Giang province, in the heartland of the Hmong community.

Dr Elizabeth Presler-Marshall is an independent research consultant whose recent work has focused on gender and adolescence. She was involved in data analysis and report production throughout the DFID-funded Transforming the Lives of Women and Girls programme and co-wrote the Ethiopia, Nepal and Viet Nam chapters.

Dr Guday Emirie is Assistant Professor of Social Anthropology at Addis Ababa University, Ethiopia, whose research work focuses on culture, early marriage, education, gender, migration and social protection. She was part of the Ethiopia research team for the DFID-funded Transforming the Lives of Women and Girls programme.

Bethelihem Gebre Alwab is a social development researcher focusing on gender, adolescent girls' well-being, and child poverty and vulnerability. She is currently a research scholar and student of development studies at the University of Antwerp, Belgium. Bethelihem was part of the Ethiopia research team for the DFID-funded Transforming the Lives of Women and Girls programme.

Matthew Maclure is a social development research consultant exploring issues of child rights, social and gender norms, and youth participation and advocacy. Matthew contributed to the Nepal decentralisation analysis in Chapter 9 of this book.

ACKNOWLEDGEMENTS

The authors wish to thank all people in all countries who kindly gave us their time and consideration, allowed us into their homes and places of work, and explained their perspectives, their lives and the challenges they faced. We also thank all who translated documents and interpreted for our teams, and the colleagues on whose research we have drawn, many of whom are referenced in this text. We are especially indebted to all the adolescent girls whose voices, concerns, hopes and dreams have educated us and inform the content of this book.

We thank the Department for International Development (DfID) for funding this research and allowing us the freedom over four years, to shape this enquiry in collaboration with our colleagues in Ethiopia, Nepal, Uganda and Viet Nam, thereby enabling a rich understanding of the lives of adolescent girls to inform the multiple actors working to improve girls' wellbeing and potential.

We would like to acknowledge all authors and the institutions which support them:

Guday Emirie, Addis Ababa University
Bethelihem Gebre
Anita Ghimire, Nepal Institute for Social and Environmental Research (NISER)
Grace Kyomuhendo Bantebya, Makerere University
Caroline Harper, ODI
Nicola Jones, ODI
Matthew Maclure
Rachel Marcus
Florence Muhanguzi Kyoheirwe, Makerere University
Elizabeth Presler-Marshall
Fiona Samuels, ODI
Tran Thi Van Anh, Vietnam Academy of Social Sciences

Bekele Tefera
Carol Watson

Our research teams wish to acknowledge the following individuals and/or institutions whose help in the production of the research and its findings has been invaluable:

Ethiopia:

Research Team: Dr. Guday Emirie, Kiya Gezahegne, Bethelhem Gebre and Kiros Berhanu
Transcription: Tarkegne Ayale, Girma Dagne, Adane Atata, Moges Kibret and Wondiye Admasu (from Addis Ababa University)
Co-operation and facilitation: Katy Webly and Tsion Tefera (Save the Children International)
Regional Government Bureaus: Amhara Bureau Heads of Education, Health, Women and Children Affairs, and Amhara Women Association
Woreda Administration Level: Woreda Head of Education, Health, Women and Children Affairs, Offices of Kelela, Kobo, Worebabo, Woreilu and Merahbet Woredas

Nepal:

Rewati Gurung, Sanju Wagle, Pranav Adhikari, Ija Giri, Roshna Gurung, Reshma Shakya and Bina Limbu

Uganda:

Dr. Ruth Nsibirano, Dr. Peace Musiimenta and Ms. Juliet Kushaba
Dr. Peace Musiimenta, Mr. Joshua Mutengu and Ms. Juliet Kushaba
Dr. Peace Musiimenta, Ms. Juliet Kushaba, Mr. Denis Khasabo and Ms. Evelyn Ejang

Viet Nam:

Research Assistants: Nguyen Phuong Thao, Dang Bich Thuy and Dao Hong Le
Managers: Prof. Nguyen Huu Minh, Director of Institute for Family and Gender Studies, and Mr Pham Ngoc Dung, Vice-director of Ha Giang Department of Labour and Social Affairs

ODI

Jessica Plummer, Book Production Manager
Catriona Foley, Project Programme Manager
Sean Willmott, Graphic Designer, for assistance in drawing the country maps.

PREAMBLE

When ODI first envisaged this research programme we aimed to develop long-term partnerships with anthropologists and sociologists with whom we could learn, in increasing depth, about the lives of adolescent girls in different country and sub-national contexts. Scholars in anthropology in developing country contexts rarely receive long-term undertakings from development funders, and our offer was well received. Over four years we worked together with the same researchers in each of four countries: Ethiopia, Nepal, Uganda and Viet Nam. This was a hugely rewarding experience for us all.

Adolescence, wherever you live, is a potentially turbulent and challenging time and no less so in the four countries where we undertook our work. Here, transitions through adolescence are fraught with difficulties, in part due to the deeply embedded gender norms which determine what a girl can and cannot do and how she must be. Each specific context came with its own factors: multi-ethnic and multi-religious communities, remoteness, variable services (if any at all) and, sometimes, a policy and cultural context without recognition of adolescence, where the transition to adulthood is short or immediate rather than prolonged.

Nevertheless, what we know from biological sciences is that adolescence is a developmental period – a time when the body and mind changes. These changes bring with them potential which in the right context, can open new opportunities. Our interest was in exploring that potential and how gendered norms might truncate opportunities and limit the development of capabilities which every young adult could aspire to own – the ability to have a political voice, to be educated, to be in good health, to have control over one's body, to be free from violence, to be able to own property and earn a livelihood, to be economically and politically empowered.

We were intrigued by the very common experiences of adolescent girls across multiple contexts. This learning and sharing enabled us to explore in much greater depth what norms are and how they operate within political and institutional spaces at national and community levels. It also allowed us to explore the changing and different conceptual understandings of gendered social relations, gender equality and the usage of the term 'norm' to capture embedded, often implicit, informal rules by which people abide, and which are bound into the values people and societies accept implicitly, accept reluctantly or actively contest.

The forces for change became increasingly clear through intergenerational work. Even where girls complained of stagnation, their grandmothers extolled the new freedoms their granddaughters had in comparison with their own young lives, illustrating a process of change over decades. The institutions, formal and informal, maintaining stasis or promoting change, the role of development interventions, the commitment or otherwise of governments and political actors, and the activities of girls themselves, supported by parents and siblings, have informed us of both the power of norms, keeping people in their place, and the potential for change, inspired from below and without.

Ultimately, we recognise that gender justice requires fundamental social change in multiple areas and at multiple levels, starting in childhood. Permanently changing discriminatory and harmful norms is necessary to ensure sustainable gender equality, without relapse back to injustice. And gender equality brings with it so much more for the benefit of whole communities in terms of enhanced health and economic outcomes and arguably a more stable and just society.

Our team is delighted to bring you this volume exploring the varied worlds of adolescent girls and the norms they experience, but norms which are constantly changing, and in this process potentially offering girls and their communities a whole new world.

Caroline Harper

INTRODUCTION

The significance of adolescence in the life course

Nicola Jones, Elizabeth Presler-Marshall and Fiona Samuels

Adolescence is increasingly recognised as being pivotal in the life course, in part because of the physical transformations brought about by puberty – which are considered second only to those experienced in infancy and early childhood in terms of their scope and speed – and in part because of the ways in which children's place in the family and broader community shifts as they approach maturity (Viner *et al.* 2015; Steinberg 2015; Patton *et al.* 2012; UNICEF 2011). Young people in the second decade of life – from 10–19 years – not only see their bodies mature but also experience significant changes in how their brains develop. These changes simultaneously facilitate the complex thinking required for adulthood but also render adolescents in need of support to avoid risky behaviours and to make decisions that will set them on a positive life trajectory (Crone and Dahl 2012). In most contexts, adolescents also progress from the relatively small, family-based world of childhood into a wider world of peers, colleagues and possibly new families. This rapidly expands both the opportunities to meet their needs but also the risks they face.

Despite remarkable progress over the past two decades – evidenced by, for instance, the narrowing gender gap in education (see Table 0.1) – the transition from childhood to adulthood remains fraught for girls in low- and middle-income countries, who largely continue to see their developmental trajectories flattened compared to those of their brothers and their male peers. This book centres on that population of adolescent girls. The editors and authors believe this focus is critical for a number of reasons. First, to enhance understanding of the diverse experiences of adolescent girls as actors of importance, both now and as future adults. Second, to disentangle the factors that shape the process of identity formation in adolescence and the extent to which young people are able to move into the future as purposive actors in their own lives. And third, to explore the implications of both secondary research evidence as well as our own primary research in four focal countries – Ethiopia, Uganda, Nepal and Viet Nam – for the types of policies and programmes

TABLE 0.1 Percentage of students who are female by education level and country

	Ethiopia	Uganda	Nepal	Viet Nam
Primary	47.4% (2014)	50.1% (2013)	50.8% (2015)	47.9% (2014)
Secondary	47.1% (2012)	46.9% (2014)	50.6% (2015)	48.8% LSS* (2015)
Tertiary	32.1% (2014)	43.7% (2011)	47.6% (2013)	50.1% (2014)

* Lower-secondary only for Viet Nam

Sources: UNESCO, *Percentage of students in primary education who are female (%)*, UNESCO, *Percentage of students in secondary education who are female (%)*, UNESCO, *Percentage of students in tertiary education who are female (%)*

that could better support adolescent girls as they transition through adolescence and into adulthood. We also reflect on the extent to which development actors are cognisant of the gender norms that hold opportunities at bay and keep girls in limited political and economic spaces.

As girls enter and progress through adolescence, the gendered norms of their sociocultural environments begin to play a heightened role in shaping their trajectories. The years of early adolescence are found to be especially important because of the ways in which norms start to become more rigidly enforced (McCarthy *et al.* 2016; Kågesten *et al.* 2016). Indeed, emerging neuroscience research suggests that the years between ages 10 and 14 may be a more 'sensitive period' for social processing than previously thought (Crone and Dahl 2012; Fuhrmann *et al.* 2015; Blakemore and Mills 2014). Critically for girls in the global South, the years of early adolescence, rather than expanding their worlds – as is common for boys and for girls in the global North – often see them narrow as they are forced to leave comparatively free childhoods in which their behaviour and movements outside the home were less scrutinised, and are compelled instead along the gendered adult pathways of their local environments (Marcus and Harper 2015). Girls who had begun to aspire to a world different from that of their mothers or grandmothers find that as their bodies mature, they are too often required to leave school and marry, abandoning not only their educational and employment plans but also mobility and friendships. In many contexts, community and family pressures related to domestic and care work burdens, and expectations around sexual purity and family honour, limit girls' possibilities in ways that often have lifelong consequences.

The role of gendered social norms in shaping adolescent trajectories

As distinct from attitudes, which are individually held, social norms are patterns of behaviour in which people engage because they believe they are expected to do so (Bicchieri 2012; Heise 2013; Mackie *et al.* 2015). Norms can either be categorised as descriptive norms, which describe what people actually do, or injunctive norms, which describe what members of a given reference group believe members ought to do (Ball Cooper and Fletcher 2012; Paluck and Ball 2010). Most social norms are what Mackie and Le Jeune (2009) call 'overdetermined' – held in place by an array of factors that include religious tradition, local custom and political interests. Whereas social scientists have approached norms from a variety of theoretical perspectives, none of which fully captures the messiness of real life, there is an emerging consensus that although 'change can be rapid and abrupt or incremental and unnoticed', it tends to be complex and non-linear, with descriptive norms often changing well in advance of injunctive norms (Marcus and Harper 2014: 34; see also Boudet *et al.* 2012; Calder 2012; Rao 2012). There is also growing evidence that it is easier to establish new norms than it is to eliminate old ones (Heise 2013).

Gender norms, which encompass a broad range of social interpretations of what it means to be a woman versus a man, or a girl versus a boy in a particular culture, tend to be especially 'sticky' and difficult to change, as we are socialised into these from birth (Boudet *et al.* 2012). Furthermore, because gendered norms come to be embedded in multiple social relations and in the ideational sphere, change can be very difficult. Indeed, noting the centrality of gender norms to our day-to-day lives, Boudet *et al.* (2012: 24) observe that they 'permeate daily life and are the basis of self-regulation'. As such, the challenge facing policymakers and practitioners is to:

> peel away the many layers of control over girls, challenge discriminatory familial and community norms, and confront male attitudes and behaviors that are damaging to girls . . . and 'invent' a value for girls by counteracting customary perceptions of girls (and the legal frameworks that often support them) and by promoting the 'novel' concept of girls' rights and capabilities apart from reproduction.
>
> *(Mensch et al. 1998: 79–80)*

In line with this call for action, adolescent girls – and the web of social norms that continue to disadvantage them due to their age and gender – have increasingly moved centre stage on international and national agendas. This is evident in events such as the UK government's global Girl Summit in London in 2014 and initiatives such as the Girls not Brides network, which has focused international attention on child marriage. Additionally, there are an increasing array of efforts to measure social norm change, including the Organisation for Economic Co-operation and Development's (OECD's) Social Institutions and Gender Index (SIGI), which attempts to rank countries based on gender discriminatory norms using data that includes national legislation and attitudinal and prevalence surveys (see Box 0.1), and the Global Early Adolescent Study,[1] which is developing new tools to measure gender norms relating to sexual and reproductive health behaviours. Momentum has been further aided by the Sustainable Development Goals (SDGs), which include a focus on tackling practices that harm girls and women, including child marriage, female genital mutilation/cutting (FGM/C) and gender-based violence (GBV).

Indeed, what we find exciting is that when we first started the research presented in this book, these issues were barely on the public agenda, yet today, there is increasing recognition that a focus on adolescent girls' well-being is essential if we are

BOX 0.1   INDICES FOR GIRLS AND WOMEN

The OECD's Social Institutions and Gender Index (SIGI) is a measure of discrimination against girls and women embedded in formal and informal institutions.[i] Ranking 160 of the world's countries, the index speaks to the underlying drivers of gender inequality, including discriminatory family codes (e.g. age at marriage, inheritance and divorce law), restricted physical integrity (e.g. sexual- and gender-based violence), son bias (e.g. missing girls and fertility preferences), restricted access to resources and assets (e.g. access to land and financial services) and restricted civil liberties (e.g. access to public space and political voice and representation). Ranking countries across domains, with risk levels ranging from 0 (no risk) to 1[i] (highest risk), SIGI also generates a composite risk profile for girls and women.

The Girls' Opportunity Index[ii] focuses in on opportunities for girls – ranking the world's countries in terms of child marriage, adolescent fertility, lower secondary school completion rates, maternal mortality (closely related to adolescent fertility) and women Members of Parliament (MPs). Of the 144 countries ranked, Sweden is first and Niger, at 144th, is last (see Table 0.2).

Source: Social Institutions and Gender Index (2014)

i While 1 indicates the highest level of risk, some sub-indices have lower real-world ceilings.
ii Lenhardt *et al.* 2016

TABLE 0.2 The Girls' Opportunity Index

	Ethiopia	Uganda	Nepal	Viet Nam
GIRLS' OPPORTUNITY INDEX	112	120	85	47
SIGI 2014 category (total risk to girls and women)	High	Medium	High	Medium
SIGI value 2014 (max of .563)	0.245	0.2163	0.3222	0.1865
Discriminatory family code value (max of .973)	0.282	0.5093	0.1813	0.3374
Restricted physical integrity value (max of 1)	0.8661	0.5635	0.4083	0.1857
Son bias value (max of 1)	0.0878	0.2991	1	0.4967
Restricted resources and assets value (max of 1)	0.5913	0.5913	0.5913	0.4076
Restricted civil liberties value (max of 1)	0.1951	0.2554	0.2554	0.6092

Source: Lenhardt *et al.* 2016

to capitalise on their developmental 'plasticity' and harness the potential of the so-called youth dividend. Moreover, whereas five years ago, examining adolescent girls' needs often meant narrowly focusing on the sexual and reproductive health of older adolescents (e.g. demographic and health survey data focuses on the 15 to 19-year-old cohort), today we see movement in all four of our focal countries towards multi-sectoral adolescent development policies and strategies.

Using a capabilities lens to understand social norm change pathways towards gender justice

The conceptual framework that serves as the basis for our research draws on the *'capabilities approach'* that has emerged over the past decade as a leading alternative to standard economic frameworks for thinking about human development, poverty, inequality and social justice. Based on Amartya Sen's (1999) theory of 'development as freedom', this approach posits development as a process of expanding 'freedoms' or 'capabilities' that improve human lives by opening up the range of things that a person can effectively be and do – such as to be healthy and well-nourished, to be knowledgeable and to participate in community life. Development, from this perspective, is about facilitating the acquisition and use of such capabilities as well as removing obstacles (such as illiteracy, ill health, lack of access to resources, or lack of civil and political freedom) to what a person can do in life (Fukuda-Parr 2003).

The capabilities approach has evolved over time into a broad normative framework for the evaluation of individual well-being and social arrangements and the design of policies and proposals about social change in society. Furthermore, through the work of feminist thinkers such as Martha Nussbaum, the capabilities approach has become a potent tool for the construction of a normative concept of 'gender justice' (Nussbaum 2000, 2003, 2011), highlighting the breadth of economic resources, political practices (e.g. guarantees of freedom of thought and expression, non-discrimination) and reform of social structures and social norms that is often essential to bring about transformative change in gender relations.

Accordingly, in this book, drawing on a gendered capabilities framework, we conceptualise adolescent girls as evolving citizens to whom rights and entitlements accrue. We also consider the full range of actors at various levels – including family, community and state – who bear responsibility for tackling discrimination and social exclusion and creating the enabling environment and adolescent-friendly services required to nurture and enhance girls' intersecting capabilities and, ultimately, to achieve gender justice.

Focusing in on the nexus between child marriage and education

The research journey underpinning this book began with a broad capabilities framework that emphasised intersections and intentionally sought to move beyond narrower sector-based silos. However, our initial results – especially when paired with national statistics on child marriage (see Table 0.3) – suggested that in order to develop a deep understanding of the complexities of adolescent girls' experiences, we needed to focus on a subset of capabilities as a window into their lives. Listening to girls' voices, we chose the nexus of two key capability domains that girls deemed to be most critical in shaping their future trajectories: education and bodily integrity – with a specific focus on child and forced marriage (see Box 0.2).

TABLE 0.3 Percentage of women aged 20–24 who were married as children

	Ethiopia (2011 DHS)	*Uganda (2011 DHS)*	*Nepal (2014 MICS)*	*Viet Nam (2014 MICS)*
Married by 15	16%	10%	10%	1%
Married by 18	41%	40%	37%	11%

DHS – Demographic and Health Survey
MICS – Multiple Indicator Cluster Survey

BOX 0.2   THE IMPACTS OF EDUCATION AND MARRIAGE ON GIRLS' CAPABILITIES

Educational vulnerabilities as pivotal in adolescent girls' trajectories

The following quotes highlight the critical importance of adolescent girls' educational vulnerabilities in their own voices:

> *They forced me to stop my education and made me marry. . . . It is because I am female that I have been forced to drop out from school. . . . I have suffered a lot as a result of dropping out of my education. The chance to attend school was given to my brother.*
>
> *(Adolescent girl, Amhara, Ethiopia)*

> *I can choose my own happy life. My parents can't provide the life I need or afford it – they can't make me happy so I have to make my own choices, and treasure my happiness. I want to finish school.*
>
> *(Adolescent girl, Ha Giang province, Viet Nam)*

> *Before, education was considered for earning money only. Now, slowly, the thinking has changed. Yes, it is a means to success, and even if nothing happens you are educated. People value education.*
>
> *(Adolescent girl, Doti, Nepal)*

My advice to mothers who have girl children is to support them and take them to school and provide for their basic needs. I advise the other children to have patience because it pays.

(Adolescent girl school graduate, Uganda)

Marrying as a child can also constrain opportunities in adolescent girls' futures

When one is married, one cannot act on one's own will. One is caught up in a kind of bondage, one is not free. . . . They mock us, they criticise us. We have to be very careful in speaking, sitting, getting up, everything. I feel we have to be very conscious when we are married. After being married, there are a lot of differences.

(Married adolescent girl, Nepal)

When a girl gets married when she is older, she can make decisions, get a job, she does not have to deal with a child who is always crying and making her cry too. When she gets married early, she is filled with admiration for what she cannot have, and she cannot make decisions in the home. Also, in marriage there is fighting and you are separated from your parents.

(Married adolescent girl, Uganda)

I hadn't finished my schooling. I didn't want to get married; I wanted to finish my studies, but my husband dragged me away.

(Married adolescent girl, Ha Giang province, Viet Nam)

If I engage in marriage, I will not compete for a job and not be able to participate in any training. . . . It is very difficult to leave the home to search for a job once I get married. This is because it is the wife who is supposed to manage the housework here. Once a girl marries, her husband doesn't allow her to move freely. In this regard, it is good to be free.

(Adolescent girl, Amhara, Ethiopia)

For most adolescent girls in the global South, marriage and education represent competing paths (Marcus and Page 2016). In all countries, the girls least likely to marry as children are those who pursue and complete secondary school (International Center for Research on Women (ICRW) 2016). In Nepal, for example, the median age at first marriage for women with no education is 16.6 years, rising to 18.5 years for women who have completed at least some secondary school (Ministry of Health and Population, New Era and ICF International 2012); in Uganda, the respective figures are 16.9 years and 20.8 years (Uganda Bureau of

Statistics (UBOS) and ICF International 2012). Furthermore, while the prevailing global pattern is for girls to marry soon after they leave school, or to leave school due to impending marriage, it is also the case that married girls have particularly poor access to school (Amnesty International 2016; Steinhaus *et al.* 2016; Hodgkinson 2016; ICRW 2016; Ghimire and Samuels 2014; Jones, Tefera *et al.* 2014; Jones, Presler-Marshall *et al.* 2014; Jones *et al.* 2016; Kyomuhendo Bantebya *et al.* 2014). The reasons for their disadvantage are many and varied. In some countries, for example, school policies specifically exclude married pupils, especially when they are pregnant. In other cases, girls themselves are reluctant to go to school when they are married, sometimes because they are stigmatised by their peers for being married and other times because, after taking time off for marriage, they find themselves older than their classmates and feel out of place. Other girls are prohibited from attending school by their husbands and their in-laws, or simply do not have the time to go to school, given the heavier domestic workloads entailed by marriage.

Marriage has long served as the traditional demarcation of womanhood and remains highly valued in many communities (Hodgkinson 2016; Fenn *et al.* 2015; Steinhaus *et al.* 2016; Boyden *et al.* 2012). In Ethiopia, for example, seeing a daughter 'flower' through marriage is considered a major parental achievement (Jones, Tefera *et al.* 2014; Jones *et al.* 2015, 2016). Indeed, the sanctity of the institution of marriage is so important that parents who are concerned that their daughters will be raped during migration often arrange for them to be married before they leave – so that they are sexually initiated within the confines of marriage – and then arrange for them to divorce, the very fact that they have been married making any future rape less stigmatising (Jones, Presler-Marshall *et al.* 2014). Marriage in Nepal and Uganda is similarly important and is considered a sign of success for both girls and their families, as it defines girls' social status in their community and further cements families into the local social structure (Ghimire and Samuels 2014; Kyomuhendo Bantebya *et al.* 2014). Indeed, in Uganda – where ever-younger girls are increasingly cohabiting without the formality of marriage – parents lament not girls' early transition into adult roles but the loss of the markers that traditionally surrounded that transition (Kyomuhendo Bantebya *et al.* 2014).

The value placed on girls' education, on the other hand, is both newer and far more contested. Commitment to girls' primary education is growing uniformly – whether because it makes girls better mothers and farmers (as with Hmong girls in Viet Nam), confers status on their eventual marital household (in Nepal) or better situates them to provide for their parents in old age (as in Uganda). The value placed on girls' secondary schooling, however, remains far more limited. Where it can help girls access paid employment, such as for Khmer girls in Viet Nam's Kien Giang province, parents are willing to 'plough harder' (Jones *et al.* 2013). Where girls remain valued for their manners and hard work (e.g. Nepal and the Hmong community), parents see little point in continued investment in education beyond lower secondary school level.

Change is slowly unfolding though, even in more isolated communities, driven by global forces that range from economic transition to the Education for All initiative, as well as national-level progress that includes innovative policies and access to role models. As more children spend more time in school – which simultaneously situates them as children and also fosters peer interaction – marriage of the youngest girls has become less common, love matches have begun to replace arranged marriages, elopement has become more common, and the age gap between spouses has begun to shrink (Ghimire and Samuels 2014; Jones, Tefera *et al.* 2014; Jones *et al.* 2016; Kyomuhendo Bantebya *et al.* 2014). Indeed, while the development community has long focused on child marriage as a form of violence perpetrated by adults on girls, recent research has suggested a growing need to recognise and programme for a diversity of marriage drivers, which include girls' own decision-making (Jones *et al.* 2016; Ghimire and Samuels 2014; Maharjan *et al.* 2012). Furthermore, while adolescent pregnancy in developing countries has long been largely driven by child marriage – with up to 90 per cent of all adolescent mothers already married – as marriage and motherhood begin to decouple (as evidenced in Uganda, for example), it is important that interventions shift to reflect this changing reality (Kyomuhendo Bantebya *et al.* 2014).

The international consensus that education is foundational to girls' empowerment – with well-documented impacts on outcomes ranging from improved employment prospects and poverty reduction to declines in child marriage, lifetime fertility and sexual and gender-based violence (SGBV) (Marcus and Page 2016; Calder and Huda 2013; Lloyd and Young 2009; UNICEF 2004; King and Hill 1997; Floro and Wolf 1990) – is not matched by any sort of uniformity in girls' educational experiences. Indeed, the exponential growth of access to and uptake of education has resulted in a growing diversity among different populations of adolescent girls (Lloyd and Young 2009). In some countries – for example, Ethiopia and Viet Nam – school continues to be taught in half-day shifts in order to accommodate the largest number of students. In other countries, such as Nepal, girls attend school full-time. Similarly, while in some countries most students attend publicly financed schools, inadequate resourcing has so impacted quality that in others (e.g. Nepal), many children attend private schools – or at least private after-school tutorial sessions. There is also tremendous variation at the individual level, with some adolescent girls still in primary school because they started late or must dip in and out of school to accommodate other demands on their time or on family resources, while others are in secondary school or studying at vocational training institutes.

School, however, is not just about reading, writing and arithmetic. Girls who attend school see not only growth in their cognitive capacities and academic skill sets, but also in their confidence and voice (Marcus and Page 2016; Willemsen 2016; Shah 2011; Lloyd and Young 2009). They have an opportunity to develop social networks with peers. Through teachers and club leaders, girls also have access to role models and supportive non-related adults, some of whom can help them navigate turning points in their lives and even provide safety nets when they are faced with forced child marriage or other challenges for which their families may not be a source of support (Marcus and Page 2016; Jones *et al.* 2015, 2016; Ghimire and

Samuels 2014). Schools also offer girls – especially in urban contexts but even in the remote mountain villages of Ha Giang province in northern Viet Nam – a window to the wider world. Whether through textbooks or the internet, education can help foster aspirations that were unimaginable even a few years ago (see Box 0.3).

The recent increase in educational opportunities for girls has, in some cases, led to increasing tensions as girls and their families attempt to negotiate the relationship between the new pathways opened up by education and the older pathways that prioritise marriage and motherhood. In communities where it is now normal for girls to attend school, what becomes of girls who are not able to do so? In Nepal those girls may find themselves forced into a polygamous marriage. How do girls and families balance educational and marital aspirations? In some Ethiopian communities, the most-educated girls are the most likely to attract educated husbands and can tempt their families with the possibility of a higher bride price if they are allowed to stay in school. In Nepal, on the other hand, young women who have pursued a university degree all too often find themselves unable to find a job – and too old to marry. In other cases, girls' and families' aspirations remain rooted in marriage, and girls still marry as children in order to attract the husbands believed to best guarantee their futures. Furthermore, as girls' education becomes more commonplace, the dichotomy between schooling and marriage is beginning to blur – in some cases (e.g. in Ethiopia) as girls negotiate with their parents, to accept a marriage but delay cohabitation until after they have completed their

---

BOX 0.3 'I HAVE A DREAM'

Chu Thi Vang is a 13-year-old Hmong girl whose family is considered 'near poor' by the Vietnamese government. While she is forced to miss school on a regular basis – in order to help her mother with work – her biggest worry in life is not herself, but rather her younger sister and her persistent case of intestinal worms. Despite her worry, however, Vang has a dream – a dream that has been nurtured by attending school and participating in an Oxfam-run club for children. She explained:

When participating in the activities, I dream of becoming a beauty queen. I asked the computer. I wrote and sent. I didn't know who answered me, but I got the information on what I should do. I asked what I should do to become a beauty queen. The answer was that you must be tall and able to walk confidently, bold enough to tell your own story, confident to talk with teachers, not to hide your own dream, you should tell other people about your dream. I really want it, so I am trying to make it come true. I try to observe how a beauty queen looks, how to become a beauty queen, how to walk.

schooling, and, in other cases (e.g. Nepal), with their in-laws, to allow them to return to school.

Geographical focus of the book

The countries selected for this programme of work included Ethiopia, Uganda, Nepal and Viet Nam. They were chosen for a number of reasons. First, we deemed it important to have countries spanning different continents in order to ensure that the research was well-positioned to identify, highlight and nuance both regional and country-specific differences and similarities. To some extent representing the regions in which they are located, these four countries have very different levels of socioeconomic development, geographical and climatic concerns, as well as religious and social institutions. They also present an interesting diversity of governance types – ranging from Viet Nam's one-party Communist state to Nepal's fledgling but highly decentralised democracy – and demonstrate a range of state–society relations, with civil society in Nepal and Uganda markedly more vibrant than that in Ethiopia and Viet Nam. We also chose these particular four countries because of their relatively high ranking on the SIGI in terms of the ways in which their social norms pose risks to girls and women (see Table 0.2).

A range of factors was taken into consideration when selecting the research sites in each country. Given that our research was qualitative, our aim was not to be representative of the whole country. Rather, we chose locations that were marginalised, socially (either due to caste, ethnicity or religion), economically (resulting from economic poverty or migration pressures) and geographically (e.g. very remote or impacted by climate change). In order to maximise the contribution our research could make towards strengthening the existing evidence base on adolescent girls in each country, the final selection of research sites was also guided by discussions with key stakeholders including policymakers, government officials and non-governmental organisations (NGOs).

In the first year of the study it was decided to juxtapose, within countries, sites that were particularly vulnerable with sites that appeared to be doing better. By comparing the most marginalised communities with 'positive deviants' we sought a greater understanding of the interplay of factors that facilitated national progress. In Nepal, for instance, we focused on remote sites in Doti in the Far West region as among the poorest in the country, comparing them with Ilam, in the Eastern region, which performs far better in terms of human development indicators. In subsequent years, the study teams returned to the more vulnerable and remote sites of the first year. However, to prevent research saturation, different communities were chosen within the same general area (e.g. in Ethiopia, our focus remained in Amhara Regional State but spread to include more districts in order to capture further nuances or local patterning of norms and behaviours around marriage and education). In the final year, when we focused on the role of programme interventions in shaping adolescent girls' lives, we again had to expand our geographical reach in some cases. In Viet Nam, for example, because there was only one programme for Hmong girls in Ha Giang province, we had to include Lao Cai province, which also has a high Hmong population.

We undertook specific analysis of communication for change programmes, cognisant of their potential for influence and aware of the somewhat limited analysis of these initiatives to date (Watson and Harper 2016; Marcus and Page 2014). In looking at change processes, researchers in each country developed analysis based on local potential and contexts. In some countries (Uganda in particular), specific communication for change initiatives were analysed, but set among other institutional, legal and political factors. Elsewhere, political ideas and institutions (Ethiopia and Viet Nam) featured more strongly. Government's capacity to manage change was also analysed, in particular looking at decentralisation structures (Nepal and Uganda). Together, these chapters provide perspectives on the very wide range of influential contexts to be considered in change processes for the benefit of adolescent girls.

Methodological approach

Because our research focused on adolescent girls, they were key study respondents – both as individuals and in groups. In addition, on account of the powerful roles of families and communities in shaping the environments in which girls must navigate decision-making around education and marriage, we also paid particular attention to the underlying structures and gendered power relations that surround girls and influence the development of their capabilities. Accordingly, our research also included a wide range of family members (e.g. girls' parents, grandparents and in-laws) and community leaders (e.g. village heads, teachers and health care providers) (see Box 0.4 for further discussion on methodological tools and Table 0.4 for a headcount of interview types). Layered into our analysis was an attempt to disentangle the roles played by macro-level factors – including economic poverty, geographical residence (whether urban, remote rural or rapid migration), governance institutions and social structures such as class, caste and ethnicity – in shaping the extent to which adolescents are able to realise their full capabilities in different contexts.

Seeking to isolate the particular impacts of gender on girls' trajectories through adolescence, in the second year of our research we included girls' brothers so that we could directly compare the experiences of sibling sets. We also focused more closely on change over time, tracing gendered roles and outcomes across generations within individual families, and on how change happens, by exploring the circumstances and inflection points that positioned some girls as positive outliers within their local communities and left others to solidly reflect older traditions.

In the final year of the study, our focus shifted to explore programmes that were targeting discriminatory social norms, paying particular attention to communications initiatives such as life skills training, radio programmes, girls' clubs and community dialogues (for more detail see also Marcus and Page 2014). We looked not only at what methods and approaches interventions were using, but also at what

BOX 0.4   QUALITATIVE METHODOLOGICAL TOOLS

In order to understand the complexity of gender norm change processes, it is necessary to capture the non-linear subtleties and nuances of norm change over time and from the perspective of different actors. Accordingly, this programme of work developed a wide range of qualitative and visual tools that facilitated the in-depth discussion necessary to explication and understanding. For example, intergenerational trios – which 'paired' girls with their mothers and grandmothers and boys with their fathers and grandfathers – allowed us to explore how life and views, particularly around gendered norms, had changed (or not) across generations. Similarly, our marital network tool allowed us to position young couples at the centre of their extended families, bringing in parents and parents-in-law to understand how roles and relationships develop and unfold. As already noted, our outlier approach also added texture to our understanding, as it allowed us to understand how some girls had made particularly significant progress – especially in education and employment – while others had remained trapped in the past. Finally, to help us understand programme impacts, we developed a 'before and after' tool that enabled girls to describe how their lives had changed through participation in various interventions (for further details see the Knowledge to Action Resource Series).[2]

TABLE 0.4 Interview types by country and instrument

Instrument	Ethiopia	Uganda	Nepal	Viet Nam
Community mappings and timelines	4+2	9+6	4+4+3	3+3
Focus group discussions – split variously into younger girls, older girls, adolescent boys, mixed adolescents, women, men and mixed adults	20+19+22	10+19+22	13+12+12	5+9+13
Individual interviews with adolescent girls and boys	12+14+21	37+8+22	32+12+22	13+8+25
Case studies, including 24 hours of observation in year 1 and as outliers in year 2	2+33	8+11	4+12+2	2+10
Life histories, marital networks and intergenerational trios	6+16+2	15+5	16+14	11+11
Key informant interviews	10+14+25	21+85+43	33+10+26	34+9+14
Total number of interviews (approximate number of respondents)	222 (765)	321 (1015)	231 (631)	170 (340)

sorts of outcomes they were producing. Accordingly, programme implementers were key study respondents in this final year of research.

Organisation of the book

Chapter 1, written by Caroline Harper and Rachel Marcus, explores the extent to which individuals can shape their own and others' destinies and asks how the development community can contribute to girls' empowerment by focusing on gender norms. Drawing on the capabilities approach to development, the authors introduce adolescent capabilities as limited by discriminatory or harmful gender norms. Exploring a rapidly growing interest in norms, the authors examine behavioural and social science approaches to both adolescence and norm change, pursuing answers to how behaviour and attitudinal change occurs. Recognising that individuals can be enabled to change the way they think and act, the authors also illustrate that changes at the level of the individual are insufficient, and that the process of empowerment requires changes in society-wide institutions as well as in the ideational sphere. The chapter illustrates that a focus on the micro-level social processes that can either uphold or lead to change in discriminatory norms can also usefully be complemented by greater attention to broader processes of social and economic change. It is a combination of agency and resources (in the broad sense of economic resources, opportunities, and a facilitating social institutional environment) that enables people, and especially girls in this context, to develop their full capabilities. Furthermore, girls' empowerment is asserted as central; norms can flex and practices can change, but without necessarily empowering girls in a sustainable way. If tangible opportunities in economic and political spheres are available, girls will themselves push boundaries to realise their full potential. Finally, the social justice agenda, with a perspective on human rights, enables some firmer footing for development actors when seeking social change, with justice for girls being the goal of all efforts in this complex area of work.

Following this we then turn to a focus on our empirical multi-country primary research findings, which highlight the complex interplay between individual agency, the manifestation of gender norms and family and community norms, along with broader formal and informal institutional and structural dynamics in shaping adolescent girls' development trajectories.

Chapter 2, by Nicola Jones, Bekele Tefera, Guday Emirie and Elizabeth Presler-Marshall, introduces the multifaceted relationship between child marriage and girls' education in Amhara, Ethiopia – one of the country's most populous and impoverished regional states. It notes that despite progress, most adolescent girls continue to face a wide variety of threats to their well-being – primarily related to 'sticky' discriminatory gender norms. On the one hand, girls in Amhara are now more likely to attend school than their male peers, rates of child marriage and arranged marriage are in rapid decline, and girls' access to contraception and divorce is improving. On the other hand, only 60 per cent of girls in the region complete primary school and well over half are married before the age of 18. Indeed, most girls – and particularly those from the poorest and most rural households – continue to see their options truncated by repressive gender norms. Such norms burden them with too much domestic and care work, leading to high rates of exam failure, which precludes further education. In addition, entrenched gender norms mean their virginity is perceived as a symbol of their worth to their families, too often resulting in pressures to enter into marriage with older men in order to safeguard their 'honour'. The chapter concludes that despite progress, most adolescent girls in Amhara continue to lack access to the voice and agency that would allow them to pursue new futures.

The third chapter, by Nicola Jones, Elizabeth Presler-Marshall, Bekele Tefera and Bethelihem Gebre Alwab, continues exploring the lives of Amhara girls, but focuses more directly on the policies and programmes that are supporting their development. Noting that both the Ethiopian government and development actors are increasingly interested in adolescent girls, the chapter builds on a political economy framework that highlights the importance of what Rosendorff (2005) terms the 'Three I's' – institutions, ideas and interests. Beginning by exploring the growing institutional support for improving girls' education and ending child marriage, the chapter then explores the way in which the ideas and interests – of girls, parents, communities, NGOs and the government – continue to limit discourse, primarily because of a lack of concerted attention to gender norms. The chapter concludes by discussing context-sensitive entry points and challenges for programmes designed to support adolescent girls and promote positive change in gender norms, drawing on examples of existent programming.

The fourth chapter turns to Uganda. Written by Carol Watson, Grace Kyomuhendo Bantebya and Florence Kyoheirwe Muhanguzi, it analyses the paradoxical nature of both change and continuity in the gender norms and practices affecting adolescent girls' transition to adulthood in the country's rural Mayuge district, where poverty is extensive, child marriage rates remain high, and adolescent pregnancies and school dropout are common. While documenting the growing value being placed on continuing education for girls, the chapter examines the increasing trends towards informal cohabitation and rising levels of adolescent pregnancy and the way in which they interact with change and stasis in gender roles and expectations within the household. The authors highlight the force of social norms around sexual maturation processes for girls and how they fuel both child marriage and adolescent pregnancy, particularly in the absence of adequate sexual and reproductive health information and services. Noting that progressive national policy thrusts are contributing to shifts in attitudes and practices, as well as generating community resistance, the chapter observes that discontinuities between the national policy framework and actual service provision at the local level are critical factors inhibiting truly transformative change on the ground. The authors conclude that integrated approaches are required to address the norms that prevent adolescent girls from developing their full capabilities.

Chapter 5, by Grace Kyomuhendo Bantebya, Florence Kyoheirwe Muhanguzi and Carol Watson, examines selected communications initiatives that aim to shift discriminatory norms around adolescent girls in rural Uganda. It sets its analysis against the backdrop of the national legal policy and programme environment for gender empowerment and adolescent girls, and highlights both the enabling aspects of progressive laws and policies along with some of the ambiguities around adolescent sexual and reproductive health rights and the reform of marriage legislation. It also highlights gaps between policy promises at the national level and action on the ground, which often result in programmes that do little to contribute to shifting the gender norms that restrict girls' capabilities. Using its case studies as a lens, the authors conclude that in order to be successful, programmes must be firmly embedded in clear national policy guidelines and frameworks supported through explicit links from national to local levels, with appropriate investment in local government and community-based structures and ongoing poverty reduction measures.

The sixth chapter moves to Asia and introduces the research undertaken among Viet Nam's Hmong community. Written by Nicola Jones, Elizabeth Presler-Marshall and Tran Thi Van Anh, the chapter explores the ways in which discriminatory gender norms continue to restrict adolescent girls' access to education, limit their marital options and compel them to take on arduous domestic workloads. It argues that despite transformative change to children's access to primary and lower-secondary education, Hmong girls continue to be largely valued for what they can produce, rather than for who they are. The authors observe that even the most motivated girls are only rarely able to attend upper-secondary school and are instead expected to focus their energies on working, first for their parents and then for their marital families. Most girls, the research found, continue to be married young to boys with whom they are barely acquainted. The authors conclude that in order to support Hmong girls to achieve the futures they are beginning to imagine for themselves, it will be necessary to focus attention on shifting the social norms that effectively entwine notions of femininity with cultural identity.

The seventh chapter, by the same authors, explores the neglected nexus of gender, ethnicity and age in Vietnamese policy and programming, and highlights the ways in which Hmong girls are made invisible by the country's lack of intersecting focus. The authors note that although Viet Nam is a regional leader in terms of policies aimed at fostering gender equality (especially in the public sphere) and has, for decades, devoted considerable resources to reducing ethnic minority poverty, until recently there has been almost no attention paid to the way in which gender, ethnicity and age work in tandem to constrain ethnic minority adolescent girls' life opportunities and broader well-being. Indeed, the chapter observes that these girls are so invisible that disaggregated data that speaks to their needs is all but unavailable. The authors then explore the ways in which policy and programming are shifting – or failing to shift – the gender norms that constrain Hmong girls' lives. They also examine three programmes aimed at Hmong adolescents, using them as windows through which to explore some of the complex interlinkages between policies and their implementation, programming, and social norm change processes. The authors underscore that priorities need to include longer-term investments in social norm change that focus on incentivising both parents and adolescent girls and are developed through engaging in dialogue with the Hmong community.

Chapter 8, by Fiona Samuels and Anita Ghimire, shifts to Nepal. It observes that despite the country's impressive progress in recent decades in promoting human rights and gender equality, adolescent girls still face discriminatory gender norms that prevent them developing their capabilities. Norms around marriage seem particularly 'sticky', such that the country has one of the highest rates of child marriage in the world. The authors look at how marriage patterns are changing for the better in Far West Nepal, where parents are now encouraging daughters to complete at least primary school before marriage, girls are beginning to have more say in who they marry, and the age gap between spouses is shrinking. The authors also observe that there is even evidence that married girls are beginning to have more access to education, as they begin to negotiate with their in-laws to stay on in school. Despite these changes, however, the chapter notes that many gendered norms remain entrenched. Son preference continues to be strong, girls' mobility and access to post-primary education continues to be restricted, and girls' value to their families remains rooted in family honour and marriage. The chapter explores how these stubbornly entrenched gender norms are threatening recent progress in surprising ways – leading, for example, to a surge in 'free choice' child marriage as adolescents who believe themselves in love elope against their parents' wishes. The authors conclude by suggesting some ways forward for programming and policy.

The final empirical chapter, by Fiona Samuels, Anita Ghimire and Matthew Maclure, analyses the effectiveness of two different models adopted by programmes to empower adolescent girls in Nepal. The first, Kishori, has been adopted by the government and uses the country's decentralised governance structures to reach girls at village level with empowerment activities. The second, funded by an international NGO but implemented by local partners, does not use these structures. The authors discuss the strengths and weaknesses of these contrasting approaches in terms of shifting discriminatory gender norms and empowering adolescent girls. The government model appears relatively more effective, largely because it enjoys community ownership – supported by its more gradualist approach that builds on economic empowerment – as well as strong links to local services. The authors also note areas for improvement, the most significant being the lack of tailored programming for local and age-related needs and the failure to integrate programming for girls with that aimed at women, men and boys. We conclude that whereas established government structures can be an important vehicle for delivering change, not least because of their coverage and legitimacy, there nevertheless remains a tension between valuing local tradition and norms on the one hand and catalysing change for girls on the other.

In the Conclusion, 'Pushing the boundaries of social order: adolescent girls and norm change', Caroline Harper and Rachel Marcus consider the identified commonalities between all our research sites and the powerful structures of patriarchy, which hold gender norms in place through a male grip on political leadership, moral authority, social privilege and control of property, and is therefore a primary factor in the ways in which girls experience their lives. Embedded into religious or moral world views and further represented in the human body itself through notions of pollution and purity, these world views are argued to emanate from a common and strong imperative to construct patterns of order to combat disorder and to build models and categories to explain and contain a complex world. This search for order and explanation is played out both through girls' bodies and concurrently in the ideational sphere, making change slow. Paradoxically, however, change processes that challenge gendered norms are also seen to be constantly in action, and flux rather than constancy appears to be the more natural order. Nuanced policy, changes to services and systems, norm-focused programmes or individual changes of attitude – all of which are essential – are seen to be insufficient. Rather, policy *combinations*, policy *implementation* and *genuine commitment* to social transformation, with strong political leadership at multiple levels, are vital to support all the other initiatives that have the potential to transform adolescent girls' lives.

Notes

1 www.geastudy.org/
2 Knowledge to Action Resource Series: Adolescent Girls and Gender Norms. Available online at www.odi.org/knowledge-action-resource-series-adolescent-girls-and-gender-norms

Bibliography

Amnesty International. (2016) *Sierra Leone: Continued Pregnancy Ban in Schools and Failure to Protect Rights Is Threatening Teenage Girls' Futures.* Press release, 8 November. Available online at www.amnesty.org/en/latest/news/2016/11/sierra-leone-continued-pregnancy-ban-in-schools-and-failure-to-protect-rights-is-threatening-teenage-girls-futures/

Ball Cooper, L. and Fletcher, E.K. (2012) *Reducing Societal Discrimination Against Adolescent Girls: Using Social Norms to Promote Behaviour Change.* New York: Girl Hub.

Bicchieri, C. (2012) *Social Norms, Social Change.* Lecture at the Penn-UNICEF Summer Program on Advances in Social Norms and Social Change, July.

Blakemore, S-J. and Mills, K. (2014) 'Is Adolescence a Sensitive Period for Sociocultural Processing?' *Annual Review of Psychology* 65: 187–207.

Boudet, A.M., Petesch, P., Turk, C. and Thumala, A. (2012) *On Norms and Agency: Conversations About Gender Equality with Women and Men in 20 Countries.* Washington, DC: World Bank.

Boyden, J., Pankhurst, A. and Tafere, Y. (2012) 'Child Protection and Harmful Traditional Practices: Female Early Marriage and Genital Modification in Ethiopia' *Development in Practice* 22(4): 510–522.

Calder, R. (2012) 'Grandmas, Pensions and FGM/C' Pathways' Perspectives on Social Policy in International Development. Issue No. 7. Available online at www.developmentpathways. co.uk/downloads/perspectives/grandmas-pensions-and-fgm-c-pp7-.pdf

Calder, R. and Huda, K. (2013) 'Adolescent Girls and Education: Challenges, Evidence, and Gaps' *Pathways' Perspectives on Social Policy in International Development.* Issue No. 13. Banbury, Oxfordshire: Development Pathways. Available online at www.development pathways.co.uk/resources/wp-content/uploads/2014/06/13-PathwaysPerspectives-adolescent-girls-and-education-pp13-1.pdf

Crone, E. and Dahl, R. (2012) 'Understanding Adolescence as a Period of Social-Affective Engagement and Goal Flexibility' *Nature Reviews Neuroscience* 13(9): 636–650.

Fenn, N., Edmeades, J., Lantos, H. and Onovo, O. (2015) *Child Marriage, Adolescent Pregnancy and Family Formation in West and Central Africa.* Available online at www.icrw.org/wp-content/uploads/2016/10/Child_Mariage_Adolescent_Pregnancy_and_Family_For mation.pdf

Floro, M. and Wolf, J.M. (1990) *The Economic and Social Impacts of Girls' Primary Education in Developing Countries.* Washington, DC: United States Agency for International Development (USAID).

Fuhrmann, D., Knoll, L.J. and Blakemore, S-J. (2015) 'Adolescence as a Sensitive Period of Brain Development' *Trends in Cognitive Sciences* 19(10): 558–566.

Fukuda-Parr, S. (2003) 'The Human Development Paradigm: Operationalizing Sen's Ideas on Capabilities' *Feminist Economics* 9(2–3): 301–317.

Ghimire, A. and Samuels, F. (2014) *Change and Continuity in Social Norms and Practices Around Marriage and Education in Nepal.* London: Overseas Development Institute (ODI).

Heise, L. (2013) *Social Norms: Introduction.* Presentation at the Expert Workshop on Empowering Adolescent Girls, 26 April, London.

Hodgkinson, K. (2016) *Understanding and Addressing Child Marriage: A Scoping Study of Available Academic and Programmatic Literature for the HER CHOICE Alliance.* Amsterdam: Amsterdam Institute for Social Science Research, University of Amsterdam. Available online at www.her-choice.org/wp-content/uploads/2016/07/Her-Choice-Scoping-Study-Final-July-16.pdf

International Center for Research on Women. (2016) *Child Marriage and Education Are Closely Linked.* Available online at www.girlsnotbrides.org/themes/education/

Jones, N., Presler-Marshall, E. and Tefera, B. (2014) *Rethinking the 'Maid Trade': Experiences of Ethiopian Adolescent Domestic Workers in the Middle East.* London: Overseas Development Institute.

Jones, N., Presler-Marshall, E., Tran, V.A. and Hamilton, J. (2013) *Expanding Capabilities: How Adolescent Khmer Girls in Viet Nam Are Learning to Juggle Filial Piety, Educational Ambition and Facebook.* London: Overseas Development Institute.

Jones, N., Tefera, B., Emirie, G., Gebre, B., Berhanu, K., Presler-Marshall, E., Walker, D., Gupta, T. and Plank, G. (2016) *One Size Does Not Fit All: The Patterning and Drivers of Child Marriage in Ethiopia's Hotspot Districts.* London: Overseas Development Institute.

Jones, N., Tefera, B., Presler-Marshall, E., Gupta, T., Emirie, G., Gebre, B. and Berhanu, K. (2015) *Now I Can Propose Ideas that Can Solve Any Problem: The Role of Community Awareness Interventions in Tackling Child Marriage in Ethiopia.* London: Overseas Development Institute.

Jones, N., Tefera, B., Stephenson, J., Gupta, T. and Pereznieto, P. with Emirie, G., Gebre, B. and Gezhegne, K. (2014) *Early Marriage and Education: The Complex Role of Social Norms in Shaping Ethiopian Adolescent Girls' Lives'.* London: Overseas Development Institute.

Kågesten, A., Gibbs, S., Blum, R., Moreau, C., Chandra-Mouli, V., Herbert, A. and Amin, A. (2016) 'Understanding Factors that Shape Gender Attitudes in Early Adolescence Globally: A Mixed-Methods Systematic Review' *PLoS ONE* 11(6): e0157805.

King, E.M. and Hill, M.A. (1997) *Women's Education in Developing Countries: Barriers, Benefits and Policies.* Baltimore, London: The Johns Hopkins University Press, for the World Bank.

Kyomuhendo Bantebya, G., Kyoheirwe Muhanguzi, F. and Watson, C. (2014) *Adolescent Girls in the Balance: Changes and Continuity in Social Norms and Practices Around Marriage and Education in Uganda.* London: Overseas Development Institute.

Lenhardt, A., Wise, L., Rosa, G., Warren, H., Mason, F. and Sarumi, R. (2016) *Every Last Girl: Free to Live, Free to Learn, Free from Harm.* London: Save the Children. Available online at www.savethechildren.org.uk/sites/default/files/images/Every_Last_Girl.pdf

Lloyd, C. and Young, J. (2009) *New Lessons: The Power of Educating Adolescent Girls.* A Girls Count Report on Adolescent Girls. Available online at www.popcouncil.org/uploads/pdfs/2009PGY_NewLessons.pdf

Mackie, G. and Le Jeune, J. (2009) *Social Dynamics of Abandonment of Harmful Practices: A New Look at the Theory.* Special Series on Social Norms and Harmful Practices Working Paper 2009–06. Florence: UNICEF Innocenti Research Centre.

Mackie, G., Moneti, F., Shakya, H. and Denny, E. (2015) *What Are Social Norms? How Are They Measured?* San Diego: UNICEF/University of California, Center on Global Justice. Available online at www.unicef.org/protection/files/4_09_30_Whole_What_are_Social_Norms.pdf

Maharjan, R.K., Karki, K.B., Shakya, T.M. and Aryal, B. (2012) *Child Marriage in Nepal: Research Report.* Kathmandu: Plan Nepal.

Marcus, R. and Harper, C. (2014) *Gender Justice and Social Norms – Processes of Change for Adolescent Girls.* London: ODI.

Marcus, R. and Harper, C. (2015) *Social Norms, Gender Norms and Adolescent Girls: A Brief Guide. Knowledge to Action Resource Series.* London: Overseas Development Institute.

Marcus, R. and Page, E. (2014) *Changing Discriminatory Norms Affecting Adolescent Girls through Communication Activities: A Review of Evidence.* London: Overseas Development Institute.

Marcus, R. and Page, E. (2016) *An Evidence Review of School Environments, Pedagogy, Girls' Learning and Future Wellbeing Outcomes.* Available online at www.ungei.org

McCarthy, K., Brady, M. and Hallman, K. (2016) *Investing When It Counts: Reviewing the Evidence and Charting a Course of Research and Action for Very Young Adolescents.* New York: Population Council.

Mensch, B., Bruce, J. and Greene, M. (1998) *The Unchartered Passage: Girls' Adolescence in the Developing World.* New York: Population Council.

Ministry of Health and Population, New Era and ICF International. (2012) *Nepal Demographic and Health Survey 2011.* Kathmandu: Ministry of Health and Population, New Era and ICF International. Available online at http://dhsprogram.com/publications/publication-fr257-dhs-final-reports.cfm

Nussbaum, M. (2000) *Women and Human Development: The Capabilities Approach.* Cambridge: Cambridge University Press.

Nussbaum, M. (2003) 'Capabilities as Fundamental Entitlements: Sen and Social Justice' *Feminist Economics* 9(2–3): 33–59.

Nussbaum, M. (2011) *Creating Capabilities: The Human Development Approach.* Cambridge, MA: The Belknap Press of Harvard University Press.

Paluck, E.L. and Ball, L., with Poynton, C. and Siedloff, S. (2010) *Social Norms Marketing Aimed at Gender Based Violence: A Literature Review and Critical Assessment.* New York: International Rescue Committee.

Patton, G.G., Coffey, C., Cappa, C., Currie, D., Riley, L., Gore, F., Degenhardt, L., Richardson, D., Astone, D., O Sangowawa, A., Mokdad, A. and Ferguson, J. (2012) 'Health of the World's Adolescents: A Synthesis of Internationally Comparable Data' *The Lancet* 379: 1665–1675.

Rao, N. (2012) 'Breadwinners and Homemakers: Migration and Changing Conjugal Expectations in Rural Bangladesh' *Journal of Development Studies* 48(1): 26–40.

Rosendorff, B. (2005) *Ideas, Interests, Institutions and Information: Jagdish Bhagwati and the Political Economy of Trade Policy.* Conference in honour of Jagdish Bhagwati on his 70th birthday. New York, 5–6 August.

Sen, A. (1999) *Development as Freedom.* Oxford: Oxford University Press.

Shah, P.P. (2011) 'Girls' Education and Discursive Spaces for Empowerment: Perspectives from Rural India' *Research in Comparative and International Education* 6(1): 90–106.

Steinberg, L. (2015) *Age of Opportunity: Lessons from the New Science of Adolescence*. New York: Eamon Dolan/Mariner Books.

Steinhaus, M., Gregowski, A., Stevanovic Fenn, N. and Petroni, S. (2016) *'She Cannot Just Sit Around Waiting to Turn Twenty'. Understanding Why Child Marriage Persists in Kenya and Zambia*. Washington, DC: International Center for Research on Women. Available online at www.icrw.org/publications/she-cannot-just-sit-around-waiting-to-turn-twenty/

Uganda Bureau of Statistics (UBOS) and ICF International. (2012) *Uganda Demographic and Health Survey 2011*. Kampala, Uganda: Uganda Bureau of Statistics and Calverton, Maryland: ICF International. Available online at https://dhsprogram.com/pubs/pdf/FR264/FR264.pdf

United Nations Children's Fund (UNICEF). (2004) *The State of the World's Children*. New York: United Nations Children's Fund.

United Nations Children's Fund (UNICEF). (2011) *Adolescence: An Age of Opportunity*. New York: United Nations Children's Fund.

Viner, R., Ross, D., Hardy, R., Kuh, D., Power, C., Johnson, A., Wellings, K., McCambridge, J., Cole, T., Kelly, Y. and Batty, D. (2015) 'Life Course Epidemiology: Recognising the Importance of Adolescence' *Journal of Epidemiology & Community Health* 69: 719–720.

Watson, C. and Harper, C. (2016) *How Communications Can Change Social Norms Around Adolescent Girls: Lessons Learned from Year 3 of a Multi-Country Field Study*. London: Overseas Development Institute.

Willemsen, L.L.W. (2016) *Embodying Empowerment: Gender, Schooling, Relationships and Life History in Tanzania*. PhD thesis, University of Minnesota.

1

WHAT CAN A FOCUS ON GENDER NORMS CONTRIBUTE TO GIRLS' EMPOWERMENT?

Caroline Harper and Rachel Marcus

Gendered social norms background

Change in gender norms, as discussed in the Introduction to this book, is almost always part of a longer-term process of wider social change, some of which can result from deliberate action but much of which flows from unpredictable events and opportunities. The extent to which individuals can shape their own and others' destinies thus depends on the wider social, political and economic contexts. For those purposively effecting change, such as politicians and activists, policymakers and implementers, understanding gender norms – the social rules and obligations and values, through which and on which societies are organised – may throw light on how social change occurs. However, stepping outside of one's own 'normal' to understand these implicit norms is always complex. This chapter explores some of the complexities and challenges of understanding adolescence, social norms and gender norms in the development context.

While undertaking field research, our Nepali team met Sneha, an adolescent girl who had been involved in life skills classes provided by a local organisation. Sneha had been persistently harassed by a neighbourhood boy who often took the bus with her to and from school, but – fearing the blame would be laid at her feet should she complain – she kept quiet. One day, taking the bus journey home, he sat next to her, and began his usual harassment, trying to touch her and verbally pestering her. One can only imagine what went through Sneha's mind, but on this day she changed – she turned to him and slapped him across the face. That moment in time must have stood still for her. Would she be scolded or worse for daring to challenge him, a boy, a soon-to-be young man? What would he do to her? In fact, the boy reacted by returning the blow and then touching her body. He felt impunity was on his side. What happened next could not have been predicted. Often such actions – standing up to a wrong – go unsupported, and retribution can be unfair and swift. On that day, though, the collective anger in the bus was on Sneha's side. The passengers held the boy, took him to the police, and in police presence he was made to apologise to Sneha. He thereafter stopped his harassment. Of course, he may seek future retribution; change comes with hard and often dangerous implications.

In recounting this story, we are not glamorising Sneha's action or the outcome, but the events here illustrate a moment where change could lead to positive new behaviour. While this harassment had been ongoing for a long while, no one took action to help Sneha, until she took action herself. Why not? Inaction – born of the acceptance of harmful behaviours and of male impunity and dominance over females – is implicit in this story.

Why did Sneha feel able to stand up to the boy after months of harassment? There are many possible factors contributing to the sudden change in her behaviour, some of which we discuss in later chapters. Sneha claims that, in part, it was because of non-formal education classes that she had been attending, during which she had become aware of her rights, and which had encouraged her to question behaviour and practices that were generally taken for granted, even if disliked. But change is usually also accompanied by a sometimes implicit absorption of a shift in gender norms – for example, seeing TV soaps that challenge stereotypes; coming into contact with role models, teachers, parents or others who represent a different view of what 'normal' may be; implementation of laws and judicial action; or the belief in self that comes with greater economic empowerment and autonomy.

Such illustrative 'norms' – the widely accepted informal social rules that govern behaviour – are simply one set of many in every society where gender discrimination often serves as a potent force against the *capability development* of adolescent girls. By this, we mean girls' potential to live the lives they want and achieve valued ways of 'being' and 'doing' (Kabeer 1999; Nussbaum 2003). Each norm that serves to restrict girls' capability development is held in place by complicit acceptance – and repeated enacting – of practices and behaviours. Much of the way adult women and girls experience gender discrimination is similar. However, girls generally have even less power and voice than adult women; they have bodies that are less able to cope with reproduction, and brains that are still developing and thus with potential to learn new norms, or imbibe old ones. Girls also have different role expectations from adult women – both the roles expected of them (specific domestic duties, for example) and those they aspire to (such as being educated). Girls also implicitly carry a reproductive value, the 'ownership' of which is not yet decided until they enter marriage.

The capabilities approach to development provides a holistic way to comprehend the goal of girls' empowerment. Arising as an alternative to standard economic frameworks for thinking about human development, poverty and social justice, it emerged out of Amartya Sen's (1999) theory of 'development as freedom' and has been further elaborated and refined from a feminist perspective by Martha Nussbaum (2003) and others. This approach understands development as a process of expanding 'freedoms' or 'capabilities' that improve human lives by expanding the range of things a person can effectively be and do – such as to be healthy and well-nourished, to be knowledgeable and to participate in community life.

Development from this perspective is about facilitating the acquisition and use of such capabilities as well as removing obstacles to what a person can do in life – obstacles such as illiteracy, ill health, lack of access to resources or lack of civil and political freedoms (Fukuda-Parr 2003). From this perspective, increasing girls' agency – the ability to define one's goals and act on them (Kabeer 1999) – is crucial, as it underpins the development of other capabilities as well as constituting an important capability in its own right. Furthermore, a capabilities approach underpins a reframing of the goals of gender equality and empowerment towards the promotion of 'gender justice' (Goetz 2007) for disempowered groups. It thus keeps the broader goal of transformation of unjust social arrangements, as well as personal empowerment, firmly in sight.

In this chapter, we describe a rising interest among policy and programme actors in adolescent girls and gender norms, and outline how the interplay between individual agency, gender norms and the wider institutional environment restricts girls' agency and their opportunities to fully develop their capabilities. We ask whether a focus on how these norms are shaped and enacted can enhance understanding of the constraints adolescent girls face, lead to more effective action to change discriminatory and harmful practices, and ultimately enhance girls' empowerment and capabilities. Importantly, not all norms are harmful or discriminatory, but where norms do contribute to harm and ill-being (and it is these harmful norms that are the focus of this chapter), attempts are being made the world over to change them.

After describing the rising interest in girls' development, we outline how practices and social roles understood as discriminatory gender norms can undermine girls' opportunities to develop agency and develop their full capabilities. We then critically examine the relevance and limitations of a social norms lens for both understanding and overcoming constraints on girls' capability development. In particular, we highlight the potential of integrating a greater understanding of power relations and empowerment, and situating norm change activities within a fuller consideration of the broader institutional environment. We conclude by outlining an analytical approach related to norms, agency, power and capability development that we believe points to a productive way of understanding the constraints that limit adolescent girls' development and ways of overcoming them.

The rise of interest in adolescent girls and introduction of norms

In 1998, Mensch et al., discussing the representation of adolescent girls in development policy, could claim that 'Girls disappear as policy subjects after receiving their last childhood immunization and do not reappear until they are pregnant and, in most cases, married' (Mensch et al. 1998: 12).

In part, this lack of past attention to adolescence in general may have reflected the fact that many societies do not distinguish adolescence as a specific life stage, considering the transition to adulthood essentially to occur at puberty or marriage. Additionally, the international community is susceptible to funding trends, with early childhood, nutrition, survival and education typically featuring large over the past 30 years.

As Mensch *et al.* prefigured in 1998, the past decade has seen a myriad of changes, with far greater attention now paid to adolescent girls and, to a lesser extent, boys (Kato-Wallace *et al.* 2016).[1]

From the early 2000s onwards a number of factors have contributed to a rising interest in adolescence. They include the growing sophistication of HIV/AIDS prevention efforts; the revitalised Education for All agenda; attention to early marriage and female genital mutilation/cutting (FGM/C) (Warner *et al.* 2014; Norwegian Agency for Development Cooperation (NORAD) 2015) and girls as future leaders (e.g. Let Girls Lead campaign);[2] and a reinvigorated and heavily critiqued (Chant 2016; United Nations 2011) consensus that investing in girls (and women) is 'smart economics', with major pay-offs for gross domestic product (GDP) growth, population control, and child health, among other socially desirable outcomes.

This growing identification of adolescent girls as 'neglected' and deserving of policy and programming attention as a specific population group has been mirrored or complemented in the past five years (2011–2016) by increased analytical attention to this group. Indeed, there is now a burgeoning body of research on adolescent girls and young women. Some of it quantifies their deprivation or documents trends in their well-being. Some aims to understand particular aspects of girls' experience, such as school violence (Leach *et al.* 2012: Parkes and Heslop 2013) or early marriage (Loaiza and Wong 2012; Warner *et al.* 2014; Brown 2012), girls' experience of disasters and their vulnerability to climate change (Plan International 2011); and some is dedicated to foregrounding adolescent girls' voices on a wide range of issues of concern to them (e.g. Walker *et al.* 2014). In some ways, this analysis mirrors earlier work in the gender and development field on 'women and . . .' and, in putting a spotlight on them, sometimes abstracts girls from the broader web of social and economic relations that surround them (Chant 2016; Cobbett 2014).

This body of girl-focused programming and analysis has engaged with gender norms in specific and arguably rather limited ways. First of all, the term 'norms' is used loosely by development actors, some of whom focus on individual behaviours, others on societal and institutional constraints. Our definition, here, takes norms to mean *the expected or accepted rules which then guide, inform and permit behaviours, practices and attitudes.* Policies and interventions can change a specific behaviour, but not necessarily the accepted rule, and the underlying values it represents. For example, family planning practices among girls may change, but girls may still be 'valued', and thus treated, in the old way. Secondly, gender norms are primarily presented as constraining, and as one of a number of barriers to be addressed, alongside factors such as 'poverty' or lack of implementation of laws. There has been less attention to the ways that girls can use gender norms as a lever for change (e.g. to point out where norms are being violated, as Sneha did, on the bus), or where they actually enable individuals to live healthy and productive lives. Although discussing the ways in which some gender norms function as 'social glue', and are socially protective and integrative, is beyond the scope of this chapter, the positive side to many gender norms must be recognised. Thirdly and more fundamentally, specific gender norms – such as those favouring early marriage – are abstracted in the policy literature and often considered in isolation (Harper *et al.* 2014) rather than as part of a web of other norms, values and ideologies that are sometimes in tension with each other.[3]

Despite socialisation to accept gender norms, the processes of brain development during adolescence actually make it a fertile time for challenging social rules and practices that young people experience as constraining (Johnson *et al.* 2009; Blakemore and Pfeifer 2012). How young men and women channel this capacity into a quest for voice and social justice is under-explored, both in the general literature on adolescence and in practice. However, the growing literature and policy emphasis on girls' agency highlights the ways in which adolescent girls often actively challenge norms that they perceive to constrain them. It also highlights how girls draw support both from peer networks and from more formally constituted organisations such as girls' clubs or community groups (Marcus and Harper 2014). These challenges may take the form of disagreement and arguing (e.g. over girls' rights to attend school, over unfair distribution of chores or an unwanted marriage) or 'running away' to avoid abuse or marriage.

In the following section, we examine the contribution of different social and gender norms insights to understanding adolescent girls' well-being, and the ways in which these insights could be enhanced.

Gender norms and barriers to adolescent girls' capability development: insights and limitations

The consideration of social norms in mainstream development discourse and action is relatively recent. International action has, until the past 20 years or so, generally regarded normative practices as largely untouchable – looking to science and technology to modernise society or focusing on markets to bring about change (Attaran 2005; Easterly 2006; Rao and Walton 2004). This has been compounded by a focus on the material manifestations of poverty (measured by income and human development indicators), accompanied by growing attention to social risks and vulnerabilities. Though a strong gender and development lobby has brought the issue of gender inequalities into the mainstream, this initially translated into a relatively narrow focus on achieving gender parity. The focus was largely limited to access to education (and more recently learning outcomes), enhancing women's economic opportunities, addressing specific health issues (such as reproductive health and HIV prevention), and increasing women's participation in governance, rather than on changing the social and cultural norms that underlie gender inequalities more generally (Jones *et al.* 2010).

More recently, recognising that economic change and technological modernisation do not necessarily always lead to substantial gains in gender equality, there is a renewed focus on the sociocultural factors that influence development strategies, including unequal gender norms. For example, within efforts to promote universal education, there is a growing emphasis on issues such as gender-based violence (GBV), which can make schools (or travel to and from school) unsafe for girls (Leach *et al.* 2012; Parkes and Heslop 2013). A strong emphasis on human rights has seen growing attention to a number of manifestations of gender inequality, such as gender-based violence, and 'harmful traditional practices' such as child marriage and FGM/C, which have risen up development agendas as legitimate areas of intervention, and which are seen as being held in place by discriminatory gender norms. Furthermore, a burgeoning interest in men, boys and masculinities is also part of this awareness of the importance of norm change.

There are many different definitions of social norms but all emphasise the importance of 'shared expectations or informal *rules* among a set of people as to how people should behave' (Marcus and Harper 2015). Most also agree that norms are held in place through social rewards for people who conform to them (e.g. acceptance and inclusion in the group, other people's approval and enhanced standing in the community) and social sanctions against people who do not (such as gossip, being ostracised or violence) (Marcus and Harper 2015; Heise and Manji 2015). Not all norms, however, are necessarily rewarded or sanctioned. However, the terms 'social norms' and 'cultural norms' are used quite widely (and sometimes loosely) in development practice as synonyms for 'culture', and used much more specifically to describe people's beliefs about typical and appropriate behaviour and shared social expectations that distinguish expected behaviour on the basis of gender or other group identity (Marcus and Harper 2015).[4]

These different strands of analysis have brought some important insights into norm change processes but also some complexity related to different ways of understanding specific norms, how they are held in place and how they change. We will here give a brief overview of the roots and emphases of contemporary approaches to social norms from behavioural science, moving on to highlight insights from sociological approaches to social norms as to how norms become embedded within society.

Behavioural science-inspired approaches to norm change

Much of the recent work on social norms draws on social psychological analysis of conformity and social convention theory (Mackie and Le Jeune 2009; Mackie *et al.* 2015) and on philosophical economics and game theory (particularly as developed by Cristina Bicchieri 2006, 2015). This body of analysis provides important insights at the micro level into what norms are and how they are held in place. To summarise and simplify, work in this tradition highlights the role that social norms – shared beliefs about what important others (one's reference group) consider typical and appropriate behaviour – play in governing behaviour. In this tradition, social norms are commonly understood as held by social groups (in contrast to attitudes, which individuals hold) and as mechanisms for coordinating behaviour that may persist even after the original circumstances in which they emerged are long gone. There is a strong focus on perceptions of other people's beliefs, which may or may not be accurate.

These perceptions of other people's views may be inaccurate because privately held attitudes can diverge from what people believe others think they should do or be. Where people risk social disapproval or worse (e.g. ostracism, loss of livelihood or violence) for not complying with a norm, they have strong incentives to follow the course of action that they believe will cement their social standing or keep them safe and free from censure or violence. For example, as Schuler (2007: 191) found in fieldwork in Bangladesh, people were increasingly sending their daughters to primary school because it was 'the done thing'. As one girl put it, '*My father thought it was unnecessary for girls to read and write but in my case he did not object. . . . None of my peers were sitting idle at home so I also went to school.*'

We found a similar normalisation of primary and lower-secondary education among Hmong communities in northern Viet Nam as evidenced in Chapters 6 and 7 in this volume.

It is argued that in order to change entrenched practices that are upheld by social norms, shifting perceptions of what others in people's reference group believe to be typical and appropriate behaviour is as important as changing individual attitudes. Tipping point and social diffusion theories suggest that this shift is often initiated by 'norm entrepreneurs', with a new norm becoming established at a point where a sufficient number of people believe an action to be typical and appropriate and are prepared to undertake it themselves (Gladwell 2004). Some theorists suggest that the primary mechanisms for achieving change are community-level deliberation, leading ultimately to coordinated agreements to change (Cislaghi *et al.* 2014; Bicchieri and Mercier 2014; Cloward 2015), and media messaging, which can aim to change attitudes or create awareness that new norms are being widely followed (where that is the case).

This body of literature, focused on micro-level social interactions, provides notable insights into why people comply with norms, and the social psychological processes that can result in norm change. In foregrounding the importance of social expectations, and people's sensitivity to social influence, these theorists unpack and shine a spotlight on the rules concerning behaviour – an influence that can be downplayed by a focus on broader cultural phenomena. These insights can be particularly useful in terms of understanding potential mechanisms to enhance girls' empowerment when they are integrated with sociological and political analysis, to which we now turn.

Sociological approaches to norm change

As described earlier, the behavioural science-inspired approach conceptualises gender norms as informal rules concerning gender. In this conceptualisation, people are usually aware of these rules, and choose whether or not to comply with them, largely based on their perceptions of what others consider acceptable. However, sociological analysis of norms also highlights that these types of choices are often not made at an individual level. Socialisation into gender norms – both in childhood and through everyday practice in adolescence and adulthood – can move gender ideologies, gendered practices and resultant gender inequalities into the realm of '*doxa*' (Bourdieu 1977, cited in Kabeer *et al.* 2011) – i.e. ideas and actions that are taken for granted and are beyond questioning. Some norms are upheld by, and entwined with, much more encompassing and profound world views, related to religion or valued cultural traditions. Bourdieu described this process as 'habitus' – patterns of behaviour created over time by an interplay between individual and group structures and free will, whereby habitus is created and reproduced unconsciously, 'without any deliberate pursuit of coherence . . . without any conscious concentration'. Habitus is, therefore, 'the way society becomes deposited in persons in the form of lasting dispositions, or trained capacities and structured propensities to think, feel and act in determinant ways, which then guide them' (Wacquant 2005: 316, cited in Navarro 2006: 16; Bourdieu 1986: 170). Habitus 'is not fixed or permanent, and can be changed under unexpected situations or over a long historical period' (Navarro 2006: 16).

For example, an older man we interviewed in eastern Uganda encapsulated this when he argued:

> *God created us differently, the men and the women. That's why culture also treats us differently. It is government which is spoiling things. How can my son cook, bathe the children, wash my clothes, or fetch water when the women and the girls are there? How can my wife build the hut when I or her sons are there? Can I call my daughter to help to slaughter the cock when God blessed me with all these sons? God would curse me if I did.*
>
> *(Kyomuhendo Bantebya et al. 2013)*

Gender norm change would entail a change in this man's entire world view. In a similar vein, some of the gender norms we encountered among Hmong communities in northern Viet Nam were bound up with beliefs about the irreversible migration of souls between a girl or woman's birth family and the family she marries into (Jones, Presler-Marshall and Tran 2014) – fundamentally determining ancestral lines and women's spiritual positioning both before and after death (Harper 1992).

As with these examples, in our view, gender norms are typically expressions of issues that are profound, and thus potentially more difficult to change than in norm change cases where simply agreeing to a new set of social rules for a particular behaviour or practice would not challenge a world view or alter the balance of power between different groups. For example, washing hands to improve hygiene, or agreeing that open defecation is unacceptable, does not (necessarily) require a challenge to fundamentally held world views, whereas releasing a daughter's reproductive rights into marriage can, for example, have implications for a daughter's relationships with ancestry and future well-being in an afterlife. Going against the norm – for example, leaving one's husband, in the case of the Hmong – can mean forsaking any relationship with the ancestors, and thus an afterlife, as she cannot return to her natal ancestors. Control over a girl's reproduction is, of course, also important for the household she marries into as it will perpetuate, through the birth of sons, the continuation of the ancestral line. Thus, much control is exercised over girls' marriage prospects.

Importantly, part of the construction of world views also involves the creation of 'cultural capital', which plays a central role in societal power relations as it 'provides the means for a non-economic form of domination and hierarchy, as classes distinguish themselves through taste' (Gaventa 2003: 6). As Bourdieu (1986: 471) argues, 'social order is progressively inscribed in people's minds' through 'cultural products' including systems of education, language, judgements, values, methods of classification and activities of everyday life. These all lead to an unconscious acceptance of social differences and hierarchies, to 'a sense of one's place' and to behaviours of self-exclusion (Bourdieu 1986: 141; powercube n.d.).

Sociological analysis thus draws our attention to the ways in which different individuals and social groups can have deep interests in particular norms and the power to enforce them. People who are economically and socially marginalised may well not be able to afford – economically or socially – not to comply with a whole range of gender norms, as the costs of social and economic ostracism may be too great. For example, research with young women garment workers in Bangladesh indicates that their need for work leads them to comply with conservative norms of dress that signal their respectability, docility and compliance with broader gender ideologies (Hossain 2011). Often, those who have the most to gain from norm change – in this case, adolescent girls – are among those who have the least power to enact change, as their right to voice is itself systematically denied by disempowering norms concerning respect for elders, particularly one's parents (Marcus and Harper 2014).

Giving up power and privilege – even where it is recognised as such – is challenging for individuals and groups alike. This may particularly be the case with gender norms where one party perceives that they gain considerably from the status quo and stand to lose out if things change (for example, with divisions of household labour, control over marriage alliances, unequal pay rates or circumcisers who stand to lose out if FGM/C is discontinued). This is not to say that change is impossible even where one party benefits considerably; there are examples of community education campaigns that have changed attitudes and resulted in boys and girls sharing domestic chores more equally (e.g. Lundgren et al. 2013; Kyomuhendo Bantebya et al. 2015). It is also the case that elites, who are socially and economically insulated from the costs of social disapproval, may be in the best position to catalyse large-scale change (Cloward 2015), as our research in Nepal found. It was, for example, local elites who were able to defy gender norms and send their daughters to study for master's degrees in Kathmandu, with the expectation that this would enhance their work prospects, rather than constituting a major risk to their reputations (Ghimire and Samuels, 2014).

Thinking and practice on norm change suggests that people change their individual practices more readily than they change their entire world view, and that working systematically on one entry point can lead to more fundamental change. For example, delaying early marriages can be a springboard to more equal gender relations in other spheres. At the same time, changing broader world views (rather than just specific norms and practices) is often more likely to be effective and sustainable than approaches that focus only on changing norms around specific practices. For example, domestic violence campaigns that emphasise fundamental values of gender equality and reframe masculinity and femininity in non-violent ways have typically been more successful than those that simply try to create new social rules about the unacceptability of violence or the acceptability of intervention (Jewkes *et al.* 2015; Michau *et al.* 2015).

Because deep-seated values and power relations can be at stake, changing gender norms can evoke considerable backlash (Balchin 2011; Kyomuhendo Bantebya *et al.* 2014). This can be manifested through verbal resistance, verbal harassment of, or violence against, people who defy gender norms, and criticism of the individuals and forces seen as spearheading change. It can also include overt or covert defiance of new laws, as in Ethiopia, where our research found people camouflaging early marriages as religious celebrations, and where, in another region, Boyden *et al.* (2013) found girls arranging their own 'circumcisions'.

Sociological analysis also brings attention to the ways in which norms are embedded in societies and upheld by various formal and informal institutional arrangements. Where a range of social institutions reinforces a norm, change may need to take place in multiple arenas – for example, a community-level decision to abandon FGM/C or child marriage may need to be reinforced by laws, schools, representatives of religious communities, local leaders and the wider community as well as the family. After initial enthusiasm and commitment to a new norm, some people backslide, whereas others need exposure to the issue when it becomes salient to them (when they have a daughter of marriageable age, for example, rather than when she is a small child). This highlights the importance of sustaining norm change efforts across time and across different institutional spaces.

A focus on the micro social processes that either uphold discriminatory norms or can lead to changes in those norms can also usefully be complemented by greater attention to broader social and economic change processes, as it is often changes in the broader institutional environment that drive changes in norms. These change processes can simultaneously create new opportunities and obstacles for girls' capability development and girls' exercise of agency. For example, our research in Nepal found that the spread of mobile phones into small rural towns was changing the way marriages were contracted. Although more girls were entering into relationships of their own choosing, this was actually driving the age of marriage down and curtailing girls' education opportunities; it was also increasing the risk of girls becoming engaged in an informal polygynous marriage with associated health, economic and psychosocial consequences (Ghimire and Samuels 2014; Chapter 8 in this volume). More positively, where people perceive an advantage in adopting new practices, they often do so, as Jensen (2010) found in northern India. Here, spreading information about white-collar work opportunities for secondary school graduates, which had increased dramatically in recent years, led to notable increased investments in girls' education, and a rise in the age at marriage.

To sum up, a behavioural science–inspired approach to gender norms provides important insights into both the processes that maintain norms and to the roles individuals can play in spreading new norms; but analysis can also be strengthened by grounding gender norms in their historical, cultural and economic contexts. In particular, a stronger understanding of how gender norms uphold power inequalities, and how power relations influence people's capacity to challenge discriminatory norms, is essential for effective and sustained norm change.

Sustainable norm change – bringing a focus on power and empowerment

Reviewing the numerous perspectives on power and empowerment is beyond the scope of this chapter.[5] However, in this section, we draw on selected writings with particular relevance to norms and to how adolescent girls experience and engage with power relations.

As already discussed, there is a danger in applying a norms lens with too great a focus on specific areas of behaviour or practice, and not enough on the gender ideologies that uphold discriminatory practices and norms. Focusing on a specific behaviour or practice can divert attention from the wider context. For example, while early marriage can be damaging for girls, it also often presents a route to social mobility, a marker of adulthood, and may be the best of very few options open to a girl if her parents have few resources (Warner *et al*. 2014; Ansell *et al*. 2009). A narrow approach to addressing norms (in situations where economic, political and social vested interests are also embedded in ideologies) may result in little or limited change. Girls may be allowed into school but not into work; they may not be given space to make marriage choices; they may be released from domestic labour, but only temporarily, returning to it upon marriage. Though these are important building blocks of empowerment and constitute real well-being outcomes, they do not necessarily, in and of themselves, constitute enduring and empowering change. Understanding norm change can thus be greatly enhanced by recognising sustainable empowerment as an outcome.

A focus on the broader economic and developmental environment (e.g. the availability of specific services and opportunities or the extent of political and public commitment to social justice) is thus important, both because it structures the environment in which norms exist and change, and it has important influences on well-being independent of norms. It is a crucial component of enhancing sustainability in changed gender norms.

The issue here is not focusing on norms for norms' sake – but as a step towards increased, sustainable and empowering agency. The most appropriate focus for norm change will vary depending on the issue. In the case of FGM/C, for example, a focus on health outcomes actually proved counterproductive, as many parents simply opted for a medicalised procedure (UNICEF 2013). In this case, focusing on the deeply embedded norm is a necessary part of change. This contrasts with early marriage, where a focus on what outcomes one is trying to achieve, such as raising the age of first birth, or providing higher education access and decent work opportunities, may be more beneficial. Focusing on the norm itself could result in reduced early marriage but also increase girls' vulnerability as they enter relationships that are not socially sanctioned (Kyomuhendo Bantebya et al. 2014), and still become pregnant too young, or they enter dangerous work environments as an alternative to marriage (Jones, Presler-Marshall and Tefera 2014). It can also deflect a focus from other drivers of early marriage such as poverty (Brown 2012). Each context is different, but in most cases, it is necessary to focus on both specific and broader norm change and related practices, alongside increasing girls' agency, capabilities and well-being.

Agency requires a sense of 'power within' and 'power to' (Rowlands 1997; VeneKlasen and Miller 2002), a sense of oneself not as powerless but as someone who can analyse a given situation, aspire to alternatives, make choices and do what is necessary to realise them, while also acknowledging the forces that have 'power over' you. It is a combination of agency and resources (in the broad sense of economic resources, opportunities, and a facilitating social and institutional environment) that enables people to develop their full capabilities (Kabeer 1999). Capabilities and agency are linked in a virtuous circle. Typically, the greater a girl's capabilities, the more agency she will have to make strategic life choices (Kabeer 1999) and realise her life goals; and the more agency she has, the more likely she is to be able to further develop her capabilities. The development of agency also fundamentally underpins girls' ability to engage in collective action in adolescence or in adulthood, whether on discriminatory gender norms or on other issues they consider important.

However, in many social contexts, adolescent girls' opportunities to develop agency are constrained and severely limited by norms that emphasise children's obedience to elders, and females' deference to males in household and public decision-making (Plan International 2014) as well as by limited exposure to the outside world, particularly for girls not attending school. These norms discourage girls from voicing their opinions even on matters of the utmost importance to their lives, such as whether they attend school, when and to whom they will marry, when they should conceive, or whether they can choose their own livelihood.

Though the extent of girls' voice (or voicelessness) varies considerably from family to family, their generally limited opportunities to speak out and assert their wishes have led girl-focused development programmes to emphasise activities that help girls develop self-confidence and communication skills. Some programmes also expose girls to role models – women who have forged their own life paths, often overcoming significant barriers to do so (Marcus et al. forthcoming; Marcus and Harper 2014). Likewise, the well-recognised disempowerment of girls has led feminist educationalists to advocate forms of schooling that help girls develop confidence and skills (Murphy-Graham and Lloyd 2015; Murphy-Graham 2012; Mlama *et al.* 2005). With greater capabilities for voice and agency, girls are in a stronger position to challenge discriminatory norms and to dislodge stereotypes about girls' poor decision-making capacity – not just in a localised environment or in relation to a single issue but over a wide range of norms and over the longer term. This can lead to a more permanent changing of norms concerning girls' influence over a number of decisions that affect them.

Conclusions

If the objective of girl-focused development activity is to enable girls to develop a range of capabilities, and ultimately to promote gender justice, a norms focus can help us to understand the persistence of certain informal institutional structures that undermine girls' capabilities. It can also help to explain why well-intentioned efforts to promote gender equality and justice – through, for example, legal reform or women's political empowerment – fall short of their goals. We argue that in order to fully understand the social and cultural forces that limit girls' opportunities for capability development, a broad approach to norms is essential. This needs to combine an understanding of the social psychological processes that hold norms in place (such as fear of sanctions for deviating from socially expected behaviour) and an understanding of how gender norms can uphold inequalities of power and access to resources and opportunities. It must take into account the often close relationship between broader cultural values and gender ideologies that speak to relations of power and inequality in society as a whole, and specific norms (such as early marriage practices). And it must recognise how norms reflect, and are affected by, the broader economic and developmental context, such as the availability of education or employment for educated women.

It is thus very important to focus on the vested interests and, in particular, the power inequalities that gender norms often sustain. Rather than just relying on individual perception and action to promote change, the real potential for change lies in the institutions of society that uphold power inequalities. Though some individual power-holders may be willing to relinquish some of the power and control they hold over women and girls and to behave differently – if they are convinced of the inherent justice of an approach – others will not, because too much is at stake or because they are comfortable with the status quo. Shifting a discriminatory *gender* norm can thus be a rather different process from establishing a new norm in areas where power relations are less central to change, such as those concerning hand-washing or smoking.

As part of the broad informal institutional environment in which adolescent girls grow up, discriminatory gender norms and broader social norms set the framework in which girls' parents, spouses/partners or the wider community make decisions and judgements about what is appropriate gendered behaviour on the part of adolescent girls, what constitutes a valuable opportunity and what is considered outside the realm of acceptable activities and life paths. As such, they have a far-reaching influence on girls' opportunities to develop capabilities and therefore must be recognised as central to processes of change and continuity.

But gender norms also directly affect girls' capability development in another way – through 'scripts' imbibed by girls themselves, concerning how much autonomy they should have and over what issues, and the social contexts and relationships in which they may (or may not) express their views. Gender norms can thus have a direct effect on girls' agency and their self-efficacy in framing and pursuing personal (or collective) goals. At the same time, girls' agency can also influence gender norms – as, for example, when girls act outside the realm of socially accepted behaviour. In these cases, girls are contributing to change – whether by refusing an arranged marriage, persuading their parents to let them attend school, or arguing for a more equal distribution of household labour or for paid work outside the home.

This close relationship between norms related to decision-making and girls' agency again points to the potential contribution that a norm-focused approach to girls' empowerment can make. This is implicitly if not explicitly recognised in adolescent girl-focused development programmes, which increasingly include processes to change discriminatory norms through work with other stakeholders (such as family members and community and religious leaders) alongside processes aimed at building girls' self-confidence, negotiation skills and ability to speak out (Marcus *et al.* forthcoming; Uganda and Ethiopia chapters).

A norms approach can thus help illuminate pathways to girls' empowerment when it places discriminatory norms and practices in their broader social, relational, economic and developmental context and acknowledges the interaction between this environment and gender norms. Norm change that contributes to girls' empowerment may be driven by the spread of new ideas via radio, television and the rise of social media, promoting alternative visions of what women's and men's lives could be like. Norm change is also driven by targeted structural political, legal and economic change, such as implementation of laws on sexual harassment, positive discrimination for political appointments, and equal pay and access to labour markets. Girl-focused practitioners would do well to draw lessons from these processes and seek to catalyse or replicate them where appropriate. For example, seeing role models, such as women parliamentarians or local council leaders, can not only change girls' aspirations and sense of what is possible (Evans 2014; Kyomuhendo Bantebya *et al.* 2014) but can also enhance parents' perceptions of their daughters' capabilities, which in turn can lead to increased investment in daughters' education and (somewhat) reduced workloads (Beaman *et al.* 2012).

This new interest in norms in development policy and practice is opening up new perspectives and opportunities for a development audience and confronting previously ignored or hidden barriers to girls' capability development. Many challenges persist, however, and some new ones present themselves. The common critique of development practice in general – that in attempting to change societies for a perceived 'better state of being', outsiders are meddling in intimate internal affairs of countries, communities, even families – is often raised. Not all norms are harmful – indeed, they underpin the functioning of all societies (Bicchieri 2006). Many norms surrounding girls' lives exist for good reason and we would do well to acknowledge this alongside seeking change where norms are harmful to girls. To understand which norms are harmful and which are not, we need to understand societies in depth and with a sense of historical change and continuity, not simply focusing on apparently detrimental norms removed from context. Development actors, researchers, policymakers and practitioners also need to understand themselves as effecting change in sometimes sensitive and nuanced aspects of others' lives – actions that are in danger of being labelled as 'meddling' in practices which can be argued to be 'different but acceptable'. The social justice agenda, with its perspective on human rights, offers some firmer footing when seeking social change, with justice for girls being the goal of all efforts in this complex area of work.

Notes

1 For example, in 2014 the UK government hosted a Girl Summit, focused on early marriage and FGM/C; prominent philanthropic foundations, such as the Gates Foundation and Nike Foundation have committed millions of dollars to transforming the lives of adolescent girls; coalitions have been set up specifically to promote girls' rights; and numerous organisations have started to focus on adolescent girls as a specific client group. These include the UN's Coalition for Adolescent Girls (collaboration with the Nike Foundation and others), the World Bank Adolescent Girls Initiative, and Girl Hub/ Girl Effect.
2 www.riseuptogether.org/en/letgirlslead/
3 For example, in relation to the capabilities of boys and young men; the critical role of ideologies and belief systems; the intersection of race and ethnicity; the intergenerational bargains and relationships inherent in marriage alliances.
4 Not all norms are gendered. Breastfeeding, for example, is not a gender norm but applies to one sex – women. When norms are interpreted differently for boys and girls, this is a gender norm – for example, schooling is available for boys and girls, but boys are often given preference and girls stay home for care economy tasks. When norms bear no relation to gender relations, such as washing hands for cleanliness, this can be termed a social norm. All of these are norms; all have some cultural embeddedness, but they are not all gender norms.
5 Powercube (www.powercube.net) and VeneKlasen and Miller (2002) provide useful overviews.

Bibliography

Ansell, N., Robson, E., van Blerk, L., Hajdu, F. and Chipeta, L. (2009) *Averting 'New Variant Famine*. Briefing Note No. 11. 'AIDS-affected young people's decision making about livelihood strategies'. Centre for Human Geography, Brunel University. Available online at https://assets.publishing.service.gov.uk/media/57a08b8bed915d622c000d43/60434_BriefingNotes_11.pdf

Attaran, A. (2005) 'An Immeasurable Crisis? A Criticism of the Millennium Development Goals and Why They Cannot Be Measured' *PLoS Med* 2(10): e318.

Balchin, C. (2011) *Towards a Future Without Fundamentalisms: Analyzing Religious Fundamentalist Strategies and Feminist Responses*. Toronto: Association for Women's Rights in Development (AWID).

Beaman, L., Duflo, E., Pande, R. and Topalova, P. (2012) 'Female Leadership Raises Aspirations and Educational Attainment for Girls: A Policy Experiment in India' *Science* 335(6068): 582–586.

Bicchieri, C. (2006) *The Grammar of Society: The Nature and Dynamics of Social Norms*. New York: Cambridge University Press.

Bicchieri, C. (2015) *Norms in the Wild: How to Diagnose, Measure and Change Social Norms*. New York: Cambridge University Press.

Bicchieri, C. and Mercier, H. (2014) 'Norms and Beliefs: How Change Occurs' in B. Edmonds (ed.) *The Dynamic View of Norms*. Cambridge: Cambridge University Press, 37–54.

Blakemore, S. and Pfeifer, J. (2012) 'Adolescent Social Cognitive and Affective Neuroscience: Past, Present, and Future' *Journal of Social, Cognitive and Affective Neuroscience* 7(1): 1–10.

Bourdieu, P. (1977) *Outline of a Theory of Practice*. Cambridge Studies in Social Anthropology Series. Cambridge: Cambridge University Press.

Bourdieu, P. (1986) *Distinction: A Social Critique of the Judgement of Taste*. London: Routledge.

Boyden, J., Pankhurst, A. and Tafere, Y. (2013) *Harmful Traditional Practices and Child Protection*. Young Lives Working Paper 93. Oxford: Young Lives.

Brown, G. (2012) *Out of Wedlock, into School: Combating Child Marriage Through Education*. London: Office of Gordon and Sarah Brown.

Chant, S. (2016) 'Women, Girls and World Poverty: Empowerment, Equality or Essentialism?' *International Development Planning Review* 38(1): 1–24.

Cislaghi, B., Gillespie, D. and Mackie, G. (2014) *Values Deliberations and Collective Action in Rural Senegal: How Participants Respond in the Human Rights Sessions of the Tostan Community Empowerment Program*. Report for the Wallace Global Fund and UNICEF.

Cloward, K. (2015) 'Elites, Exit Options, and Social Barriers to Norm Change: The Complex Case of Female Genital Mutilation' *Studies in Comparative International Development* 50(3): 378–407.

Cobbett, M. (2014) 'Beyond "Victims" and "Heroines": Constructing "Girlhood" in International Development' *Progress in Development Studies* 14(4): 309–320.

Easterly, W. (2006) *The White Man's Burden: Why the West's Efforts to Aid the Rest Have Done So Much Ill and So Little Good*. New York: Penguin.

Evans, A. (2014) 'Co-education and the Erosion of Gender Stereotypes in the Zambian Copperbelt' *Gender and Development* 22(1): 75–90.

Fukuda-Parr, S. (2003) 'The Human Development Paradigm: Operationalizing Sen's Ideas on Capabilities' *Feminist Economics* 9(2–3): 301–317.

Gaventa, J. (2003) *Power After Lukes: A Review of the Literature*. Brighton: Institute of Development Studies.

Ghimire, A. and Samuels, F. (2014) *Change and Continuity in Social Norms and Practices Around Marriage and Education in Nepal*. London: Overseas Development Institute.

Gladwell, M. (2004) *The Tipping Point: How Little Things Can Make a Big Difference*. Boston: Little, Brown and Co.

Goetz, A-M. (2007) 'Gender Justice, Citizenship and Entitlements – Core Concepts, Central Debates and New Directions for Research' in M. Mukhopadhyay and N. Singh (eds.) *Gender Justice, Citizenship and Development*. Ottawa: International Development Research Centre, 15–57.

Harper, C. (1992) *The Social Life of the Green Mong Textile: Commercialisation and Alternative Discourses of Value in Thailand*. PhD Thesis: University of London.

Harper, C., Jones, N., Presler-Marshall, E. and Walker, D. (2014) *Unhappily Ever After: The Fight Against Early Marriage*. London: Overseas Development Institute.

Heise, L. and Manji, K. (2015) *Introduction to Social Norms*. Briefing note for DFID. London: Department for International Development.

Hossain, N. (2011) *Exports, Equity, and Empowerment: The Effects of Readymade Garments Manufacturing Employment on Gender Equality in Bangladesh*. Background Paper for the World Development Report 2012.

Jensen, R. (2010) *Economic Opportunities and Gender Differences in Human Capital: Experimental Evidence for India*. NBER Working Paper 16021. Cambridge, MA: National Bureau of Economic Research.

Jewkes, R., Flood, M. and Lang, J. (2015) 'From Work with Men and Boys to Changes of Social Norms and Reduction of Inequities in Gender Relations: A Conceptual Shift in Prevention of Violence against Women and Girls' *The Lancet* 385(9977): 1580–1589.

Johnson, S., Blum, R. and Giedd, J. (2009) 'Adolescent Maturity and the Brain: The Promise and Pitfalls of Neuroscience Research in Adolescent Health Policy' *Journal of Adolescent Health* 45(3): 216–221.

Jones, N., Harper, C. and Watson, C. (2010) *Stemming Girls' Chronic Poverty: Catalysing Development Change by Building Just Social Institutions*. Manchester: Chronic Poverty Research Centre.

Jones, N., Presler-Marshall, E. and Tefera, B. (2014) *Rethinking the 'Maid Trade': Experiences of Ethiopian Adolescent Domestic Workers in the Middle East*. London: Overseas Development Institute.

Jones, N., Presler-Marshall, E. and Tran, T.V.A. (2014) *Early Marriage Among Viet Nam's Hmong: How Unevenly Changing Gender Norms Limit Hmong Adolescent Girls' Options in Marriage and Life*. London: Overseas Development Institute.

Kabeer, N. (1999) 'Resources, Agency, Achievements: Reflections on the Measurement of Women's Empowerment' *Development and Change* 30(3): 435–464.

Kabeer, N., Khan, A. and Adlparvar, N. (2011) *Afghan Values or Women's Rights? Gendered Narratives About Continuity and Change in Urban Afghanistan*. IDS Working Paper No. 387. Brighton: Institute of Development Studies.

Kato-Wallace, J., Barker, G., Sharafi, L., Mora, L. and Lauro, G. (2016) *Adolescent Boys and Young Men: Engaging Them as Supporters of Gender Equality and Health and Understanding Their Vulnerabilities*. Washington, DC: Promundo; New York: United Nations Population Fund (UNFPA).

Kyomuhendo Bantebya, G., Kyoheirwe Muhanguzi, F. and Watson, C. (2013) *Adolescent Girls and Gender Justice: Understanding Key Capability Domains in Uganda*. London: Overseas Development Institute.

Kyomuhendo Bantebya, G., Kyoheirwe Muhanguzi, F. and Watson, C. (2014) *Adolescent Girls in the Balance: Changes and Continuity in Social Norms and Practices around Marriage and Education in Uganda*. London: Overseas Development Institute.

Kyomuhendo Bantebya, G., Kyoheirwe Muhanguzi, F. and Watson, C. (2015) *Communications for Social Norm Change Around Adolescent Girls: Case Studies from Uganda*. London: Overseas Development Institute.

Leach, F., Slade, E. and Dunne, M. (2012) *Desk Review for Concern: Promising Practice in School-Related Gender-Based Violence (SRGBV) Prevention and Response Programming Globally*. University of Sussex: Centre for International Education.

Loaiza, Sr E. and Wong, S. (2012) *Marrying Too Young: End Child Marriage*. New York: United Nations Population Fund (UNFPA).

Lundgren, R., Beckman, M., Chaurasiya, S., Subhedi, B. and Kerner, B. (2013) 'Whose Turn to do the Dishes? Transforming Gender Attitudes and Behaviours Among Very Young Adolescents in Nepal' *Gender and Development* 21(1): 127–145.

Mackie, G. and Le Jeune, J. (2009) *Social Dynamics of Abandonment of Harmful Practices: A New Look at the Theory*. Special Series on Social norms and Harmful Practices Working Paper 2009–06. Florence: UNICEF Innocenti Research Centre.

Mackie, G., Moneti, F., Denny, E. and Shakya, H. (2015) *What Are Social Norms. How Are They Measured?* UNICEF/UCSD Centre on Global Justice Project Cooperation Agreement Working Paper 1.

Marcus, R. and Harper, C. (2014) *Gender Justice and Social Norms – Processes of Change for Adolescent Girls.* London: Overseas Development Institute.

Marcus, R. and Harper, C. (2015) *Social Norms, Gender Norms and Adolescent Girls: A Brief Guide.* Knowledge to Action Resource Series. London: Overseas Development Institute.

Marcus, R., Page, E., D'Arcy, M. and Gupta-Archer, N. (2017) *Girls' Clubs, Life Skills Programmes and Girls' Wellbeing Outcomes: A Rigorous Review.* London: Overseas Development Institute.

Mensch, B., Bruce, J. and Greene, M. (1998) *The Unchartered Passage: Girls' Adolescence in the Developing World.* New York: Population Council.

Michau, L., Horn, J., Bank, A., Dutt, M. and Zimmerman, C. (2015) 'Prevention of Violence Against Women and Girls: Lessons from Practice' *The Lancet* 385(9978): 1672–1684.

Mlama, P., Dioum, M., Makoye, H., Murage, L., Wagah, M. and Washika, R. (2005) *Gender Responsive Pedagogy: A Teacher's Handbook.* Nairobi: Forum for African Women Educationalists (FAWE). Available online at www.ungei.org/files/FAWE_GRP_ENGLISH_VERSION.pdf

Murphy-Graham, E. (2012) *Opening Minds, Improving Lives: Education and Women's Empowerment in Honduras.* Nashville, Tennessee: Vanderbilt University Press.

Murphy-Graham, E. and Lloyd, C. (2015) 'Empowering Adolescent Girls in Developing Countries: The Potential Role of Education' *Policy Futures in Education* 7 November: 1–22.

Navarro, Z. (2006) 'In Search of Cultural Interpretation of Power' *IDS Bulletin* 37(6): 11–22.

Norwegian Agency for Development Cooperation (2015) *Evaluation of Norway's Support to Women's Rights and Gender Equality in Development Cooperation, Ethiopia Case Study Report.* Oslo: Norwegian Agency for Development Cooperation.

Nussbaum, M. (2003) 'Capabilities as Fundamental Entitlements: Sen and Social Justice' *Feminist Economics* 9(2–3): 33–59.

Parkes, J. and Heslop, J. (2013) *Stop Violence Against Girls in School: A Cross-Country Analysis of Change in Ghana, Kenya and Mozambique.* London: ActionAid.

Plan International. (2011) *Weathering the Storm: Adolescent Girls and Climate Change.* Woking: Plan International.

Plan International. (2014) *Because I Am a Girl: The State of the World's Girls 2014. Pathways to Power: Creating Sustainable Change for Adolescent Girls.* Woking: Plan International.

powercube. (no date) Available online at www.powercube.net/other-forms-of-power/bourdieu-and-habitus/

Rao, V. and Walton, M. (2004) *Culture and Public Action.* Stanford, CA: Stanford University Press.

Rowlands, J. (1997) *Questioning Empowerment: Working with Women in Honduras.* Oxford: Oxfam.

Schuler, S.R. (2007) 'Rural Bangladesh: Sound Policies, Evolving Gender Norms, and Family Strategies' in M. Lewis and M. Lockheed (eds.) *Exclusion, Gender and Education: Case Studies from the Developing World.* Washington DC: Center for Global Development, 179–203.

Sen, A. (1999) *Development as Freedom.* Oxford: Oxford University Press.

United Nations Children's Fund (UNICEF). (2013) *Female Genital Mutilation/ Cutting: A Statistical Overview and Exploration of the Dynamics of Change.* New York: United Nations Children's Fund.

United Nations. (2011) *World Youth Report. Youth Employment: Youth Perspectives on the Pursuit of Decent Work in Changing Times*. New York: United Nations.

VeneKlasen, L. and Miller, V. (2002) *A New Weave of Power, People & Politics: The Action Guide for Advocacy and Citizen Participation*. Rugby: Practical Action Publishing.

Wacquant, L. (2005) 'Habitus' in J. Becket and Z. Milan (eds.) *International Encyclopedia of Economic Sociology*. London: Routledge.

Walker, D., Samuels, F., Gathani, S., Stoelinga, D. and Deprez, S. (2014) *4,000 Voices – Stories of Rwandan Girls' Adolescence: A Nationally Representative Survey*. London: Overseas Development Institute and Girl Hub Rwanda.

Warner, A., Stoebenau, K. and Glinski, A. (2014) *More Power to Her: How Empowering Girls Can Help End Child Marriage*. Washington, DC: International Center for Research on Women.

PART 1
Ethiopia

2

'STICKY' GENDERED NORMS

Change and stasis in the patterning of child marriage in Amhara, Ethiopia

Nicola Jones, Bekele Tefera, Guday Emirie and Elizabeth Presler-Marshall

Summary

Ethiopia's place on today's international stage is far removed from the place it held only a generation ago. However, our research, located in eight districts in Amhara Regional State and including approximately 800 respondents over three years, found that despite progress, most adolescent girls continue to face a wide variety of threats to their well-being, primarily related to 'sticky' discriminatory gender norms. On the one hand, girls in Amhara are now more likely to attend school than their male peers, rates of child marriage and arranged marriage are in rapid decline, and girls' access to contraception and divorce is also improving. On the other hand, only 60 per cent of girls in the region complete primary school and well over half are married before the age of 18. Indeed, most girls – particularly those from the poorest and most remote rural households – continue to see their options truncated by repressive gender norms that burden them with too much domestic and care work, leading to high rates of exam failure. In addition, entrenched norms see girls' virginity as a symbol of their worth to their families. Pushed into marriage with older men to safeguard their 'honour', many adolescent girls continue to largely lack access to the voice and agency that would allow them to pursue new futures.

Introduction

Despite ranking 173rd out of 186 countries on the Human Development Index (HDI), Ethiopia has made remarkable progress since the turn of the millennium (United Nations Development Programme (UNDP 2013). The world's poorest country in 2000, with a poverty rate of 44 per cent, high growth rates have slashed poverty rates to only 26 per cent in 2013 (UNDP 2015a), even as its population climbed 50 per cent in the same period. Although poorer than many of its sub-Saharan neighbours, with a per capita income of only $550 (compared with a regional average of $1,699) (World Bank 2015), Ethiopia's place on today's international stage is far removed from the place it held only a generation ago. Ethiopian girls and young women, however, continue to face a wide variety of threats to their well-being, primarily related to 'sticky' discriminatory gender norms that see them as little more than symbols of family honour and a critical source of domestic labour. These norms leave many girls unable to focus on their schooling, likely to marry as children, pushed into early and high fertility and with little power to protect themselves from domestic violence because of their limited access to the assets that facilitate independence. Our research found that although there is evidence of rapid change on some fronts, especially in girls' uptake of primary education, other restrictive gender norms are more stubbornly entrenched.

The national context for girls

Ethiopian girls, like their male peers, have seen significant improvements to their well-being over the past generation, especially in terms of access to education and reproductive health care. However, the Gender Inequality Index (GII) ranks Ethiopia 121st out of 151 countries (UNDP 2015b) and the Social Institutions and Gender Index (SIGI) rates it 'high' in terms of gender discriminatory institutions, largely due to pervasive violence against women and women's lack of access to assets (SIGI 2015).

Despite remarkable and accelerating progress, child marriage continues to threaten many Ethiopian girls – with girls in some regions more at risk than those in others (see Box 2.1). Though the practice is illegal under national law,[1] with significant penalties in place since 2005,[2] the country ranks 18th in the world in terms of incidence (International Center for Research on Women (ICRW) 2015). Two-fifths of all women in their early twenties married before the age of 18, 8 per cent of girls aged 15–19 were married before the age of 15, and the median age at first marriage for women aged 15–49 is 16.5 years (Central Statistical Agency (CSA) and ICF International 2012). Girls who are uneducated, rural and poor tend to marry significantly earlier than their peers who are urban, educated and well-off (ibid.; see also Erulkar *et al.* 2010). Girls also tend to marry men who are significantly older; the average gap between spouses is seven years and for the youngest girls it can be much larger. Nearly 15 per cent of all married girls – and 22 per cent of rural married girls – are more than ten years younger than their husbands (Erulkar 2013). Not surprisingly, given the relationship between child marriage and adolescent pregnancy, Ethiopian women tend to begin childbearing early. Of those aged 20–49, one-third were mothers before the age of 18 (CSA and ICF International 2012).

Girls also face restricted access to education and employment. The International Labour Organization (ILO) (2013), for example, estimates that while only 3.4 per cent of boys aged 7–14 are entirely out of school, nearly 10 per cent of girls the same age are being denied their right to an education. Kept at home to provide free

BOX 2.1   THE AMHARA CONTEXT FOR GIRLS

Amhara Regional State has the country's lowest median age at first marriage – 15.1 years (for women aged 20–49) (CSA and ICF International 2012). With 56 per cent of all women in their early twenties having been married before their 18th birthday, Amhara also has the second highest rate of child marriage in Ethiopia (United Nations Population Fund (UNFPA) 2012).

Erulkar *et al.* (2010), in their 2009 survey of nearly 700[3] Amhara girls and young women, found even higher child marriage rates. For example, of young women aged 18–24, 39 per cent had been married by the age of 15 and more than 63 per cent by the age of 18. Indeed, the Amhara rate of early adolescent marriage was approaching twice that of the next highest region (Benishangul-Gumuz with 23.9 per cent). The same survey also found that Amhara had the country's highest rates of arranged marriage (more than 94 per cent) and the second highest rate of early adolescent sexual debut (20 per cent of girls aged 15–24 had had sex before the age of 15, almost exclusively within the confines of marriage).

On the other hand, though Amhara girls are especially vulnerable to child marriage, which typically – but not always – ends their access to education, most are increasingly likely to attend school and do well there. Their primary enrolment and completion rates are higher than those of girls in other regions and higher than those of Amhara boys (see Table 2.1) (Ministry of Education 2015).

TABLE 2.1 Educational statistics

	Girls in Amhara	Boys in Amhara	Girls nationally	Boys nationally
NER[i] grades 1–4	109.5	114.3	103.9	111.8
Grade 5 completion rate[ii]	93.3	83.5	75.2	77.2
NER grades 5–8	58.3	49	50	49
Grade 8 completion rate	60.5	53.2	52.2	53.4
NER grades 9–10	22.2	17.5	20.9	19.6
10th grade exam *failure* rate[iii,iv]	52%	32%	55%	39%
NER grades 11–12	5.6	5.5	5.5	5.5

Source: Ministry of Education 2015, 2014

i Figures are for the 2013/2014 school year as reported in the Education Statistics Annual Abstract (Ministry of Education 2015). Ratios greater than 100 are possible because they are based on population figures from the 2007 census, which is a decade out of date at this point.

ii Completion figures are for the 2012/2013 school year (Ministry of Education 2014), as they were not reported by region in the 2013/2014 Education Statistics Annual Abstract.

iii Authors' calculations, using the figures reported in the 2013/2014 Education Statistics Annual Abstract (Ministry of Education 2015). Passing scores are those greater than 2.0 (out of 4.0) and only students who sat the exam were included in calculations.

iv At the 12th-grade level, 4.6 per cent of Amhara girls, but less than 1 per cent of boys, failed preparatory school-leaving exams.

Like their peers, however, Amhara girls remain highly unlikely to complete their education. More than half fail exams at the end of 10th grade and the net enrolment rate (NER) for preparatory school (11th and 12th grades) is only 5.6 per cent (ibid.). There are also stark differences in enrolment by wealth quintile, with well-off children far more likely to attend school than their poorer peers[4] (Gurmu and Etana 2013; World Bank 2005).

labour for their parents – and to safeguard their reputations for purity – girls are especially unlikely to attend secondary school. Their net enrolment for first cycle (9th and 10th grades) is only 21 per cent and their net enrolment for preparatory (11th and 12th grades) is under 6 per cent (Ministry of Education 2015). Girls also see less return on their education in terms of employment and wages. Indeed, the 2013 Labour Force Survey found that, per year of education, women who had graduated from preparatory school (12th grade) had the highest rate of unemployment – 32 per cent for female graduates versus about 17 per cent for male graduates (CSA 2014).

Locating our research

Our research, which involved nearly 800 respondents over three years,[5] was conducted in Amhara Regional State, one of Ethiopia's largest but most disadvantaged regions (see Figure 2.1). Amhara has a population of approximately 20 million, who are overwhelmingly rural, mostly Ethiopian Orthodox Christian[6] and prone to food insecurity driven by deforestation, drought and increasing land fragmentation. Our research sites – which included *woredas*[7] in North Gondar, North Shoa, West Gojjam, South Wollo and North Wollo zones – were chosen because they are diverse in terms of demographics and geography, and we wanted to explore the relative importance of livelihood patterns and opportunities and of religious and sociocultural norms on girls' vulnerabilities to school dropout and child marriage. Sites for the third round of research (2014) were specifically chosen because of the child marriage programming in place there.[8]

Change and stasis: the 'sticky' nature of gender norms

Our primary research with Amhara adolescent girls concurs with the broader literature that gender norms tend to be especially 'sticky' because of the way in which they are enacted in myriad small ways on a daily basis, beginning in childhood and persisting over time (Boudet *et al.* 2012). It found that even as arranged child marriages become less common – and girls' education becomes more common – the emphasis on girls' sexual purity and unpaid contribution to domestic and care work continues to limit the capabilities and life trajectories of most.

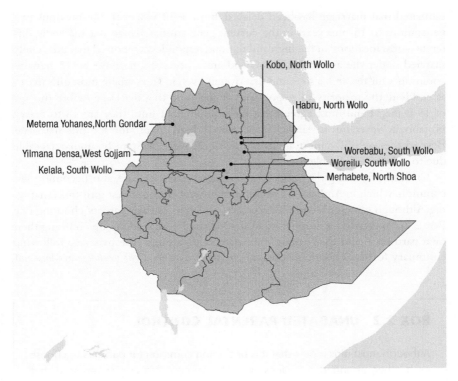

FIGURE 2.1   Amhara research sites

Source: Author

Changes in the uptake of education

Reflecting the push for Education for All,[9] which has included investments in educational infrastructure,[10] policy changes aimed at prioritising girls' education, and greater efforts by local authorities to ensure children's regular attendance, our research found that most parents agreed that schooling is important for girls as well as boys. Indeed, as reflected in enrolment statistics, it is increasingly common for families to send girls, rather than boys, to school – especially in lowland areas where the latter are engaged in herding and other agricultural activities. As a 14-year-old girl from Kobo reported, '*I live with my father, mother, one sister and two brothers. I am the eldest child for my parents. I am attending school, but my immediate younger brother is not going to school since he is looking after animals*'.

Changes in the patterning of marriage

Our research found that while child marriage remains common enough that girls often defined mid-adolescence as the time when girls marry, overall respondents estimated that marriage has been delayed, from 4–12 years[11] in the previous two generations to 15-plus years in the current generation. Change was markedly different across locations: in the highland regions, respondents reported that girls rarely married under the age of 18; in lowland areas, however, marriage by 15 remains common. Our research also found that overall, even in areas where most girls marry as children, the majority of respondents understood that marriage before the age of 18 is illegal and most agreed that girls should wait until they are 18 to marry. Notably, however, our research also identified a hard upper limit for girls' marriage. Beyond the age of 20, most adults felt that girls were likely to be unmarriageable due to a deficit of eligible men.

Critically, from a girl's perspective, arranged marriages are also becoming less common, which in Amhara[12] is working to prevent the youngest girls from marrying. Although some girls continue to marry strangers of their parents' choosing (see Box 2.2), an increasing number of adolescents and young adults are choosing their own partners – and then asking their parents to 'arrange' the marriage following customary forms. Where previously '*a girl didn't have the right to choose her husband*'

BOX 2.2   UNABATED PARENTAL CONTROL

Although most girls report that it is becoming common for partners to choose each other, arranged marriages are still common. A few girls reported that their father threatened to kill them if they did not do as they were told.

Hirut is 17 years old and from North Gondar. She was forced by her father to drop out of school and get married:

> *I was good at my lessons when I was a grade 7 student, but things were out of my control. . . . I was engaged to a young boy . . . but only found out one year before my wedding ceremony. I was not told directly. As I knew the situation, I reacted to my father, but he told me that he would kill me if I refuse their decision.*

Later, once Hirut and her new husband had moved into their own home, her father took control again. He found out that her young husband had sold the livestock he had given them upon marriage and demanded that they divorce. He threatened them and shot at them with a gun. Hirut left the marriage in fear of her life.

In an attempt to finally gain independence from her father's control, Hirut stole 500 birr from him, escaped her home and migrated across the border to Sudan to begin a new life as a domestic worker: '*I couldn't live here. I planned to commit suicide if I stayed longer here. Later on I decided to go there [Sudan] than dying here. . . . Life became totally meaningless for me*'.

(grandmother), these days, according to young women, *'children do not accept their parents' decision in matters of marriage'* (mothers in focus group discussion), especially if they are better educated than their parents. Indeed, several adolescents in a focus group discussion noted that *'if the daughter's parents refuse to approve the proposed marriage (then) she escapes from the area to a place chosen by her partner'*, meaning that *'parents . . . seldom go against their children's will'*.

What is driving change?

Outside of policy and programming aimed at improving girls' educational outcomes and eliminating child marriage (which will be discussed in greater detail in Chapter 3), there are a variety of macro-, meso- and micro-level factors working to shift the gender norms that keep Amhara girls from realising their full human capabilities.

Education

'An educated girl is expected to lead a country and lead a home' (Father of adolescent girl).

Changes in the availability of schooling – and the environment within schools – have had significant impacts, both on girls' educational outcomes and their odds of child marriage. Whereas impact pathways are many and tangled, in Amhara, girls' increased participation in education is leading to rapid shifts in gender norms.

For example, access to schooling and exposure to successful graduates is feeding girls' aspirations for stable jobs of their own (and parents' aspirations for their daughters). Across the research sites, as more girls are educated at higher levels and take up important positions as local health workers, teachers or government officials, younger girls (and their parents) see those achievements and set their own hopes higher. As one *kebele* (see note 7) manager observed, *'Students who complete grade 10 . . . also become role models for the others following them. So the attitude of the society, especially the youth, has changed to giving attention to education'*. This is helping a small but growing number of girls make the transition to secondary school, with parents firmly behind the idea of an adult marriage. Indeed, in sites where there are university graduates, girls are increasingly interested in pursuing even tertiary education. One female university graduate, for example, said she told girls that *'joining a university is the same as going to heaven'*.

Critically, our research also found that improvements in boys' and men's education are supporting improvements in girls' trajectories. For some girls, having educated brothers or uncles has been key to their remaining unmarried and in school. A 21-year-old university student, for example, told us that when she was forced to leave school to herd cattle for her parents, *'my uncle intervened and urged my father to change his mind'*. Similarly, a 15-year-old girl reported that when her parents were considering marrying her off, *'my brother advised my mother to reject the offer as he wished for me to attend school'*. Her brother now provides *'educational materials like the*

English-Amharic dictionary', which '*motivates me to attend my education seriously*', she explained.

For other girls, shifts in the aspirations of future husbands are driving change, as they further incentivise parents to leave their daughters in school. Respondents agreed that '*men don't want to marry an illiterate girl*', as educated wives are better able to contribute to the household income. Therefore, if a family aspires for an educated husband and son-in-law, it must commit to educating its daughters as well.

Changes within schools are also working to keep more girls in school – and prevent them from getting married. For example, at most schools, teachers increasingly monitor girls' attendance on a day-by-day basis and when they are absent, go to their homes to find out why. Several girls and young women told us they had managed to avoid marriage, and stay in school, because teachers disrupted their parents' plans. Most schools now also run girls' clubs, which sometimes even provide extra tutorial support to help compensate for girls' lack of homework time (discussed later in the chapter). Though many clubs are under-resourced and lack access to the gender-focused curricula that help girls develop voice, most are ensuring that girls know that child marriage is illegal and that teachers and *kebele* leaders will support them to refuse it. As a result, girls increasingly know where to turn for help when they wish to report a planned marriage – either their own or a friend's – albeit often at the risk of significant cost to themselves. One 15-year-old girl explained, '*My parents attempted to get me married, but I rescued myself by reporting the case to the local kebele administration. As a result, my father was sent to prison for two days*'.

Rights-based discourses embedded in school curricula are also driving changes in gender norms. Shifts were especially apparent in interviews with boys and young men. Though most reported that the proverb '*women to the kitchen, men to the court*' continues to resonate with local realities, a surprising number supported more gender-equitable relationships. One 16-year-old boy, for example, told us that '*discrimination in terms of responsibilities should be stopped and there should be cooperation in all of the jobs among women and men*'. Similarly, a young married man reported that he and his wife make all decisions jointly: '*We both discuss the issue and arrive at a decision that satisfies both of us*'. Girls were also increasingly aware of their rights. Though norms dictating obedience kept many girls quiet, as already noted, a growing number are refusing to leave school and submit to an unwanted marriage – even when it means their parents go to jail.

Land fragmentation

For most girls, increasing land fragmentation, driven by explosive population growth, has worked to simultaneously encourage education and discourage child marriage. As Rahmato (2013: 126) notes, 'family holdings are not just small but getting smaller' and are 'increasingly fragmented', with many families already subsisting on 'micro-plots' (see also Bezu and Holden 2014). Our research found that because of this, parents increasingly understand the value of an education that will allow their children greater access to the cash economy and a more stable income.

Also, because parents have traditionally gifted young couples with land as a wedding present, many parents prefer to delay their daughters' marriages so that they can hold on to their land for longer. A recent shift towards smaller families, also driven by land fragmentation, is further working to reduce the pressure on girls to marry as children, as early pregnancy is increasingly associated with high fertility and seen as unsustainable.

On the other hand, for girls with access to their own land, now or in the future, land fragmentation is working to encourage child marriage.[13] Respondents reported that for '*daughters of the rich . . . there would be competition to marry her. As a result, she might be betrothed even while she was just a baby*' (father) (with strict rules on sexual contact, see Box 2.3). Girls with no land, they noted, are unlikely to marry as children. Girls who have already inherited land or other assets are especially likely to marry as children, because it is felt that they are incapable of managing their own assets and need a husband to work on the land. One girl in a focus group discussion, for example, told us that when she inherited land she first rented it out and continued her education. However, with a queue of young men interested in marriage, she was pressured by her family into leaving school in order to acquire a husband.

Contraception

Improved access to contraception is also supporting girls' access to school and, for some, helping them remain unmarried. Our research found that most girls had some degree of information about reproductive health, mostly gleaned from school textbooks as well as from health extension workers (present in every community), health centre staff, school clubs, non-governmental organisations (NGOs) and (in a few cases) their mothers. They also, in most *kebeles*, had good access to free contraception, regardless of their age, marital status or husbands' approval.

Whereas in the past girls were expected to have children as soon after marriage as possible, as '*an infertile woman can't have a home*' (father), today most of the married girls we interviewed agreed that couples are choosing to use contraception to delay first pregnancies until they are more financially secure. Given that land

---

BOX 2.3 INFORMAL PROTECTION MECHANISMS FOR CHILD BRIDES

Gaido is a traditional contract between families in the Gojjam area that protects young wives from sex and pregnancy. It mandates that husbands will not have sex with their wives, even when they live in the same household, until the girl is mature – usually around the age of 15 – and specifies fines and other punishments for abrogation. Historically, these were oral contracts but they are increasingly taking written form.

fragmentation has left many young couples with little land of their own, girls and young women told us their husbands are mostly supportive of contraception – with some even seeing it as a way to support their wives' continued school attendance.

Although premarital sexual relations are comparatively uncommon in Amhara, owing to the heavy emphasis on girls' sexual purity (discussed later in the chapter), for some unmarried girls it appears that access to contraception is allowing them to remain unmarried, as it prevents the pregnancies that would necessitate an immediate marriage. Girls reported that contraception was freely available from the age of 13.

Divorce

Improved access to divorce for girls and women is also working to keep girls in school and to mitigate the impacts of child marriage. Though divorce in Amhara has long been common, with up to 45 per cent of all first marriages culminating in divorce (Tilson and Larsen 2000) and some women respondents in our research having been divorced three or four times, there is a growing realisation that child marriages are especially likely to end in divorce – and poverty – because the young girls '*lack maturity*' and have traditionally had '*no choice*' (grandmother). Girls told us that as a consequence of shifting attitudes, it is easier for them to convince their parents to delay arranging a marriage and simpler to '*insist on divorce*' and enlist the help of '*the elderly people who were our witnesses when we made our marriage*' to divorce quickly in the event of abuse (30-year-old divorced woman).

Girls also told us they used divorce as a tool to secure their futures. Some, for example, chose to marry in mid-adolescence and divorce immediately, so that they would have fewer restrictions on their mobility. Others, usually those married as young children, told us they had initiated a divorce in early adolescence, when they might otherwise be expected to move in with their husbands, so that they could stay in school.

What is maintaining stasis?

Despite progress on many fronts, our research found that gendered norms which emphasise girls' sexual purity – and make them responsible for helping their mothers to shoulder the burden of domestic and care work – are keeping most adolescent girls from the futures they would like to have.

Sexual purity

The notion of sexual purity is key to understanding the limits placed on Amhara girls' lives. It drives child marriage, forces girls to leave school, keeps them confined to home and shapes the expectations placed on them from early childhood. Many parents – and girls, too – are deeply worried that if girls' reputations become sullied, then their options for marriage will shrink. In a world where marriage is the best way to ensure girls' economic security, and a premarital pregnancy can preclude a good marriage, this is a potent fear that fundamentally situates child marriage as a form of protection.

> *If a girl was to be pregnant before marriage, her parents 'would say that she has to leave the house or they would kill her. She might not have been pregnant voluntarily. But the people of the village always assume that she did it voluntarily'.*
>
> *(Adolescent girl)*

Even more important, however, is the reality that girls' reputations are central to their families' social status. This drives parents – some of whom mistakenly believe that menstruation is caused by sex – to insist that their daughters are married off before puberty. Most girls, carefully socialised to be obedient and submissive, do as they are told, which includes lying to officials about their age when asked if they are old enough to legally marry. They know that '*the community considers girls that disobey their parents as rude and immoral*'. Girls who push back and refuse to accept a child marriage risk being seen by their parents as '*the enemy*' of the family and mercilessly harassed. A 14-year-old reported of her same-aged friend, whose parents made her lie about her age: '*I know a girl who married, claiming that she was 18 years old*'. She continued, '*The parents of the girl are very strict. If somebody tells them they saw her with a boy, they beat her. When the marriage proposal came she agreed to it because she wanted to be free from all the pressure they put her in*'.

Traditionally, unmarried adolescent girls have been subject to a variety of insults. Some have been called '*kumoker*', which translates to 'unworthy of marriage' or 'still standing'. This insult is rooted in the notion that girls are waiting for a husband to propose to them and that if they are single then it must be because they are unwanted. Other unmarried girls, particularly those who are seen in public with boys – even at school – are called '*shermuta*' (whore). One adolescent girl told us: '*Before I married, there were some boys who used to insult and throw stones at me. Now, nobody does that to me*'.

In addition to worrying that their daughters will find boyfriends, parents (and girls) are also worried about rape. Many reported that they saw child marriage – or at least child betrothal – as a way of protecting their daughters, as girls who 'belong' to other men are believed to be less vulnerable (and especially because rape after marriage has less dire consequences culturally). Some girls told us they did '*not experience sexual abuse before marriage because I married early*' and others reported that '*engagement rings make them less vulnerable . . . because she already had someone else*'. Most agreed that despite recent improvements, rape remains a real risk, especially when girls are sent to '*fetch water and collect firewood*', but also at school, where teachers can heavily '*pressurise*' girls to have sex.

Whereas in some *kebeles*, religious leaders strongly condemn child marriage – and refuse to officiate if the girl is under 18 – in others, the importance of girls' sexual purity to religion means that religious leaders are especially likely to seek child brides themselves. Because it is seen as vital for deacons to marry girls who are virgins, it is widely believed that '*if a girl's leg touches the ground when she sits on a chair, she is ready for marriage'.* According to one priest, this means that most deacons marry girls aged no older than 16, and often considerably younger.

'Idleness' and work

Noting that Amhara girls are rarely given the opportunity to be 'idle' (see Box 2.4.), marriage is seen as particularly important when girls have left school, because their parents and the wider community perceive girls to be 'waiting for trouble' and likely to engage in illicit relationships that would cost them their virginity and destroy their family's reputation. Although girls are increasingly likely to attend school, and stay in school longer than boys, many children from poorer households drop out of primary school due to opportunity costs and being unable to afford school supplies, while secondary school remains out of reach for most girls. Regardless of when they leave school, it is 'idle' girls who are at highest risk of child marriage – whether to placate their parents or escape them.

BOX 2.4   GIRLS' WORK

In our community, most of the family work burden falls on girls, though some school-attending 'good' boys are willing to share their school-attending sisters' work burden at home. When girls are getting the chance to attend school, their academic performance is lower than that of boys since girls do not have sufficient time to do school-related activities or to study at home like their brothers because when a female student returns home from class, a lot of work is awaiting for her.

(School-attending younger adolescent girls' focus group discussion, Kelala)

I am not attending my schooling properly. I am in grade 7. I am busy doing cooking food, feeding these children and doing other tasks in the house. Bearing such a responsibility at this age is a big problem.

(14-year-old girl, Kelala)

I dropped out from grade 6 because of the work burden at my parents' home. My main duties include cleaning the house, looking after my younger sister, taking care of my aged grandparents and sick uncle, fetching water, collecting firewood and cow dung for fuel, weeding and gathering sorghum heads, taking lunch for my father when he works on the farm. I also support my elder brother in running his tea shop.

(15-year-old girl, Kobo)

Girls' school-leaving is often driven by academic failure that is frequently related to their heavy work burdens, as both their attendance and their focus are compromised because they must support their mothers' agricultural, domestic and care work. Mothers in our research, even those who were members of the Women's Association, were clear that when their daughters came home from school they were not allowed to '*sit with a book*'; after '*a whole day in school*' they were instead expected to '*start work*'. Adolescent boys, however, reported that they were comparatively immune from these expectations. They observed that while they were allowed to focus on homework, their sisters were '*unable to study . . . because there were many things to manage at home*'.

In Ethiopia, as girls progress through school, access gets more difficult. Children must sit national exams at the end of 8th, 10th and 12th grades in order to continue in school. Rural children are rarely well prepared for these exams. Indeed, some evidence suggests that rural children's learning outcomes have actually fallen in recent years in tandem with burgeoning enrolment (Woldehanna and Pankhurst 2014). Exam failure rates are consequently high – especially, as noted earlier, for girls at secondary level.

The cost of school also makes it challenging for girls to progress to and through secondary school. Unlike primary school, which has no tuition fees, the registration fee for 9th and 10th grades is 100 birr. Furthermore, as most *kebeles* have only primary schools, secondary students must either travel long distances each day or rent lodging closer to school – something few rural families can afford. Girls are often perceived as an especially poor family investment since they are expected to leave home and become part of their husbands' families. The only option for many is, as one 18-year-old young man studying in 9th grade observed, for '*students to be engaged in daily labour for one year and earn money so that they can go to secondary school the next year*'. Even this is increasingly difficult for most families though. With high rates of youth unemployment, even for students who have completed 10th or 12th grade, '*the community lacks hope in formal education*' (15-year-old girl).

> *Parents believe that boys could get government employment when they complete a higher level of education, that is contrary to their expectation of girls' education. Some parents tend to think that education will not take girls anywhere.*
>
> *(Married, out-of-school girl)*

However, even more important, from the parents' perspective, is the fact that secondary school attendance exposes adolescent girls to risks that are mitigated by keeping them close to home. Where girls must walk long distances to school, they are at risk of rape. Similarly, where girls must live away from their families, they are inadequately supervised. Parents in all of our study areas expressed reluctance to consider secondary school for their daughter because they were concerned for their '*safety*' and '*virtue*'. Indeed, reported one girl, '*The absence of a high school in Metema Yohanes has become a cause for early marriage*'. She explained, '*Had there been a school in the kebele, girls could have continued their education under the strict follow-up of their parents'.*

Outside of migration (see Box 2.5), which provides an increasing number of girls with access to their own incomes, our research found that rural girls have few remunerative opportunities, leaving them with little ability to refuse marriage. Adolescents reported that while their parents and other relatives often gifted them with livestock, boys are far more likely to keep theirs, as they are better able to negotiate

---

BOX 2.5 MIGRATION

Migration is a widespread phenomenon in Amhara. Until autumn 2014, when international migration was outlawed (due to persistent human rights abuses of migrants), it was common for adolescent girls to migrate, within the country or to the Middle East, primarily to undertake domestic service. Girls as young as 13 migrate, often after either completing primary school – or failing their 10th-grade exams (discussed in more detail later) (Jones *et al.* 2014).

The impact of migration on girls' educational trajectories and marriage patterns is highly variable. In some communities, especially those that are largely Ethiopian Orthodox Christian, migration is working to prevent child marriage. It not only offers migrants themselves an alternative to marriage, as it enables them to earn their own income, but it affords older sisters the economic independence that allows them to protect their younger sisters. One adolescent girl, for example, told us that when her parents tried to arrange her marriage, in 5th grade, *'My sister objected to the idea of marriage and took me with her. I stayed with my sister until I completed my elementary education'*. Furthermore, because migrant girls' remittances would go to their husbands if they are married – but their parents if they are unmarried – increased migration has tended to reduce parents' zeal for child marriage.

In other, predominantly Muslim communities, migration emerged as a primary driver of child marriage. Some parents reported that because married girls are perceived to be less vulnerable to rape, they preferred to marry their daughters before they allowed them to migrate. Other parents told us that marriage was a necessary precursor to migration because it guaranteed that their daughters were 'deflowered' in the context of marriage – meaning that if they were raped, it would have fewer ramifications for their purity.

For some girls, migration serves as a route out of an unwanted or abusive marriage. Several adolescents mentioned acquaintances who had migrated to other areas in order to end their marriages (see also Erulkar and Mekbib 2007; Erulkar *et al.* 2010). Research with migrant girls in Ethiopia's cities has found that some flee marriage only to end up as sex workers (Van Blerk 2008; Girma and Erulkar 2009).

with their parents in times of financial stress. Livestock gifted to girls, on the other hand, is often among the first assets liquidated by parents as a coping mechanism.

Economics

In some cases, gender norms are being supported by economic drivers. As already noted, in the case of land-holding girls, their relative wealth can result in school-leaving and child marriage, as they find themselves in demand in the local marriage market. For poorer girls, on the other hand, marriage into a better-off family can be a route to a more secure future with '*land and cattle*' (17-year-old girl married at 13). A *kebele* manager, for example, reported that '*Men who have money lure poor girls into marriage*'.

Marriage can often be a coping mechanism that helps impoverished households withstand shocks, because it means that '*my parents have less mouths to feed*' – and, in some cases, brings in bride price (married 15-year-old girl). However, we found that increasingly, in a context of growing scarcity of land, girls who do not stand to inherit land are less likely to marry young and may instead leave school to engage in paid domestic work in rural towns or larger urban centres, either in Ethiopia or abroad. In a minority of cases, our research also found that child marriage can be a way of acquiring an adult man's labour for households that have experienced paternal death. Given the land fragmentation discussed earlier, landless young men can find it advantageous to marry into a family with land, even if it means taking on the bulk of agricultural labour work – either instead of or with a girl's father.

Backlash

Our research uncovered evidence of a backlash that is slowing norm change. Some respondents were highly critical of the focus on 'rights', claiming that the discourse was '*eroding tradition*', encouraging disobedience, and resulting in confusion and tensions across generations and among the genders. One father, for example, explained, '*Currently, the students claim everything that it is their democratic right. . . . They misuse their rights to their disadvantage and to the disadvantage of their parents and the community*'. Girls with more traditional attitudes agreed that rights-based slogans – which students must parrot back in class and which are broadcast over loudspeakers during school breaks – are sowing dissent. One married in-school girl, who had clearly benefited from recent programming, told us that rights-based education was not supporting girls' well-being because '*it is after the coming of the notion of equality that people stopped respecting each other*'.

Overall, though we found no evidence that this backlash was keeping girls out of school, it did appear to be driving some child marriages underground. With laws and community discourse alike discouraging the practice, parents determined to uphold tradition either forced their daughters to lie about their age so that they could be publicly married, or arranged 'secret' marriages under the guise of religious or community festivals.

Conclusions and policy implications

Ethiopia has made tremendous progress recently in enhancing women's and girls' rights. Largely the result of improved access to education, contraception and divorce, the gender norms that restrict adolescent girls' lives are evidencing significant shifts. Girls in Amhara are now more likely to attend school than their male peers and the rates of child marriage and arranged marriage are in rapid decline. That said, our research reveals that the trajectories of many girls – particularly those from the poorest and more remote rural households – continue to be truncated by repressive gender norms that burden them with too much work, leading to high rates of exam failure, and see their virginity as a symbol of girls' worth to their families. In the case of better-off girls in rural areas – especially now that women are able to inherit land – child marriage remains a key vulnerability in the context of increasing land fragmentation and population growth.

To continue to improve girls' trajectories, Ethiopia must invest in policy and programming that helps girls and boys, and men and women, to more equitably share both domestic work and opportunities for schooling and paid employment. Interventions might include more investment in educational infrastructure at the secondary school level, in-kind support or tuition subsidies for girls' schooling or free boarding facilities so that girls could safely attend secondary school without fear of sexual harassment or rape. Evidence also suggests, given the centrality of girls' sexual purity to community respect, that it will be necessary to directly address the discriminatory norms which leave young girls vulnerable to stigma and abuse when they choose to delay marriage until adulthood. Given evidence that pervasive rights-oriented campaigns may encourage stealth and backlash, our findings suggest the importance of government investments in supporting local role models and facilitating the community conversations that foster local ownership of new ideas. By working with community and religious leaders, and investing in the girls and women already positioned to demonstrate alternatives to child marriage, we believe that it is possible to capitalise on the norm shifts already seen in girls' education to further shift the norms surrounding girls' sexuality and broader value.

Notes

1 The Revised Family Code of 2000 set the minimum age of marriage at 18.
2 The Revised Penal Code of 2005 calls for both fines and jail terms – they vary by the age of the girl and by the perpetrator's role in the marriage. For example, men who marry girls under the age of 13 are subject to jail terms of up to seven years, while men who victimise girls between the ages of 13 and 18 face maximum terms of three years. Officiators of child marriage are also subject to terms of up to three years (see www.wipo.int/edocs/lexdocs/laws/en/et/et011en.pdf).
3 The full survey included more than 5,000 girls and young women aged 12–24 and seven of the country's nine regions.
4 Within Amhara, gross enrolment rates for the poorest quintile are up to 30 per cent lower than those of the wealthiest quintile (World Bank 2005). Nationally, the wealthiest girls are 1.3 times more likely to attend school than those from middle-income families (Gurmu and Etana 2013).

5 Between 2012 and 2014.
6 Just over 80 per cent of Amhara people are Orthodox; the rest are almost entirely Muslim.
7 A *woreda* is a 'district' level administrative area. There are four layers of government administration in Ethiopia: region, zone, *woreda* and *kebele* (ward).
8 We also wanted to ensure complementarities rather than overlap with a good practice mapping exercise we undertook for UNICEF Ethiopia – see Jones, Tefera, Presler-Marshall *et al.* 2016.
9 Education for All is a global movement, spearheaded by the United Nations Educational, Scientific and Cultural Organization (UNESCO), which aimed to meet the educational needs of all children and adults by 2015.
10 The government has built more than 1,000 new primary schools in Amhara alone in the past five years; it has also built more than 100 new secondary schools.
11 There is tremendous diversity in marriage customs, even within Amhara. Girls are sometimes raised by their own parents and do not move in with their husbands until puberty. Other girls are raised by their in-laws as if they were their own biological daughters.
12 Recent research in other regions found that free choice marriage may be increasing the odds of young adolescent marriage, with Oromo girls as young as 13 'choosing' to marry their 'first love' without their parents' permission (see Jones, Tefera, Presler-Marshall *et al.* 2016; Jones, Tefera, Emirie *et al.* 2016).
13 While land in Ethiopia is held by the national government (per the 1995 Constitution), women's legal access is equal to that of men. Since the 2003 Land Use Proclamation, land use certificates have been issued jointly to both husbands and wives and documentation has included photos of both partners. Amhara's institutional capacity in regard to land certification is considered among the strongest – about 52 per cent of land holdings are jointly titled, 27 per cent are registered to women and 21 per cent to men (International Fund for Agricultural Development (IFAD) 2013; UN 2013; Girma and Giovarelli 2013).

Bibliography

Bezu, S. and Holden, S. (2014) 'Are Rural Youth in Ethiopia Abandoning Agriculture?' *World Development* 64: 259–272.

Boudet, A., Petesch, P., Turk, C. and Thumala, A. (2012) *On Norms and Agency: Conversations about Gender Equality with Women and Men in 20 Countries*. Washington, DC: World Bank.

Central Statistical Agency (CSA). (2014) *Key Findings on the 2013 National Labour Force Survey*. Addis Ababa: CSA.

Central Statistical Agency (CSA) and ICF International. (2012) *Ethiopia Demographic and Health Survey 2011*. Addis Ababa and Calverton, Maryland: CSA and ICF International. Maryland. Available online at http://dhsprogram.com/pubs/pdf/FR255/FR255.pdf

Erulkar, A. (2013) 'Early Marriage, Marital Relations and Intimate Partner Violence in Ethiopia' *International Perspectives on Sexual and Reproductive Health* 39(1): 6–13. Available online at www.guttmacher.org/pubs/journals/3900613.html

Erulkar, A., Ferede, A., Ambelu, W., Girma, W., Amdemikael, H., GebreMedhin, B., Legesse, B., Tameru, A. and Teferi, M. (2010) *Ethiopia Young Adult Survey: A Study in Seven Regions*. Addis Ababa: Population Council.

Erulkar, A. and Mekbib, T. (2007) 'Invisible and Vulnerable: Adolescent Domestic Workers in Addis Ababa, Ethiopia' *Vulnerable Children and Youth Studies* 2(3): 246–256.

Girma, H. and Giovarelli, R. (2013) *Lesson 2: The Gender Implications of Joint Titling in Ethiopia*. Focus on Land in Africa. Available online at www.globalprotectioncluster.org/_assets/files/field_protection_clusters/Etiophia/files/HLP%20AoR/Ethiopia_Brief_Gender_Implications_Joint_Land_Titling_2013_EN.pdf

Girma, W. and Erulkar, A. (2009) *Commercial Sex Workers in Five Ethiopian Cities: A Baseline Survey for USAID Targeted HIV Prevention Program for Most-at-risk Populations*. Addis Ababa: Population Council.

Gurmu, E. and Etana, D. (2013) 'Socio-economic and Demographic Determinants of Children's Primary School Enrolment in Ethiopia' *Eastern Africa Social Science Research Review* 29(1): 1–30.

International Center for Research on Women (ICRW). (2015) *Child Marriage Facts and Figures.* Available online at www.icrw.org/child-marriage-facts-and-figures

International Fund for Agricultural Development (IFAD). (2013) *Strengthening Women's Access to Land in Ethiopia.* Available online at www.itacaddis.org/docs/2013_09_24_08_25_22_WomenAndLand_Ethiopia_FactSheet.pdf

International Labour Organization (ILO). (2013) *Decent Work Country Profile: Ethiopia.* Geneva International Labour Office. Available online at http://www.ilo.org/wcmsp5/groups/public/---dgreports/---integration/documents/publication/wcms_237881.pdf

Jones, N., Presler-Marshall, E. and Tefera, B. (2014) *Rethinking the 'Maid Trade': Experiences of Ethiopian Adolescent Domestic Workers in the Middle East.* London: Overseas Development Institute. Available online at www.odi.org/publications/9045-rethinking-maid-trade-experiences-ethiopian-adolescent-domestic-workers-middle-east

Jones, N., Tefera, B., Emirie, G., Gebre, B., Berhanu, K., Presler-Marshall, E., Walker, D., Gupta, T. and Plank, G. (2016) *One Size Does Not Fit All: The Patterning and Drivers of Child Marriage in Ethiopia's Hotspot Districts.* London: Overseas Development Institute. Available online at www.unicef.org/ethiopia/Hotspots.pdf

Jones, N., Tefera, B., Presler-Marshall, E., Gupta, T., Emirie, G., Gebre, B. and Berhanu, K. (2016) *What Works to Tackle Child Marriage in Ethiopia: A Review of Good Practice.* London: Overseas Development Institute. Available online at www.odi.org/publications/10453-what-works-tackle-child-marriage-ethiopia-review-good-practice

Ministry of Education. (2014) *Education Statistics Annual Abstract 2005 E.C. (2012/2013).* Addis Ababa: Ministry of Education.

Ministry of Education. (2015) *Education Statistics Annual Abstract 2006 E.C. (2013/2014).* Addis Ababa: Ministry of Education.

Rahmato, D. (2013) 'Food Security and Safety Nets: Assessment and Challenges' in D. Rahmato, A. Pankhurst and J. van Uffelen (eds.) *Food Security, Safety Nets and Social Protection in Ethiopia.* Oxford: African Books Collective, 111–144.

Social Institutions and Gender Index (SIGI). (2015) *Ethiopia.* Available online at http://genderindex.org/country/ethiopia

Tilson, D. and Larsen, U. (2000) 'Divorce in Ethiopia: The Impact of Early Marriage and Childlessness' *Journal of Biosocial Science* 32(3): 355–372.

United Nations (UN). (2013) *Realizing Women's Rights to Land and Other Productive Resources.* New York, Geneva: United Nations. Available online at www.ohchr.org/Documents/Publications/RealizingWomensRightstoLand.pdf

United Nations Development Programme (UNDP). (2013) *Human Development Report 2013. The Rise of the South: Human Progress in a Diverse World.* New York: United Nations Development Programme. Available online at http://hdr.undp.org/en/2013-report

United Nations Development Programme (UNDP). (2015a) *National Human Development Report 2014 Ethiopia: Accelerating Inclusive Growth for Sustainable Human Development in Ethiopia.* Addis Ababa: United Nations Development Programme. Available online at http://hdr.undp.org/sites/default/files/nhdr2015-ethiopia-en.pdf

United Nations Development Programme (UNDP). (2015b) *Gender Inequality Index.* Available online at http://hdr.undp.org/en/content/table-4-gender-inequality-index

United Nations Population Fund (UNFPA). (2012) *Marrying Too Young: End Child Marriage.* New York: United Nations Population Fund. Available online at www.unfpa.org/sites/default/files/pub-pdf/MarryingTooYoung.pdf

Van Blerk, L. (2008) 'Poverty, Migration and Sex Work: Youth Transitions in Ethiopia' *Area* 40(2): 245–253.

Woldehanna, T. and Pankhurst, A. (2014) *Education and Learning: Preliminary Findings from Round 4 in Ethiopia*. Oxford and Addis Ababa: Young Lives. Available online at www.younglives.org.uk/publications/CR/preliminary-findings-from-round-4-ethiopia/education-and-learning-ethiopia-round-4

World Bank. (2005) *Education in Ethiopia: Strengthening the Foundation for Sustainable Progress Country Study*. Washington, DC: World Bank. Available online at http://documents.world bank.org/curated/en/488571468255255324/Education-in-Ethiopia-Strengthening-the-foundation-for-sustainable-progress

World Bank. (2015) *Data*. Available online at http://data.worldbank.org/

3

THE POLITICS OF POLICY AND PROGRAMME IMPLEMENTATION TO ADVANCE ADOLESCENT GIRLS' WELL-BEING IN ETHIOPIA

Nicola Jones, Elizabeth Presler-Marshall,
Bekele Tefera and Bethelihem Gebre Alwab

Introduction

Ethiopia has seen significant progress with regard to legislation and policy to promote girls' and women's well-being and empowerment in recent decades. Gender equality and women's empowerment have been on the agenda of the Federal Government of Ethiopia since it came to power in the early 1990s. This is reflected in the incorporation of women's rights and child protection issues in the 1994 Constitution of the Federal Democratic Republic of Ethiopia and the development of the 1993 Ethiopian Women's Policy, which aims to streamline gender into all government sectors and give women special emphasis in health, education and social welfare programming.

In the case of policies and programmes to advance the well-being of adolescent girls specifically, the government has made significant strides over the past two decades in narrowing the gender gap in education (especially at primary level) and in establishing health extension services down to *kebele* (village) level, which provide girls and women alike with free sexual and reproductive health services (Ministry of Education 2015; Ministry of Health 2015; UNESCO 2015). More recently, the government included a high-level commitment to eradicate harmful traditional practices (HTPs) in its Second Growth and Transformation Plan and has established, with development partners and non-governmental organisations (NGOs), a National Alliance to End Child Marriage and FGM by 2025.

These important steps notwithstanding, the extent to which these national-level commitments and programmes are making a difference in the lives of adolescent girls is uneven at best. Part of the problem is the 'stickiness' of gender norms (see Chapter 2). Equally important are the complex political economy dynamics surrounding the implementation of policies and programmes for adolescent girls. We begin this chapter by outlining our political economy approach, which draws

heavily on Rosendorff's (2005) 'Three I's' approach of 'institutions, ideas and interests', and providing a brief discussion of the key contours of the Ethiopian political
and governance context. Next, using findings from three years of primary research
in eight districts in three zones of Amhara Regional State (see Figure 2.1), we
apply the 'Three I's' framework to Amhara girls' situation. Our discussion reflects
in particular on the extent to which social communication initiatives have been
able to negotiate these political economy dynamics. The chapter concludes with a
discussion on what will be needed if change interventions for adolescent girls are
to have maximum traction in what is increasingly a challenging political economy
environment.

The 'Three I's' political economy framework

Women and girls worldwide do not share equal social and economic rights with
men and boys, nor do they have the same access to productive resources. Gendered
political economy approaches examine the material basis of relationships that govern the gender unequal distribution of resources, benefits, privileges and authority
within societies (True 2012; Holmes and Jones 2013). In this chapter we focus on
the ways in which power relations affect adolescent girls' ability to realise their full
human capabilities and, more specifically, how they shape their vulnerability to a
curtailed education and to child marriage. In order to explore these dynamics, we
draw on Rosendorff's (2005) 'Three I's':

*   **Institutions** – both formal and informal – (e.g. elections and party politics, the
    legislature, the judiciary, community-level religious and traditional decision-
    making structures) and how they facilitate, or present opportunities for or
    constraints to addressing adolescent girls' capability deprivations.
*   **Ideas** held by elites and the public regarding gender roles and social norms,
    and the acceptability of different forms of gender discrimination faced by ado-
    lescent girls vis-à-vis their male peers.
*   **Interests** of key actors who are likely to gain or lose from shifts in policy, prac-
    tice or behaviour (e.g. political elites, community leaders, civil society champi-
    ons, heads of household) related to adolescent girls' roles and opportunities and
    the relative balance of power between them. These same interests can result in
    backlash or co-option of efforts to provide redress (True 2012).

Ethiopian context

National governance contours

The Federal Democratic Republic of Ethiopia has been governed by the Ethiopian People's Revolutionary Democratic Front (EPRDF) since 1995. The EPRDF
has promoted a policy of ethnic federalism, dividing the country into nine semi-
autonomous regions and two chartered cities, meaning there are four layers of

sub-national government administration: region, zone, district (*woreda*) and ward (*kebele*). While in theory there is considerable decentralisation, in practice this is more limited, especially in recent years (Abbink 2010).

The importance of local variation

National- and regional-level statistics highlight the country's low standing in terms of gender equality, high poverty levels, the strength of its recent economic growth, its relatively flat income structure and the highly pyramidal age structure of its population (see Chapter 2). This picture, however, misses the local-level variation that shapes girls' lives. The eight research sites in which we worked are very different from one another – even though they are all in Amhara Regional State. Some are almost entirely Muslim (Kelala and Worebabo), whereas others are predominantly Ethiopian Orthodox (Yilmana Densa and Metema Yohanes). Some are drought prone and food insecure (Habru and Kobo), whereas others are food secure (Woreilu and Merhabete). Metema and Woreilu are relatively urban, whereas Kelala and Worebabo are very rural. Merhabete and Habru are recognised as hotspots for child marriage; Worebabo and Woreilu are recognised as hotspots for girls' migration. Not surprisingly, our research – which included an assessment of social communication programming in three *woredas* (see Box 3.1) – found that understanding

---

BOX 3.1 COMMUNICATION PROGRAMMES AIMED AT SHIFTING DISCRIMINATORY SOCIAL NORMS HINDERING AMHARAN ADOLESCENT GIRLS' CAPABILITY DEVELOPMENT

Of the three communication programmes we assessed, two were broadly aimed at improving girls' sexual and reproductive health (SRH) practices. The first, implemented by Hiwot Ethiopia in Merhabete *woreda*, includes a community dialogue initiative designed to sensitise communities to the risks of child marriage and early and closely spaced pregnancies. It works with girls to improve their access to and utilisation of SRH services; with providers to encourage the provision of youth-friendly services; and with community leaders to build support for delayed marriage and continuing education.

The second programme we assessed, implemented by the Amhara Development Association (ADA) in Woreilu *woreda*, relies primarily on girls' clubs and a menstrual management scheme – both of which endeavour to keep girls in school and thereby delay marriage and motherhood. The programme works at three levels: empowering individual girls with life-skills training; helping schools to better identify and meet the needs of female students; and working with communities to create environments which support girls to stay in school.

The third programme was the Department for International Development (DFID)/Girl Hub-funded social marketing initiative Yegna and its community radio component, focused on outcome differences in two *woreda*s: rural Habru and more urban Yilmana Densa. Yegna is a serial drama that was designed to create role models and highlight relevant social issues for girls in order to stimulate discussion in communities and create a safe, informed and inspiring conversation about the value of girls. The ultimate goal is for radio programming to be paired with group activities so that girls can listen together in school-based clubs or with their caregivers in community safe spaces. But this is yet to be realised in some of the more rural areas.

differences in local contexts can be key to understanding the specific vulnerabilities facing girls – and shaping programming to address them.

The 'Three I's' framework as applied to adolescent programming in Ethiopia

Institutions

The first of Rosendorff's 'Three I's' is 'institutions'. This focuses on how institutions and institutional arenas create or restrict opportunities for change. In Ethiopia, and in many ways especially in Amhara, government institutions are largely driving change for adolescent girls. Top-down policy in regard to gender, education and health is overall quite favourable and commitment on behalf of the federal government to ending child marriage is strong. On the other hand, implementation is limited by poor data and inadequate fiscal space, and national law has significantly restricted the engagement of NGOs who have often been key catalysts for change at the community level. Moreover, the regional government has not taken decisive action in order to tackle the ways in which migration is truncating some girls' schooling and limiting their longer-term capabilities.

Institutional strengths

Gender inequality

Ethiopia's poor standing on international gender indices notwithstanding, gender equality is enshrined in the Ethiopian Constitution. Article 35 provides women with rights and protections equal to those of men and specifically covers women's right to equality in marriage, to property (with an emphasis on land and inheritance issues) and to equal employment. The Ministry of Women, Children and Youth Affairs[1] is tasked with 'gender mainstreaming in sector and development programs, advocacy and capacity-building initiatives' (Ministry of Health 2015: 19) and has recently developed a framework for engaging men and boys on gender issues. Furthermore, the ministries of Health, Education and Justice each have gender units, and Ethiopia's Second Growth and Transformation Plan, finalised in late 2015, identifies gender equality as a multi-sectoral, cross-cutting issue.

The Amhara Region's Five-Year Strategic Plans, which have focused mainly on promoting economic growth in the region, have maintained for more than a decade that unleashing the potential of women is central (Bureau of Finance and Economic Development 2006). This is broadly reflected across *kebeles*, where adolescents and parents increasingly report – and, in the case of girls, genuinely believe – that '*educating a girl is educating a country*'. It can also be seen in the way that Amhara has made SRH services (including contraception) freely available to adolescent girls.

Child marriage

Ethiopia evidences a great deal of institutional commitment to eliminating child marriage. For example, the revised Federal Family Code sets the minimum age for marriage at 18 years for both sexes (Article 7) and has done away with betrothal, which would lead to the creation of an alliance between families when children are young. In addition, the 2005 Criminal Code stipulates penalties for violators, including fines and jail terms.

As noted in Chapter 2, recent progress towards eliminating child marriage appears, from the limited data available,[2] to be impressive. The 2011 Demographic and Health Survey (DHS), for example, found that the proportion of young women aged 15–19 who had been married by the age of 15 was less than half that of their slightly older peers (8 per cent compared to 16.3 per cent for young women aged 20–24) (Central Statistical Agency (CSA) and ICF International 2012). The rate of marriage by age 18 is also falling, though not as steeply. Whereas 56.2 per cent of women aged 25–29 were married by age 18, only 41 per cent of women aged 20–24 were married by 18 (ibid.).

Our research in Amhara suggests that although the region is best known for having the lowest average age of first marriage in the country (15.1 for women aged 20–49), the upcoming DHS and census are likely to find that progress in the region has been especially rapid, particularly for the youngest girls. Indeed, the Finote Hiwot End Child Marriage programme, in Amhara's East and West Gojjam zones, had to revise its targets downward to account for existent trends.[3] Whereas it initially aimed to prevent 200,000 child marriages, current targets call for 37,500 (DFID 2014). In addition to acknowledging the impact of NGO programming on child marriage rates, local informants attribute Amhara's recent success to improvement in girls' education, the efforts of health extension workers and the near-total penetration of the Women's Development Army (discussed on page 69).

Education

Given that Ethiopia remains one of the world's poorest countries, the speed with which it has scaled up educational opportunities is laudable. A regional-level informant explained, '*Access has improved very fast since 1991*,[4] *when the current government took power*'. In just the past five years, for example, the government has built 5,000 primary schools (there are now more than 32,000), 1,000 secondary schools (there are now more than 2,300) and 900 Technical and Vocational Education and Training (TVET) centres (there are now about 1,300) (Ministry of Education 2015). Enrolment has exploded, especially at the primary level, and while most Ethiopian women (nearly two-thirds) are illiterate, their daughters are increasingly on track for a brighter future. UNESCO reports that only 16.4 per cent of primary-aged Ethiopian girls are now out of school – a rate substantially lower than in several other low-income sub-Saharan countries[5] (2016) – and that the net intake rate of 7-year-olds has approached 100 per cent (2015).

Mindful of the fact that girls' primary graduation rates remain low (32.8 per cent as reported by UNESCO 2015[6]), and their transition to secondary school quite uncommon, the government has introduced a variety of policies explicitly aimed at girls' education. For example, girls with lowered pass marks on national-level school exams,[7] are provided with 'tutorial support' to partially compensate for the irregular attendance that often results from their heavy domestic work burdens, and have access to girls' clubs, which aim to develop their leadership skills (Ministry of Education 2010). The government is also prioritising hiring more female teachers[8] to serve as role models, and has called for 'building of low cost hostels' in selected *woredas* to help girls transition to secondary school (ibid.: 16).

As noted in Chapter 2, on a regional basis Amhara girls are comparatively well-situated in terms of education. Because the '*BoE (Bureau of Education) has moved towards facilitated girl's education*' (regional-level informant) – meaning that local governments are especially likely to force parents to send their daughters to school – Amhara girls are now more likely than boys to attend, and complete, primary school. Furthermore, because '*girls have access to tutorial classes in all schools*', teachers '*actively work with parents . . . about reducing girls' workload at home*', '*schools are required to have separate toilets for girls and boys*' and '*gender clubs are established in all schools*' (regional educational informants), girls are also now substantially more likely to enrol in first-cycle secondary school (9th and 10th grades) (net enrolment rate (NER) of 22.2 per cent versus 17.5 per cent) and marginally more likely to enrol in preparatory school (11th and 12th grades) (NER of 5.6 per cent versus 5.5 per cent) (Ministry of Education 2015) (see Box 3.2). Notably, however, while Amhara girls are more likely to attend school than their male peers, and are outperforming national averages (which include the developing regions[9]) at almost every level, compared to their Tigrayan peers, Amhara girls' progress has been limited. For example, while the NER for first-cycle secondary school for Amhara girls is 22.2 per cent, for Tigrayan girls it is 54 per cent. Similarly, Tigrayan girls are nearly

---

BOX 3.2   THE ROLE OF SCHOOLS IN COMBATING CHILD MARRIAGE

When I was 14 or 15 years old my parents decided to marry me to someone in the community. The school director informally heard about this. The director called me alone outside and asked me why I was absent from the school. I told him that my parents were going to marry me off and the wedding day was approaching. Then he called my parents and warned them that if they continued they would be imprisoned. Then my parents feared they would face imprisonment and they cancelled the marriage and decided to return me back to school. The school director saved me from child marriage.

If I had not participated in the training and discussions about child marriage, child childbirth, rape, venereal diseases, HIV/AIDS, I would not have completed my secondary education or I would have married as a child and had my own baby when I was still a child myself.

(In-depth interview with 19-year-old girl)

---

twice as likely as Amhara girls to enrol in preparatory school (20.9 per cent versus 5.6 per cent) (ibid.). These differences are in part linked to Tigray Regional State's stronger enforcement record.

The impact of health extension workers

Ethiopia's more than 38,000 health extension workers have played a nearly heroic role in transforming the health landscape for Ethiopian women and girls, reducing both child marriage and adolescent pregnancy. Introduced by the government in 2003 as a way of rapidly scaling up the health services required to make progress towards the Millennium Development Goals (MDGs), the Health Extension Programme uses 10th-grade graduates to deliver a free package of 16 basic health interventions, including contraception (Ministry of Health 2015; Workie and Ramana 2013). Nationally, the contraceptive prevalence rate rose nearly 85 per cent between 2005 and 2011 (to 27.5 per cent) (ibid.) and the 2011 DHS found that nearly all married women (97 per cent) had heard of at least one modern method of family planning (CSA and ICF International 2012). Indeed, while Ethiopia's median age at first birth is low (19.2 for women aged 25–49), its adolescent pregnancy rate is also low by regional standards. The most recent DHS found that 'only' 12 per cent of Ethiopian adolescents aged 15–19 were mothers or pregnant with their first child (compared to 19 per cent for Senegal, 23 per cent for Tanzania and Nigeria, 25 per cent for Malawi and 34 per cent for Sierra Leone) (ibid.).

Amhara has one of the highest contraceptive acceptance rates in the country – 91 per cent (Ministry of Health 2015) – and research has found that adolescents on average have a good understanding of sexual health and contraception (Melaku *et al.* 2014; Abajobir and Seme 2014). Adolescents in our research explained that '*Health workers come to our school and teach us about reproductive health. They explain to us the dangers of marrying below years. They also teach us about HIV transmission*' (17-year-old boy). Adolescent girls in our sample also often highlighted that health extension workers are one of the few trusted adults to whom they can turn for advice outside of their family. They also noted that access to contraception is largely good – even for unmarried adolescents – because they are stocked by community health posts.[10] Furthermore, local informants reported that health extension workers also gather figures on cancelled marriages – with several thousand cancelled last year on a regional basis (informant from the Bureau of Women, Children and Youth Affairs). Though the ultimate aim from a rights perspective is for the marriages not to be arranged at all, cancellation of child marriages can nevertheless be viewed as an important intermediate progress indicator.

The Women's Development Army

The Women's Development Army (WDA) grew out of the Health Extension Programme in 2011 and is now being extended across the country. By mobilising families, especially women, 'to scale-up best practices gained from the HEP [Health Extension Programme] and ensure wider community participation in facilitating community ownership', the WDA is working to help communities 'produce their own health' (Ministry of Health 2015: 22). Though implementation remains variable, due to the fact that the programme is still in its infancy, the ideal WDA organises all of the *kebele*'s women into groups of around 20–30 members. These groups meet at least twice a month to discuss topics ranging from sanitation to vaccination to HTPs (including child marriage). Nested under these larger groups are '1:5' groups (composed of one leader and five members), which meet in some cases on an almost daily basis for coffee ceremonies.

Though still nascent in Ethiopia's developing regions, the WDA is well-established in Amhara. There are, according to key informants, 122,000 WDA groups throughout the region – with membership approaching 3.3 million women. Indeed, households in Amhara are more likely to have completed the health extension training package delivered through WDAs than those in any other region (more than 60 per cent) (Ministry of Health 2015). Building on this success, the '*Bureau of Women has formed a coalition of sectors at the regional level which goes down to the kebele and got* (village*) levels*', reported a regional-level informant. '*Working through the 1:5 groups, their aim is to send girls to school and protect them from early marriage by following up with schools to ensure that girls have access to reproductive health services in schools, separate toilets, etc.*'

Institutional weaknesses

Budget deficits

While higher-level institutions are largely working to support change for Amhara's girls, there remain a variety of institutional shortcomings that are slowing progress.

Under-resourcing, for example, is a critical problem. Not only are *kebele* and *woreda* leaders given insufficient resources (such as motorbikes) with which to monitor child marriage and girls' education in more distant villages, but rural children are also rarely well-prepared for national-level exams. This is partly because class sizes tend to be very large but also because the out-of-pocket expenses entailed by ostensibly free primary education force many children to take a non-linear approach to schooling. For example, many enrol late and it is not uncommon for children, particularly the poorest, to drop in and out of school in order to save money for school-related fees (such as uniforms and books).

Continued under-investment in secondary school is a primary driver of girls' school-leaving and – because girls are likely to marry when they have no other options – child marriage (see Box 3.3) However, while the government has built some secondary schools, it continues to prioritise primary schools. In Amhara, there are 21 times as many primary schools as there are secondary schools (7,704 versus 362). Furthermore, most secondary schools are located in urban areas, meaning that should a rural family wish to send their daughter on to 9th grade, they must have, and be willing to commit, significant financial resources given the cost of boarding. Our research found no evidence of the 'low-cost hostels' that were planned in 2010.

Restrictive laws

In some cases, federal law is directly working to slow change for adolescent girls. For example, the 2009 Proclamation to Provide for the Registration and Regulation of Charities and Societies has significantly limited the role of NGOs in the country, especially at the community level. The law restricts fundraising activities and operations, and imposes stricter requirements for registration, including stipulating that

---

BOX 3.3   THE FRAUGHT TRANSITION TO SECONDARY SCHOOL

I have paid 100 birr registration fees. I bought exercise books, textbooks, and pens and pencils. I also rented a house in Kobo town for 100 birr per month, where I am attending my secondary education. . . . In addition, the school has asked students to contribute money to buy a plasma television to receive lessons that are broadcast to all secondary schools.

Last year, I worked for the safety net public works programme before I went to Kobo town to attend my secondary education. This year, the untimely rain has destroyed the crops. So I am afraid that this may not be a good year for me to continue with my secondary education because my parents may force me to stop my education due to economic problems.

(15-year-old girl, grade 9, Kobo)

charities and civil society organisations (CSOs) must secure a letter of recommendation from the Ministry of Foreign Affairs, which can slow work down by years (Amnesty International 2012). The law further requires that NGOs which receive more than 10 per cent of their financing from foreign sources refrain from engaging in all human rights and advocacy activities, including those related to child marriage specifically and gender more broadly (ibid.). Those activities are instead required to rely on government channels. Our research found that where WDAs are functioning well, they are well-positioned to work with NGOs to directly tackle girls' education and child marriage (see also Jones, Tefera, Emirie et al. 2016; Jones, Tefera, Presler-Marshall et al. 2016). WDAs provide the structure, and NGOs help ensure that gender messaging is not lost in the welter of other development topics. Where WDAs are weak, however, or where hostility towards government interventions precludes women's heartfelt commitment to the education provided by WDAs, the lack of NGO programming can have decidedly negative consequences for girls. That is, the enforcement of girls' rights to an education and protection from early marriage is not prioritised by communities, and community leaders turn a blind eye to violators.

Lack of data

Change is also slowed by a lack of data. The last census is quite dated (2007), the DHS is not designed to capture either local variation or distinguish between types of child marriage,[11] and very few girls have birth certificates. Although the Ethiopian government adopted a comprehensive law governing the institutional and operational framework of vital events registration (which includes registration of birth, death, marriage, divorce and other recognised vital events) in July 2012, implementation remains nascent in large part due to limited institutional will. This has made it all but impossible in many areas to enforce the marriage law; with no way to ascertain a girl's age, 'marriage approval committees' are often forced to simply take parents' word and, according to our respondents, parents often lie.

Limited local capacity

While noting significant variation just within the eight *woredas* in which our research was conducted, it is apparent that lower-level institutions across Amhara's zones, *woredas* and *kebeles*, are often far less effective at supporting adolescent girls, especially once they have left the more watchful environment of primary school (either because they have dropped out or because they have transitioned to secondary school) (see Box 3.4). In part due to the lack of resources already discussed, but also due to limited capacity and poor communication and coordination, at the more local levels there are simultaneously issues with gaps and duplication. Bureau of Justice officials too often have inadequate resources to investigate in detail reports of child marriage, especially as, unlike the Bureau of Women, Children and Youth Affairs and the Bureau of Education, they have no staff at *kebele*

BOX 3.4   LOCAL VARIABILITY IN INSTITUTIONAL COMMITMENT TO ADOLESCENT GIRLS

While the past two years have seen WDAs established throughout Amhara, our research found that some groups are working better than others. For example, Woreilu and Yilmana Densa had strong, well-established groups that were being used to disseminate information about child marriage to mothers. Habru and Metema, on the other hand, had groups that were less well-established. Critically, in terms of shaping programming, there were indications during our field visit that members of Merhabete's WDA – which had previously been a strong group actively working against child marriage – were experiencing meeting fatigue and that the group was at risk of becoming less effective.

Similar variation was seen in girls' clubs. While all eight *woredas* have girls' clubs, and most were very active, the club in Habru was markedly under-resourced and the club in Yilmana Densa can best be described as functional but not active. Woreilu's girls' club, on the other hand, is used as a model because of how it has included boys in programming and is using student 1:5 groups to cascade information from club members to the rest of the student body.

Differences between *woredas* are also evident in schooling outcomes. Kelala, for example, has the highest number of out-of-school children in the region, with girls unlikely to progress even to second-cycle primary school because they first marry and then migrate. In Kobo, Yilmana Densa and Merhabete, however, teachers go door-to-door checking up on absent girls. In Woreilu, girls' enrolment, even in secondary school, is quite high.

Exam pass rates are also highly variable. In Kobo and Worebabo, for example, less than 75 per cent of registered girls passed their 8th-grade exams in 2015. In Yilmana Densa and Metema, more than 90 per cent passed. Similarly, while only 19 per cent of registered girls in Kelala passed their 10th-grade exams in 2015, nearly 40 per cent of girls in Woreilu passed and more than 70 per cent of girls in Kobo passed.[12]

---

level who can follow up on the ground. As such, they openly admit that their focus is on prevention rather than prosecution. In addition, while the WDA 1:5 group structure facilitates the spread of messages down to the grassroots, because officials from various sectors are relying on the same platform, there are growing concerns about meeting fatigue and, in turn, potential dilution of messages.

Lower-level institutions such as schools and police, especially in Wollo, are also paying inadequate attention to migration and the way in which it pulls girls out of school and, in some cases, pushes them into marriage (see Chapter 2). In Worebabo, for example, an educational informant reported that migration is a greater cause of girls' school-leaving than child marriage, while in Metema, adolescents reported that brokers regularly transport trucks full of migrants out of the country (see also Jones *et al*. 2014).While the risks of migration are well understood, we found that, in a context of rural poverty recently made worse by land fragmentation, adolescents and often their parents see migration (either internal or cross-border) as the only way to a more secure future.

Ideas

The second of Rosendorff's 'Three I's' is 'ideas'. Political economy analysts emphasise the centrality of ideas (e.g. Hickey and Bracking 2005) and the ways in which belief systems and ideas shape behaviour and distribution of power. Such ideas can be manifested in weak or discriminatory legislative and policy frameworks, high state tolerance or lack of punishment for violators, a mismatch between the goals of national officials and 'street-level bureaucrats', and/or low levels of awareness of policy provisioning among service providers, law enforcement and judicial actors.

In the case of child marriage and girls' education in Amhara, the ideas held both by ordinary citizens and elites shape discursive space. Traditional gender roles, which position men as social superiors, emphasise girls' sexuality as well as leave them with an outsized share of domestic responsibilities that constrain their options on a daily basis. However, the ideas held by government and NGO actors also work to limit progress. On the one hand, rote messaging – which typically focuses on age at marriage and a relatively narrow set of health risks facing adolescent girls (including the risk of fistula for younger brides) – has proved valuable in kick-starting processes that can drive change. On the other hand, those same narrow messages are all too often working to slow transformative change by precluding the spread of the participatory programming that facilitates ownership, builds girls' confidence and strengthens their voice.

As noted in Chapter 2, nascent shifts aside (see Box 3.5), ideas about traditional gender roles are central to understanding most Amhara girls' lived realities. A continued emphasis on girls' virginity, which is seen as central to families' social standing and is supported by a wide variety of common misunderstandings,[13] encourages child marriage. Similarly, customs such as assigning girls many hours of domestic work each day leave them vulnerable to school failure and reinforce the idea that girls' education is worthless. Girls themselves are also deeply constrained by these gender norms, which leave many to replicate the trajectories of their mothers and grandmothers despite the emergence of alternative options and the new pathways being forged by their peers. Some girls, for example, continue to believe that '*bad girls . . . are among those who go to school*' and are '*not willing to work*'. Others, despite equitable divorce laws that offer them some protection from poverty should they choose to leave their husbands, are loathe to do so because they believe that their husband '*beat me because he loved me*' (17-year-old girl).

The ideas held by government elites also reinforce stasis. By bundling child marriage with female genital mutilation/cutting (FGM/C), violence against women

---

BOX 3.5   NEW NOTIONS FOR MEN AND BOYS

I taught my children how to prepare food and bake injera [traditional bread]. I told them that we have no option but to share responsibilities of taking care of house chores together. When the girl fetches water, one of her brothers bakes injera and the other keeps the cattle. The old culture was that it was shameful for man to help his wife in preparing food, even if he would eat that food. Now this old culture is non-existent.

(Ahmed, 63)

Discrimination in terms of responsibilities should be stopped. The culture of giving on-the-field tasks to men and household tasks to women should be abandoned. There should be cooperation in all of the jobs among women and men.

(Seid, a 16-year-old boy)

Source: In-depth interviews with men and boys from Yilmana Densa and Worebabo

---

and other HTPs, government agendas have effectively de-emphasised child marriage. Not only has it moved off-centre in terms of targeting, meaning that messages risk being diluted and muddied, but the broader platform further discourages differentiation. Child marriage, even within Amhara, has very diverse drivers. Some girls marry because they are forced to do so, others because they 'choose' to – sometimes due to adolescent passion and other times merely exhausted by being tormented about their virginity. Key to eliminating child marriage by 2025 is a concerted focus on the local specifics. For example, we found that in some communities, where fistula is common, adults were particularly responsive to links between child marriage and girls' health. In other communities, messages about poverty reduction and countering high rates of divorce and gender-based violence (GBV) were more likely to resonate.

The government's failure to distinguish between what is necessary versus sufficient is also working to slow change. For example, federal and regional governments are committed to girls' clubs as a vehicle for educating girls about their rights and preventing child marriage. Furthermore, our research is clear that where clubs offer hands-on programming that increases girls' confidence and voice, those clubs can be transformatory. However, we also found that all too often, girls' clubs are supplied not with curricula that could guide even less-prepared teachers on how to use the methods girls need in order to imagine – and chase – different futures, but with loudspeakers and slogans. Similarly, while community-level programming centres around encouraging mechanistic declarations of abandonment of child marriage, our research suggests that because gender norms are among the 'stickiest', genuine change tends to be non-linear and requires long-term commitment that builds ownership (see also Boudet *et al.* 2012; Jones, Tefera, Emirie *et al.* 2016; Jones, Tefera, Presler-Marshall *et al.* 2016).

Interests

So to the third of Rosendorff's 'Three I's': 'interests'. Although institutional-level commitment to ending child marriage in Ethiopia is currently high, the pervasive ideas about gender norms discussed in the previous section serve to limit the longer-term interests of some actors, especially those who perceive that they will be on the losing end of any shift in the relative balance of power. This means that although the policy environment is strong, uptake and implementation are often weak and inconsistent. Where government officials – from the federal to the *kebele* level – understand the links between child marriage, girls' education and poverty, policy interest in girls tends to remain high because meeting their needs serves broader development goals (especially vis-à-vis reducing fertility and poverty rates because women who marry as adults are less likely to be poor and tend to have fewer children). On the other hand, where officials fail to see the harm in child marriage – either because of traditional protections such as *gaido*[14] or because recent progress means that girls are now marrying by choice at age 15 rather than by force at age 10 – legal enforcement remains rare, especially when coupled with social concerns such as *kebele* officials' desire to maintain the friendship and respect of their constituents. There is particular concern among some researchers that recent progress towards reducing child marriage will see attention – and resources – diverted elsewhere, similar to what was seen after the early successes of the 1970s literacy campaigns in Ethiopia (see Box 3.6).

NGO interests are also complex. Whereas NGOs play an important (albeit relatively small-scale) role in promoting social change communication around

---

BOX 3.6   THE RISK OF BACKSLIDING

In Metema, Worebabo and Yilmana Densa, female focus group participants reported that traditional marriage practices, including child marriage, have been on the rise since *kebele* officials – incorrectly believing that child marriage had been abandoned – stopped monitoring and penalising these activities two years ago. One reported,

> There was serious supervision on early marriage by the school and government offices; as a result, the practice was abandoned. However, there has been no more supervision over the past two years because the government believed that the attitude of the society had changed towards early marriage.

adolescent girls' education and the risks of child marriage, their programming is also often siloed due to funding and organisational incentive structures and does not adequately reflect community need. Some NGOs, for example, serve only girls – and overlook the role of broader communities, parents, and men and boys that evidence indicates is critical for genuine norm change (see also Box 3.7). Others focus only on one type of intervention without recognising the web of need that makes it unlikely that a single intervention can return results. For example, while we found that Hiwot Ethiopia is working well with both adolescents and parents in Merhabete *woreda*, serving the former in age-segmented groups and targeting

---

BOX 3.7 INTENSIVE TRAINING IN SMALL GROUP FORMATS REAPS HIGH DIVIDENDS

Hiwot Ethiopia has transformed the lives of Tsige and her daughters by helping them to understand the value of educating girls and eliminating child marriage in their community.

Tsige is 30, has been divorced for 15 years, and was married young enough that her oldest daughter is in late adolescence. Afraid to remarry, she supports her family by selling *areke* (an alcoholic beverage). Once a week, Tsige meets with dozens of other women to learn about topics ranging from HTPs to sanitation. She explained that they have come to understand not only that girls should not marry as children, but also that they should only marry men they choose. The intensive trainings take time, she concluded, but they lead to '*changes in the attitude of the people*'.

Another way in which Hiwot Ethiopia has changed lives in Tsige's family is through its focus on girls' education. Tsige never had the opportunity to go to school, but she is determined, because of the '*discussion held at the kebele level*', that her daughters will complete their education. When her elder daughter failed to pass to grade 11 in the national exam, Tsige decided to enable her to continue to learn in private college. Now she is taking technical and vocational training in Alem Ketema [the *woreda*/district town].

Tsige's daughter attends Hiwot Ethiopia's girls' club, which has helped her put schooling first. '*After she started to engage in the discussions . . . she has focused on her education. She does not want to miss classes.*' She also '*tells me that she does not want to marry before she completes her education and gets a job*'.

Tsige especially likes the way that Hiwot Ethiopia has helped the community integrate the new trainings into the 1:5 governmental structure, which brings neighbours together in small groups so they can discuss what they have learned. She says that while some people cannot come to the larger meetings, or do not understand in so large a group, '*people can well understand things in small group such as 1:5 structure*'.

women for mother-to-mother education (see Box 3.7), the girls' club intervention in Woreilu *woreda* implemented by the Amhara Development Association (ADA) is largely ignoring the parents and religious leaders who drive child marriage. On the other hand, while ADA's programming was highly successful in improving girls' school attendance and performance – in part because it offered girls practical and emotional support, especially to deal with 'shameful' menstruation – we found that Yegna used a predominantly urban model that failed to resonate in rural Habru, where girls did not have access to discussion groups to help them map new ideas onto their daily realities. As a key informant at the Women's Association noted about Yegna's Melat character, '*The way they train for the music contest is also a reflection of urban life rather than the rural one*'. While we acknowledge that programming which attempts to address all segments of society can end up fragmented and of poor quality, shifting social norms requires a breadth in which too few NGOs are currently invested.

The interests of community and religious leaders are also not necessarily aligned with national policy. On the one hand, respondents in some communities reported that local priests '*do not preach things which can hurt the society*', emphasising instead that girls must not marry until they are age 18 or older. For example, in Worebabo, respondents told us that religious officials would not permit child marriage because they understood that they would be held legally accountable were they to do so. In Yilmana Densa, on the other hand, study participants reported a far more mixed relationship between church leaders and child marriage, with leaders willing to take on the school officials trying to prevent child marriage and insist on child brides for themselves. A local informant reported:

> *We went to a rural area to teach about early marriage as a harmful traditional practice. There was a 13-year-old girl in grade 6. There was a deacon in grade 8 and he wanted to marry her. The school was against their marriage. However, the deacon insisted on the marriage, saying 'no one can take her away from me'. And the wedding ceremony continued to be prepared.*

The interests of parents, and sometimes even girls, are also variable. Where parents aspire for their daughters to become educated and employed – driven either by external factors such as land fragmentation or internal factors such as memories of their own lost opportunities – their commitment to new ideas such as free choice, adult marriage and girls' education is remarkable, especially given resource constraints. On the other hand, where they feel they will be social outcasts if they fail to uphold tradition and/or are heavily reliant on their adolescent daughter's domestic and care work contributions, it is difficult for them to accept new ideas. Girls have conflicting interests as well. Whereas as a group they are increasingly committed to economic independence, some approach this broader goal by plotting how to achieve a university education while others leave school as soon as they are old enough to '*try their luck*' with migration – or, as adolescents in pursuit of independence, believe they can no longer tolerate living with their parents.

Conclusions and policy implications

Our findings from three years of primary research across Amhara Regional State have helped to clarify the complex ways in which the political economy dynamics of policy and programme implementation are mediating well-being outcomes for adolescent girls. Given the multiple institutions, interests and ideas involved in policy and programme delivery, our research has underscored the importance of coordinated efforts that bring together governmental and non-governmental actors at national and subnational levels. Though social communications programming can play an important role in starting to shift discriminatory social norms, broader structural shifts which require national government investments are critical.

For example, if adolescent girls are to realise their full educational capabilities and the other capability domains that are often closely linked (including voice and agency), improving girls' physical and financial access to secondary school is essential, as is expanding labour-saving technologies (e.g. water pumps). Simultaneously, given that our research and that of other analysts has highlighted that exam failure drives not only school-leaving but also migration and child marriage, greater efforts are needed to improve educational quality to ensure that rural children are on a more equal footing in terms of the all-important national exams. Given that land fragmentation is increasingly rendering agriculture an unsustainable path, efforts must also be directed at developing the rural labour market opportunities that would encourage families to invest in girls' secondary education and then allow girls to become economically independent. At the subnational level (*woreda* and *kebele*), complementary changes are needed in terms of monitoring girls' attendance, providing them with clubs that emphasise life skills training and offer both tutorial support and menstrual management, while also linking girls at risk of child marriage to reporting chains that culminate in rigorous enforcement of the marriage law. Within this broader set of policy and programme imperatives, as our findings have highlighted, NGOs can play a vital supporting role in working with local officials, health extension workers, WDAs and school-based clubs to catalyse and foster coordination and focus.

Critically, in order to shift the 'sticky' gender norms that restrict girls' lives, our research has also highlighted that communications programming must have broader aims – working not only to end child marriage and improve girls' education but also to shift the gender norms that underpin girls' disadvantage. Girls need the voice and confidence that develops through participatory experiences which encourage them to identify their own goals and think through the barriers to achieving them. Boys, as brothers and as future husbands, need programming that helps them develop more equitable attitudes and behaviours, teaching them to cease taunting girls about menstruation and offer to do their fair share of household chores. Parents and community and religious leaders also need targeted messaging that is locally tailored, focusing on health risks or poverty, depending on which themes are most likely to resonate with daily reality in a given context.

Notes

1 This ministry was split in 2015 into the Ministry of Youth and Sport and the Ministry of Women and Children. At the time of writing, it is unclear where adolescent girls will fall.
2 As the last census was in 2007 and the last full DHS was in 2011, the most recent progress is not yet statistically visible.
3 The DFID (2014) annual review noted that 'The calculations driving this change were based on the analysis of the 2011 DHS raw data in which the zonal data (only available since 2013) reported significant declines in the incidence of child marriage in the target regions.'
4 1999 in the Gregorian calendar.
5 Rates in Gambia (28.1 per cent), Burkina Faso (33.8 per cent), Mali (40 per cent), Niger (43.1 per cent) and Eritrea (61.5 per cent), for example, are much higher (UNESCO 2016).
6 The Ministry of Education (2015) reports girls' primary graduation rate to be 46.7 per cent.
7 For example, boys must achieve a minimum of 2.71/4.0 on their 10th-grade exams in order to enter preparatory schools. Girls must score over 2.4.
8 On a national level, only 44 per cent of first-cycle primary teachers, 29 per cent of second-cycle primary teachers and 18 per cent of first-cycle secondary teachers are female. Amhara's figures are slightly higher (51 per cent, 33 per cent and 23 per cent, respectively).
9 The Ethiopian government has designated some regions (such as Gambella) as 'developing' due to their low levels of development.
10 Ethiopia's health care system is layered. In Amhara, each health post serves about 7,000 people. Each health centre serves about 25,000 and each hospital serves about 450,000.
11 In Amhara, many girls have traditionally been married as infants or toddlers – and then divorced before adolescence. The threats facing these girls are minimal compared to the girls married in later childhood or early adolescence, who were often expected to begin cohabiting with their husbands (see Jones, Tefera, Emirie *et al.* 2016; Jones, Tefera, Presler-Marshall *et al.* 2016).
12 Kobo's girls were less likely to pass their 8th-grade exams than girls in the other *woredas* in which we worked, but of girls who transitioned on to secondary school, Kobo's did quite well.
13 For example, it is believed that menstruation indicates that a girl has lost her virginity.
14 *Gaido* (also *guido*) is a custom wherein young married girls are protected (by their in-laws) from sexual intercourse until the onset of puberty.

Bibliography

Abajobir, A. and Seme, A. (2014) 'Reproductive Health Knowledge and Services Utilization Among Rural Adolescents in East Gojjam Zone, Ethiopia: A Community-based Cross-sectional Study' *BMC Health Services Research* 14: 138.

Abbink, J. (2010) *Political Culture in Ethiopia: A Balance Sheet of Post-1991 Ethnically Based Federalism.* The Netherlands: African Studies Centre.

Amnesty International. (2012) *Ethiopian Parliament Adopts Repressive New NGO Law.* Available online at www.amnesty.org/en/news-and-updates/news/ethiopian-parliament-adopts-repressive-new-ngo-law-20090108

Boudet, A., Petesch, P., Turk, C. and Thumala, A. (2012) *On Norms and Agency: Conversations About Gender Equality with Women and Men in 20 Countries.* Washington, DC: World Bank.

Bureau of Finance and Economic Development. (2006) *Amhara National Regional State: The Third Five-Year (2005–2010) Strategic Plan.* Bahir Dar: Bureau of Finance and Economic Development.

Central Statistical Agency (CSA) and ICF International (2012) *Ethiopia Demographic and Health Survey 2011.* Addis Ababa, Ethiopia and Calverton, Maryland, USA: Central

Statistical Agency and ICF International. Available online at http://dhsprogram.com/pubs/pdf/FR255/FR255.pdf

Department for International Development (DFID). (2014) Annual Review Finote Hiwot, End Child Marriage Programme, Summary Sheet.

Hickey, S. and Bracking, S. (2005) 'Exploring the Politics of Chronic Poverty: From Representation to a Politics of Justice.' *World Development* 33(6): 851–865.

Holmes, R. and Jones, N. (2013) *Gender and Social Protection in the Developing World: Beyond Mothers and Safety Nets*. London: Zed Books Limited.

Jones, N., Presler-Marshall, E. and Tefera, B. (2014) *Rethinking the 'Maid Trade': Experiences of Ethiopian Adolescent Domestic Workers in the Middle East*. London: Overseas Development Institute. Available online at www.odi.org/publications/9045-rethinking-maid-trade-experiences-ethiopian-adolescent-domestic-workers-middle-east

Jones, N., Tefera, B., Emirie, G., Gebre, B., Berhanu, K., Presler-Marshall, E., Walker, D., Gupta, T. and Plank, G. (2016) *One Size Does Not Fit All: The Patterning and Drivers of Child Marriage in Ethiopia's Hotspot Districts*. London: Overseas Development Institute. Available online at www.odi.org/publications/10455-one-size-does-not-fit-all-patterning-and-drivers-child-marriage-ethiopia-s-hotspot-districts

Jones, N., Tefera, B., Presler-Marshall, E., Gupta, T., Emirie, G., Gebre, B. and Berhanu, K. (2016) *What Works to Tackle Child Marriage in Ethiopia: A Review of Good Practice*. London: Overseas Development Institute. Available online at www.odi.org/publications/10453-what-works-tackle-child-marriage-ethiopia-review-good-practice

Melaku, Y., Berhane, Y., Kinsman, J. and Reda, H. (2014) 'Sexual and Reproductive Health Communication and Awareness of Contraceptive Methods among Secondary School Female Students, Northern Ethiopia: A Cross-sectional Study.' *BMC Public Health* 14: 252.

Ministry of Education. (2010) *National Girls' Education Strategy Federal Democratic Republic of Ethiopia*. Addis Ababa: Ministry of Education. Available online at http://info.moe.gov.et/gendocs/MOEGE.pdf

Ministry of Education. (2015) *Education Statistics Annual Abstract 2006 E.C. (2013/2014) Federal Democratic Republic of Ethiopia*. Addis Ababa: Ministry of Education.

Ministry of Health. (2015) *Health Sector Transformation Plan, Federal Democratic Republic of Ethiopia*. Addis Ababa: Ministry of Health.

Rosendorff, B. (2005) *Ideas, Interests, Institutions and Information: Jagdish Bhagwati and the Political Economy of Trade Policy*. Conference in Honour of Jagdish Bhagwati on his 70th Birthday, New York, 5–6 August.

True, J. (2012) *The Political Economy of Violence Against Women*. Oxford: Oxford Studies in Gender and International Relations.

United Nations Educational, Scientific and Cultural Organization (UNESCO). (2015) *Ethiopia: Education for All 2015 National Review*. Available online at http://unesdoc.unesco.org/images/0023/002317/231724e.pdf

United Nations Educational, Scientific and Cultural Organization (UNESCO). (2016) *UIS. Stat*. UNESCO Institute for Statistics. Available online at http://data.uis.unesco.org

Workie, N. and Ramana, G. (2013) *The Health Extension Program in Ethiopia*. Washington, DC: World Bank.

PART 2
Uganda

4

THE PARADOX OF CHANGE AND CONTINUITY IN SOCIAL NORMS AND PRACTICES AFFECTING ADOLESCENT GIRLS' CAPABILITIES AND TRANSITIONS TO ADULTHOOD IN RURAL UGANDA

Carol Watson, Grace Kyomuhendo Bantebya and Florence Kyoheirwe Muhanguzi

Introduction

Uganda has made significant progress over recent decades in reducing poverty, expanding education (through policies of universal primary and secondary education) and creating an enabling legal and policy environment for gender equality, adolescent development and women's empowerment. The legal minimum age of marriage is 18 years, and the national adolescent reproductive health policy commits the government to protecting adolescents' rights to appropriate information and services (Ministry of Health 2004). The government also recently adopted a comprehensive strategy on the elimination of child marriage and teenage pregnancy (Ministry of Gender, Labour and Social Development and UNICEF 2015). However, progress has been uneven and implementation of national policies at the local level is often weak (see Chapter 5). Gender-specific vulnerabilities persist, particularly in remote rural regions where discriminatory norms and practices combine with constrained service provision and uncertain economic opportunities to limit the development of adolescent girls' capabilities and circumscribe their life trajectories as they transition to adulthood. National statistics (see Box 4.1) reveal a sobering picture of continuing challenges for adolescent girls – all of which were reflected in the findings of our first two years of research.

This chapter analyses the paradoxical nature of change and continuity in the gender norms and practices affecting adolescent girls' transition to adulthood in rural Uganda, based on findings from qualitative research and available statistics in three sub-counties in the district of Mayuge, where poverty is extensive, child marriage rates remain high, adolescent pregnancies are common, and school dropout rates are significant.[1]

BOX 4.1 SOBERING NATIONAL STATISTICS IN UGANDA

- Though the poverty rate has dropped from 56 per cent in 1992 to 19.7 per cent in 2012/2013, 43 per cent of people continue to live close to the poverty line, with rates varying by region and urban/rural location (Ministry of Finance, Planning and Economic Development 2014).
- Only two-thirds (66 per cent) of girls and slightly more boys (68 per cent) complete primary school. Thereafter, gender disparities sharpen as fewer than half of all girls (46.6 per cent) enrol in secondary school and only a third (34 per cent) of those enrolled actually complete secondary education (the respective figures for boys are 53.4 per cent and 52 per cent) (Ministry of Education and Sports 2012).
- Pregnancy and early marriage – both of which are strongly linked to poverty – contribute to high dropout rates for girls as they continue along the educational pathway. At the national level, a quarter of dropouts at secondary level are due to early marriage, while more than half (59 per cent) are due to teenage pregnancy (Ministry of Education and Sports 2012).
- More than a fifth of girls aged 15–19 in Uganda have been married (Amin *et al.* 2013) while more than a third (39 per cent) of women aged 20–49 have given birth by the age of 18 (Uganda Bureau of Statistics (UBOS) 2012a). Teenagers from the poorest households have rates of pregnancy (34 per cent) that are more than double the rates for their counterparts from the wealthiest households (16 per cent) (ibid.).
- Nearly a fifth of deaths among girls aged 15–19 are related to maternal causes, as are nearly a quarter (23 per cent) of deaths among women aged 20–24 (ibid.).
- The limited data available indicates continued high levels of gender-based violence (GBV), with more than a quarter of young women (29.1 per cent) reported to have experienced physical and sexual violence (UNICEF 2013).
- Economic discrimination against girls and women also persists, partly due to the challenges involved in trying to combine productive and reproductive roles, with reproductive responsibilities for household and children continuing to fall solely on the shoulders of women and girls.

Setting and context

Mayuge (see Figure 4.1) is situated in the East Central region of Uganda. It is one of the poorest districts in the country with a poverty rate of 24.5 per cent, and one where progress in reducing poverty has been slowest.[2] Environmental degradation and rapid population growth have contributed to land fragmentation and declining yields, leading to significant livelihood challenges for its largely rural small-holder

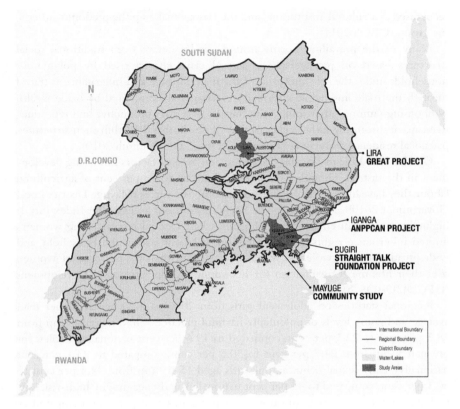

FIGURE 4.1 Map of Uganda showing study districts

Source: Map adapted from original supplied by the Uganda Bureau of Statistics

farming and fishing communities (Republic of Uganda 2015; Ministry of Finance, Planning and Economic Development 2014). Youth unemployment has become a particular challenge, with few formal sector jobs available; at the same time, child labour in the informal sector is on the rise, fuelled by the need for labour on sugar cane plantations, rice farms and fisheries, while the development of urban trading centres has thrown up new social challenges (Mayuge District Local Government 2010a, 2010b, 2011, 2012, 2013).

Capacity to fully implement national policies at the local level remains severely constrained. Social service infrastructure (schools, health centres) is expanding but remains limited and the quality of services is low. Only 47 per cent of births take place in district health facilities; sexual and reproductive health services, including family planning, have not been prioritised in district budgets or staffing; and school learning environments remain poor (Mayuge District Local Government 2010a, 2010b, 2011, 2012, 2013).

The district is religiously and ethnically diverse. About two-thirds of its population are Christian and a third Muslim. Mayuge is one of several districts that make up the cultural region of Busoga, one of the pre-colonial entities that is currently

recognised as a cultural 'institution', and the Basoga make up the predominant ethnic group (UBOS 2011).

Many of the prevailing norms around gender derive from traditional social
structures based on patriarchally organised clans characterised by polygynous
households under the sole authority of the man. Lineage and inheritance is traced
through the male line, while customary marriages are cemented by bride wealth
symbolising (among other things) the transfer of a girl's productive and reproductive capacity from the father's clan to that of her husband. Within such structures,
patrilocal residence patterns are the norm (Otiso 2006; Kaduuli 2010).

Gender-based inequality and discrimination are key factors hindering development in the district. Though women contribute up to 76 per cent of agricultural
labour, they have little control over land and other resources (Mayuge District Local
Government 2010b, 2011, 2012). The Social Institutions and Gender Index (SIGI)
highlights significant challenges for Uganda's East Central region, citing women's
limited inheritance rights, unequal division of labour within the household, and
widespread domestic violence, which affects more than 60 per cent of women
over their lifetime (Organisation for Economic Co-operation and Development
(OECD)/UBOS 2015).

Regional statistics on adolescent girls from 2006 to 2011 reveal higher than
average and rising levels of potentially harmful practices: child marriage (up from
18.3 per cent to 22.1 per cent, compared to 19.6 per cent nationally); adolescent
pregnancy (up from 24.7 per cent to 30.5 per cent, compared to 23.1 per cent
nationally); early sexual debut among girls aged 15–19 (up from 44.4 per cent to
50.1 per cent, compared to 44 per cent nationally); and engaging in 'high-risk' sex,
including multiple partners (up from 14.1 per cent to 18 per cent, compared to
11.9 per cent nationally). Educational indicators show that a quarter of girls aged
15–19 are illiterate and more than a third (38.7 per cent) were not in school in
2011 – compared to 21.6 per cent of boys (Amin *et al.* 2013).

District-level statistics show that while access to both primary and secondary school is expanding, primary completion rates overall remain low, at around
30–35 per cent (district education official, Mayuge); girls start dropping out in the
primary cycle, beginning during the fifth year (ages 12–13) and rising sharply after
the seventh year (around ages 14–15). Causes include pregnancy and early marriage,
lack of resources to pay for indirect school fees and materials, and parental reluctance to invest in daughters' education, as well as poor quality teaching and gender-
insensitive school environments (Mayuge District Local Government 2010b and
interviews with key informants).

Change and continuity in marriage norms and practices and their consequences for girls

Persistent and rising trends of early marriage

Early marriage was a feature of traditional agrarian society in Busoga, where
customary marriages were arranged between clans as a means of cementing the

social structure. Upon reaching adolescence, young girls were considered ready for marriage and prepared for this by their extended families. Our study confirmed the continuing high prevalence of child marriage: many girls in the study communities were married or cohabiting by the age of 16, and some even as early as 12 or 13. Intergenerational discussions further suggested that child marriage may be on the rise; this was often explained in relation to what is seen to be the earlier onset of sexual activity. As one 80-year-old grandmother observed: '*In my day, most girls got married around 16, when they knew what to do in marriage and were not just experimenting. These days, girls get married even younger – at 13, 14, 15 years. They no longer wait to grow older, but just get married*'. This captures a sense not only of the current early age at marriage, but also of the lack of preparedness for it on the part of young girls. Early marriage is described as being more common among out-of-school girls, but is also clearly linked to school dropouts. Despite laws against early marriage (and potential punishment under 'defilement' laws, which criminalise sex with or between minors under the age of 18), the practice remains common.

While there was near unanimity among our study participants that early marriage may not be good for either the girl or her family, they attribute its prevalence to a number of factors. These include parental desire for bride wealth; premarital pregnancy precipitating marriage; conditions of poverty or mistreatment of girls at home (particularly by step-parents); peer pressure; films that provoke 'experimentation' with adult relationships; and continuing perceptions within local communities that sexual maturation equals readiness for marriage. As one girl explained during a focus group discussion, '*Young girls get married as soon as they grow breasts – even at age 12; at 15 years old it is already too late*'.

Girls' sexual maturation is seen to mark the abrupt dividing line between girlhood and womanhood, with no transitional period in between. Cultural taboos against shedding menstrual blood in the father's homestead are still quite strong and reinforce the urgency of early marriage: while boys, upon reaching puberty, construct their own huts in the family compound, girls often remain with their parents. Girls' 'transient' position within their natal households – where, unlike boys, they will not inherit property and are expected to move out permanently – also contributes to the pressure to marry early.

The growing phenomenon of informal cohabitation

One of the most striking changes in marital patterns in our study communities is the rise of informal living arrangements among young people who – foregoing customary practices of introductions through parents and family accompanied by the payment of bride wealth – are 'running off' to live together, either without their parents' knowledge or against their wishes, with no bride wealth involved. The practice is commonly referred to as 'marriage through the window' (*kawundo kakubye edirisa*) and was estimated by our study participants to account for more than half of all new marriages in their communities. Adults – mothers as well as fathers – tend to explain the phenomenon as a function of reduced parental control over children and the multiplication of opportunities for young people to meet each other outside of the confines of family:

> *A girl boards a bus to Tororo and on the same bus she meets a man – a total stranger – but before you know what is happening, they are married. Or they go to a video hall (kibanda) and come out with a girl ready for marriage.*

Others take the view that laws against child marriage are driving the practice underground, resulting in more informal arrangements. Many lament this growing trend as a sign of the loss of 'traditional' values: '*In the olden days,*' explained one man,

> *it was before the formal introductions were made that parents could find out about the background of the intended spouse, to see if he was suitable for their daughter. Only afterwards would the negotiations between families be made. Today, such introductions are optional. . . . Our children have lost the culture.*

The rise of informal unions has entailed a shift in marriage as an institutional arrangement between families – and indeed entire clans – to one that is more of an agreement between individuals. Formal bride wealth no longer cements such unions, although parents often demand 'compensation' from the boy and his family after the fact. '*Afterwards,*' explained one of our primarily male key informants at sub-county level, '*the boy may bring the girl's parents an "appreciation" in the form of an envelope with money*'. This is sometimes referred to as a 'fine' and is one of the overall changes seen to be affecting the bride wealth system, although it remains in force for customary marriages.

The growing trend towards informal unions has also contributed to a diminished role for the '*senga*' – the paternal aunt who was traditionally responsible for preparing the girl to assume her roles as wife and mother and, as such, was an important conduit of cultural values and expectations around marriage. '*Girls used to get educated by sengas about marriage issues, but now girls just go for marriage without learning these things*', said an 18-year-old unmarried girl with a baby, explaining that now, '*these things have changed because we have copied the Western culture*'. The loss of this traditional transmission of knowledge and family-based preparation for marriage has not, for the most part, been replaced by other forms of preparation or access to sexual and reproductive health (SRH) information for girls, either through the school system or health centres.

Cohabitation, although increasingly common, is not a legally recognised form of marriage in Uganda, so there is no legal protection for girls that enter into such relationships. These informal unions are particularly volatile and can easily break up, leaving the girl with children to bring up but with no financial support from the father. As a male cultural leader explained, '*Such "marriages" are highly unstable, leading to a situation of multiple marriages or cohabitation arrangements in serial form*'. Another key informant explained that '*Boys who marry young girls find they cannot sustain them economically, so they abandon them and run off*. Girls themselves recognise the risks:

> It is bad and risky because the parents do not know where you went. In case of serious problems, the man will just dump you at home when your parents are away, or, when you die the man can just dump your corpse at your home and run.

Some girls within these relationships would prefer to be formally married – something they are planning to do at a later stage, craving the perceived security and respect accorded to couples through formalisation ceremonies. As one girl said: '*I am not happy with this type of marriage because they [the in-laws] have not gone to my parents but we are preparing to go there*'.

Increased individual choice of partner

The trend towards informal cohabitation is contributing to a growing tendency for young people to exercise more free choice in the selection of their potential spouse, which, to some extent, is being seen more in customary marriages as well. In some cases, when parents are set on 'marrying off' their daughters against their will, individual girls are finding the courage to resist and run away – often establishing informal marriages with boys of their own choosing as the only perceived viable option.

Many respondents felt that greater individual choice is a positive development. '*In my mother's time*,' said a 19-year-old unmarried mother of two, '*they gave girls away without their consent, but I expect to choose my own husband*'. '*In earlier days*,' said a 73-year-old grandmother, '*girls couldn't refuse – they would force you into marriage. Children can now choose their marriage partners, which is a good thing because no one is crying*'. This reflects an appreciation of the heightened agency of adolescent girls, as expressed by some adults as well as girls themselves. Others harbour reservations: '*Our marriage passed through the elders*,' reported one of the fathers-in-law, '*but girls these days decide which man to marry. . . . Today, it is by chance that you get a good girl who is well-behaved and will bring respect at home*'. This reflects adult concern for the breakdown of parental – often patriarchal – control systems and a shift away from collectivist systems to a much more individualistic culture; but it also reflects parental concern for a daughter's welfare in contracting a union with a 'stranger'. There are additional questions around whether 'agency' exercised under conditions of limited options is actually always a positive assertion of choice or, rather, a desperate response to circumstances.

Strong gender norms within the household confronted with changing realities

Ideals of femininity and masculinity over the life cycle as expressed by our study participants – male and female – underscore the strongly held cultural values around gender and the norms that govern social relations and behaviour. These are rooted in the gendered division of labour within the household, discriminatory legal norms around property, and ascribed gender roles and responsibilities in both the economic and social domains.

Our study participants confirmed that, as in other parts of Uganda, the man is expected to be the head of household, the main decision-maker and the overall breadwinner. His authority cannot be contested by his wife, as reflected in the common saying among the Basoga that '*What a man says a woman says also*'. Women and girls have little control over resources and are mainly responsible for reproductive tasks as well as subsistence farming. Adolescent girls, whose mobility is more restricted than that of boys, are expected to stay close to home to help their mothers with household tasks, which are seen as an important initiation into the responsibilities they will later be expected to assume as married women. The consequences of not fulfilling this role are weighty, as one girl explained (in a group discussion with married, out-of-school girls): '*If you fail to be an ideal woman, the man will marry another woman and you may also get diseases because the man will become a womaniser*'. It is generally considered absurd for a man or boy to take on domestic roles: '*A man cannot wash clothes because – why did he marry a woman?*' asked an adolescent girl. '*God created us differently, the men and the women*', an older man explained, '*How can my son cook, bathe the children, wash my clothes or fetch water when the women and girls are there?*'

Some of these norms stem from, and at the same time uphold, structural features of the household. An 18-year-old married girl noted that,

> The man is the head of the family and controls all the family resources – land, goats, tree plantations and other household assets such as a bicycle and crops. He makes decisions in everything and no one can stop him. I only decide on the household utensils – saucepans, plates, cups, my clothes.

Inheritance continues to be from father to sons; indeed, a girl's position within the household is considered 'transitory' as she will, upon marriage, leave to join her husband's clan, prompting one girl to comment: '*It's like everybody wants you to get out of the way. Tell me, what's wrong with being a girl?*' Lack of inheritance rights and access to 'in vivo' transfers that sons may benefit from mean that a daughter cannot build up her own economic assets, unless, for example, she gets an education and can work outside the home. The unequal gendered division of labour within the household, which burdens women with most of the care work – coupled with restricted mobility – limits their capacity to engage in and benefit from other activities, including education or productive economic opportunities.

However, our study respondents noted some changes in actual practices, and identified many difficulties in adhering to notions of the ideal man or woman. They noted that some husbands and wives consult on major family decisions, and a number observed that women's increasing entry into the labour market – reinforced by government efforts to promote 'women's rights' – are contributing to changes in gender relations at the household level. Some welcomed these changes, as this

19-year-old girl explained: '*Before, women stayed at home and were ruled by men. . . . But today, women work and have liberty*'. Others consider these trends responsible for increased marital instability, sexual immorality and domestic violence. Men, in particular, complain of feeling like '*empty trousers*' as their traditional breadwinning role and authority within the household come under threat. In parallel, some men are seen to be '*abandoning*' their household responsibilities and '*relinquishing*' their breadwinner role to women – instead, hanging out in trading centres where they gather to drink, gamble and talk about '*important issues*' while leaving women alone with the full care of the household. Male power within marriage has, in a sense, 'fractured', creating a sense of hopelessness or alienation among some men, which is seen to be contributing to domestic violence, reported to be common in the study communities. Such changes reflect a breakdown in social norms around male responsibility, as well as the reduced power of clans to sanction unacceptable behaviours.

Rising rates of adolescent pregnancy and childbirth outside of marriage

Most study participants acknowledged high rates of adolescent pregnancy and childbirth as a significant problem in their communities and perceived that pregnancy outside of marriage is a growing phenomenon: '*It was not common in our time for girls to produce babies before marriage*,' said one grandmother, '*but these days it has become a custom*'. Virginity before marriage was said to be highly valued in the past – surrounded by a number of sanctions for those who did not adhere to the expectation and rewards to those who maintained it. '*It was important to be a virgin,*' explained a 50-year-old mother, '*so a girl would protect herself so much! Some girls may have entered marriages as non-virgins, but it was kept hidden – a secret – and was very embarrassing*'. Sengas played an important role in advising girls about maintaining virginity and in providing proof of it in the form of bloody sheets on the marriage night, upon which the *senga* would be rewarded with a goat. Our research revealed that norms around virginity may be easing somewhat in the study communities though, more or less in response to behavioural practices. '*You cannot find an 18-year-old virgin today*', observed one unmarried schoolgirl whose view was echoed by others in the group discussion. '*These days girls are running with boys all over the place*', added a male Protestant pastor.

Adolescent girls in our study sites had very little knowledge about SRH issues, including sexual maturation and how to prevent pregnancy. Mothers, for the most part, seemed reluctant to take over the role of the *senga* in explaining such 'bedroom' issues to their daughters, and most schools do not provide SRH education due to continuing perceptions in the community that doing so will encourage young people to engage in sexual relations. The lack of quality health services in the district, coupled with the ambiguity surrounding the provision of adolescent-friendly SRH services (in a context where all sexual relations involving children under 18 – consensual or not – are classified as 'defilement' and therefore illegal) severely restricts adolescent girls' access to the information and services they need to protect themselves against unwanted pregnancies. A male non-governmental organisation (NGO) representative explained that under-18s cannot easily get condoms from health services: '*It is very difficult because they shouldn't be having sex at that age*'.

In the context of early onset of sexual activity in the absence of appropriate SRH information and services, there is now a certain resigned acceptance of premarital pregnancy: '*Yes, daughters giving birth while still at home is embarrassing,*' commented the male Protestant pastor, '*but people are now used to it, though it was bad in Busoga culture. You might get embarrassed today but tomorrow it is your neighbour's daughter*'. Nevertheless, while the sanctions around premarital pregnancy are generally becoming less extreme, it continues to be a source of shame and stigmatisation – for girls and their parents. Some families, particularly in Muslim communities, uphold premarital virginity as a strong social norm to be guarded at all costs, including through early marriage. As one girl in a focus group discussion with married girls explained: '*Giving birth before marriage is seen badly in the community. You are referred to as "second hand", "scrap"'*. *It has always been like this and to avoid it, Muslim families marry off their daughters before or as soon as the onset of menstruation.*'

The physical consequences of early pregnancy can be severe: because young girls are not yet physically mature, they risk dying during delivery, developing fistula (which can lead to stigma, exclusion and divorce), or delivering through C-section – after which, according to the primarily male district technical staff we spoke to, they may be rejected by their partner as '*sexually weak*'. Abortion is illegal, so those who seek recourse to 'silent' abortions not only face significant health risks but also legal risks and social censure. Once they become pregnant, girls often fail to get proper care in the absence of appropriate health services. Thereafter, the social and economic consequences set in, as teen pregnancies contribute to school dropout and diminishing prospects for economic empowerment, reinforcing the intergenerational cycle of poverty.

Study participants offered a variety of explanations for the rising phenomenon of adolescent pregnancy and motherhood outside of marriage. These ranged from a loosening of morals to a loss of culture, to excess liberty for young people and, according to a group of adult women, '*too many exciting things like videos, discos*'. One woman explained that, due to a combination of all these factors, '*Girls begin playing sex, "scratch themselves" at an early age and sleep with men and get pregnant, and men mistreat them so much*'. Another woman was convinced that '*It started when girls started interacting with boys in schools. When they are schooling, they start other things and before you know it, the girl is seven months pregnant*'. Others attributed it to girls' desire for money from boys: '*Today, the girls we have go on begging boys to give them money – they don't fear men*'. Transactional sex for material gain such as 'air time', soap, watches, even 'chapatti' was reported by many of our study participants: '*Girls engage in sexual encounters at an early age because they need and want things that their parents cannot afford*', explained one adolescent in a group discussion with girls and boys.

High levels of GBV, including rape and 'defilement', were also identified as problems contributing to the high rates of adolescent pregnancy in the district, though precise statistics are unavailable and such cases often go unreported. Study participants said that girls have no safe spaces in the communities: in homes where the mother has remarried, they are at risk of being abused by their stepfathers; at school, they may be sexually harassed or defiled by their teachers; in the wider community, they are prey to older men, including (of late) the moto-taxi (*boda boda*) drivers. The village well/borehole, the rice paddies, the road to school, the trading centres, beaches/fish landing sites and the 'lonely' forests and gardens – all were described as high-risk spaces for adolescent girls. As a male NGO representative explained, '*Gender-based violence arises out of cultural beliefs of male power over women*'.

Changing values around education for girls but continuing challenges

A clear trend emerging from our research is that girls today have greater opportunities for schooling compared with their mothers and grandmothers, and there is greater social value placed on education for girls. This is largely attributed to national policies designed to expand education and, in particular, universal primary education. This in turn has fuelled girls' aspirations for education, which is seen as important both in and of itself and as a means to pave the way for a better life for themselves and their families. As one adult woman put it,

> *I expect my children to help me in old age and this cannot happen if they are not educated. If a girl is still enrolled in school after age 18 she stands a high chance of getting a job to be able to help me and to take care of her needs. An educated girl also makes a better wife and mother.*

Men and boys often agree. As one boy in a group discussion said, '*An educated girl makes a good wife because she can make informed decisions and take better care of the children*'.

Grandmothers spoke with regret about the education they had missed out on: '*We never saw these papers you are writing on*', said one. '*In my day, none of us went to school, which was only for the rich and for boys*'. Girls spoke with determination about continuing their studies, with one commenting: '*They used to say educating a girl was a waste of time, but I see a speaker of Parliament being a woman*'. Some also noted that bride wealth for educated girls was higher than for uneducated girls, reflecting the increased value of education for both parents and in-laws. Yet though most study participants expressed the positive links between an educated girl and a good wife, some expressed cautionary views: '*Education makes a girl a better woman because "they go with respect"*', noted one grandmother. '*Nevertheless, when they reach home, they don't know how to make the local brew*'. One boy confessed that '*I fear marrying a girl who is more educated than me, because she might not respect me*'.

Girls in any case face many gendered risks along the path to educational attainment, including lingering social norms that mean parents prefer to invest in their sons' education, particularly at higher levels. A male district official noted that,

> There is a shift from thinking that girls are ready to marry the instant they grow breasts, towards thinking that they should be given time for school. Nevertheless, parents also want quick cash [through bride wealth] and wonder why they should waste time on a girl's education when they will just go to some other family.

Some girls also face harassment within schools, including by teachers, with girls often powerless to resist their advances: '*When a teacher talks to the girl, she cannot say no*', explained a male district planning official. '*They call them masters*'. Abuse of schoolgirls by teachers has been identified in many parts of Uganda and was cited frequently by study participants. Parents, who are fully aware of such problems, say, '*When we complain, the culprit teachers are merely transferred*'. Some fathers and mothers take the threat of such harassment as justification for pulling their adolescent daughters out of school as a protective measure.

Many girls drop out of school when they reach puberty due to lack of appropriate hygiene facilities or because, at this time, they are thought to have '*grown out of school*'; others drop out due to pregnancy which, for most, means the end of their education due to a lack of clear re-entry policies and support: '*Once you get pregnant, that is the end of school for you*', said a 17-year-old girl with a baby. Community attitudes maintain that allowing pregnant girls or new mothers to continue with schooling would set a '*bad example*' for other girls, though there is emerging evidence that this may be changing. In spite of universal secondary education policies, girls in our study communities faced a continuing lack of full educational opportunities, with long distances to schools increasing the opportunity costs and risks of experiencing violence while travelling to and from school, while technical training opportunities remain practically non-existent for girls and boys alike. Moreover, the limited options for formal sector employment in the district make the opportunity costs of trying to complete secondary school all the more onerous and risky. As one district official explained:

> Some people see no value in education in general, given high unemployment. The father pays school fees but is jobless, so he gets demoralised and also loses morale at the example of educated people in the district who remain unemployed.

Complex drivers and paradoxical processes of change and continuity

Our study identified multiple drivers of both change and continuity in norms and practices around gender equality, education and marriage for adolescent girls in Mayuge.[3] These operate at different levels, but also intertwine in paradoxical processes that at times promote and at other times prevent positive change, and can even accentuate negative outcomes for girls.

Socioeconomic transformations coupled with persistent poverty

One cluster of drivers contributing to our observed paradoxes stems from broad-based processes of socioeconomic transformation underway in our study communities. These entail a shift from a purely rural subsistence economy to one that is increasingly based on cash, but with incomplete market penetration and poor integration, which leaves livelihoods extremely insecure and contributes to high levels of household poverty. Such conditions affect adolescent girls in a number of ways, contributing, among other things, to (1) the rise in informal marriages among young people as girls seek young men engaged in the cash economy who can provide for their needs better than their own parents; (2) transactional sex encounters for the same reasons – often with older men, or 'sugar daddies' (in what one study respondent called sex *'for the price of a chapatti'*), encounters which in turn fuel premarital pregnancies and expose girls to sexually transmitted illnesses; and (3) a persistent tendency, among some parents at least, to consider their daughters as sources of bride wealth (or compensation in the case of informal marriage) to contribute to the alleviation of household poverty.

At the broader societal level, some socioeconomic transformation is seen to be contributing to positive changes through a heightened value placed on education, which is seen as one of the few paths to secure livelihoods and jobs both for boys and girls. Nevertheless, households in our study communities have limited economic options, struggling to maintain rural livelihoods in the face of land fragmentation, environmental degradation and the farming of suboptimal plots. The lack of alternative sources of employment means that adolescent boys and girls alike have uncertain futures.

Strong legal and policy environment but weak implementation locally

A second cluster of drivers of change and continuity in gender norms and practices emanates from the legal and policy environment on women and children's rights, education, and adolescent and sexual health. Here, again, forces for positive change towards greater gender equality intermingle with more reactionary forces, while constraints in implementation lead to significant challenges on the ground.

The promotion of women and children's rights in Uganda represents a positive step forward in terms of greater respect for the rights of boys and girls and overall gender justice; however, many study participants pointed to the negative effects of this in terms of its perceived contribution to the breakdown in family structures and authority. A clear backlash was apparent, among parents in general and fathers in particular.

So, too, the constitutional guarantee of 18 years as the legal age for marriage and efforts to enforce the law on 'defilement', prohibiting sexual relations with under-age children, are intended as strong reinforcement of the rights of adolescent girls to remain unmarried. However, as we have seen, these measures may be contributing to driving the practice of early marriage underground, while also fuelling the rise of early informal cohabitation arrangements. In both cases, girls are denied the right to access SRH services, particularly contraception. Moreover, strong resistance at community and national levels to a proposed marriage and divorce bill – which, among other things, would have given women greater rights in relation to cohabitation, bride price and divorce – is symbolic of the strength of norms and vested interests around issues of marriage and gender, rendering progress towards gender justice both complex and difficult.

National education policies promoting universal primary education have served as a positive force for change, opening up opportunities for girls and boys alike, enhancing girls' educational aspirations, and placing greater value on girls' education. But poor educational quality, inadequate protection for girls in school, and lack of policy attention to pregnant girls and young mothers continue to deprive many girls of their right to education. At the same time, continued limitations in implementing secondary education policies, coupled with neglect of vocational training – both of which could be most transformative for girls – have left a void at these levels of education. Meanwhile, national policies on adolescent SRH face significant challenges given the criminalisation of sexual activity before the age of 18; there are also challenges in implementing such policies at local level, given community attitudes which hold that providing this kind of information to adolescents promotes sexual activity.

Sociocultural forces in flux

These broad-based socioeconomic transformations, alongside national policy thrusts around gender equality, children's rights and expanded education, are seen to be contributing to broader sociocultural changes brought about through a complex nexus of forces that many study participants labelled 'Westernisation' or 'modernisation', which are seen to be driving out 'traditional' norms and values. Though some new trends are welcomed, many community members expressed a general sense of cultural unravelling – '*a sense of chaos*' – whereby old values are breaking down and younger generations are adopting behaviours considered to be 'immoral', influenced by what many regard as the most negative aspects of Western culture. Study participants pointed to the rise of trading centres, video halls and discos – even smartphones – conveying 'inappropriate' images as responsible for a general breakdown in morals and a laxity in relations between young men and women, which is seen to be facilitated by national policies promoting gender equality and children's rights. Even education is suspect: '*Modern education has taught children to forget their cultural behaviours,*' noted a male clan leader, '*and older men and women have lost control over their own children who say, "Leave us alone. What do you know, you old man/woman?"*' Within this shifting terrain of competing norms, adolescent girls become, as one man described it, '*the targets of culture*' as some sections of society seek to hold onto and reinforce more traditional cultural values.

Mediating sites and institutions both promote and impede positive change

Our research revealed the foundational but changing role of the household, which serves as the main site where young girls and boys internalise the roles society has set out for them and begin the culturally guided transition to adulthood. As one of our key informants noted,

> *It is not about understanding the girls themselves, but understanding the context in which they live, because norms guide the socialisation process. Within the first seven years of life, girls are already indoctrinated into the idea of being subject to men. This starts in the household and is reinforced in the community.*

Nevertheless, while some parents in our study communities struggled to maintain the household as a site of socialisation into traditional gender norms, others hoped to serve as springboards for positive change through, for example, supporting their daughters' education in the face of economic difficulty and in opposition to social norms favouring boys. As one rare 'outlier' girl in our research communities testi-fied: '*I attribute my staying in school till university level among other children in the family to the support and advice I got from my mother and father*'.

The same duality of positive and negative forces was seen to operate within schools. As institutions reflecting the wider society of which they are a part, schools sometimes served as sites for gender discrimination and risks for girls but some-times offered powerful avenues and opportunities for empowerment, including female teachers acting as role models and encouraging girls to develop new aspira-tions. As norms around education for girls beyond primary level begin to expand and take hold – and if more schooling opportunities are provided and the quality of education improves – the very idea of 'adolescence' as a space for girls to study rather than marry may contribute to further shifts in community norms and values around child marriage.

Cultural and religious institutions and leaders remain the guardians of ethnic and religious values in the ideational sphere, which they urge community members to apply in practice. Many of these institutions and leaders, however, seemed to be struggling in the face of the larger forces of socioeconomic and cultural change described earlier; their authority is now being challenged as cultural controls and sanctions are lost. '*That was in the past, but now there is no culture*', explained one key informant in Mayuge. '*Actually, cultures have been washed away*'. A male clan coordi-nator and cultural leader felt strongly that young people '*should not go about wildly in these modern ways. . . . My worry is how we can preserve our culture while at the same time adapting to current developments*'. Most of our respondents agreed that such adaptation was not a smooth process. As one local government official poignantly asked, '*Once culture breaks down, how do we go back?*'

Local government structures and the justice system – mandated to serve as the key purveyors and enforcers of national laws and policies on universal education, women and children's rights and early marriage – are struggling to make inroads on these issues. Nevertheless, public trust and confidence in such institutions is weak, as is public recourse to them. This is partly due to severe capacity gaps limiting quality service provision, but also due to a perception of widespread collusion – for example, in the case of arrests for early marriage – between police and parents for 'compensation' money paid by the boy's parents.

Local political structures that have promoted greater female representation are providing powerful role models to girls who now see, for example, that the work of a female Member of Parliament (MP) is respected. Girls can therefore begin to imagine a world in which their own voice is heard. Moreover, a number of NGOs and community-based organisations active in the district are helping to strengthen or expand services through interventions that could have a potentially transformative if still limited impact on the women, girls and communities involved in their projects (see Chapter 5).

Conclusions and policy implications

In the midst of the complex forces of change and continuity in gendered norms and practices around transitions to adulthood in Mayuge, and in spite of much positive progress, adolescent girls continue to experience a host of risks and vulnerabilities. The paradoxical nature of the change processes underway and their often ambiguous effects on girls have emerged as key research findings.

Though cultural values and attitudes towards some issues – for example, girls' virginity – seem to be easing, social stigma persists and lack of access to appropriate SRH information and services results in high levels of teenage pregnancy. Some girls appear to have freer choice of marriage partner within customary unions or are entering into informal unions with partners they themselves have chosen. However, this latter is often done at an early age in the absence of other opportunities or in response to difficult conditions at home, resulting in highly unstable unions which present their own risks, thus limiting the potentially transformative power of increased 'agency' in this instance. Educational opportunities – particularly at the primary level – have expanded for girls and boys alike, but secondary education remains a challenge and schools themselves often reproduce the gender discriminatory attitudes and practices that characterise much of the wider society. Changes in rural livelihoods are beginning to open up new forms of participation in the monetary economy for some, but opportunities remain limited; girls in particular lack both the education and vocational skills necessary to fully engage with new economic opportunities, and they continue to face disadvantage due to patrilineal inheritance systems. Policies for women's empowerment are being promoted, but community backlash threatens progress, contributing to domestic violence and leading to further imbalances in the gendered division of labour as men use such policies to justify the abandonment of their traditional roles as family providers.

Overall, households and the processes of household formation are being buffeted by forces and structures within the wider community and environment that are setting up potent and contradictory processes. These are leading to tensions and cracks in normative systems at all levels, often with negative consequences for girls. Our analysis suggests that both gender norms themselves and the broader drivers of change and continuity in such norms need to be addressed in order to pave the way for positive transformation. This should go alongside further investment in the mediating institutions that can help to empower adolescent girls and contribute to shifting harmful norms and practices.

Community dialogue processes can be useful in raising awareness of the need to change discriminatory gender norms and practices – drawing in and deepening engagement by local cultural and faith-based leaders, mothers and fathers, and boys and girls in collective efforts to confront the challenges in achieving gender justice. National policies promoting the rights of women and children should be accompanied by appropriate programmes to enable them to claim these rights, along with further community sensitisation and strengthened legal services to protect them. At the same time, further investment in social infrastructure and quality service delivery at district level is critical to ensure that schools and health centres can play potentially transformative roles, within a policy framework that promotes positive change.

As an overarching priority, clear plans and investments are needed to support overall socioeconomic development in the district so as to counter household poverty as a driver of child marriages, adolescent pregnancies and school dropouts. Specific measures for the economic empowerment of girls and women would help ensure that adolescent girls themselves become more empowered to contribute to positive changes in both norms and practices, guided by more visible female role models from within their communities and beyond. To be successful, such processes will require political will to manage the conflicting interests and ideas that continue to surround efforts to promote gender equity and empowerment, as well as consensus on devoting sufficient resources to effect truly transformative change.

Notes

1 The study in Mayuge was conducted by researchers at Makerere University and ODI over two years (2012 and 2013). It combined extensive documentary review, key informant interviews at national and subnational levels, and interviews and discussions with community members (girls/boys/women/men), drawing on a variety of innovative and participatory research instruments. Full reports of findings can be found in Kyomuhendo Bantebya *et al.* 2013 and Kyomuhendo Bantebya *et al.* 2014.

2 East Central region is one of two regions carved out of the earlier, larger, Eastern region in 2006; numerous statistical indicators continue to be collected for the larger entity, as is the case for poverty indicators and some educational statistics.

3 Analysis of drivers of change and continuity draws on the conceptual framework developed for the study as a whole which depicts how both positive change in social norms and forces maintaining discriminatory gender norms may be mediated by a variety of

factors, operating through different institutions and sites to affect adolescent girls' capability development (Marcus 2014).

Bibliography

Amin, S., Austrian, A., Chau, M., Glazer, K., Green, E., Stewart, D. and Stoner, M. (2013) *The Adolescent Girls Vulnerability Index: Guiding Strategic Investment in Uganda*. Kampala and New York: The Ministry of Gender, Labour and Social Development of the Government of Uganda, Population Council, and UNICEF. Available online at www.ungei.org/index_5160.html

Kaduuli, S.C. (2010) *Kwandhula: Cultural Engagement and Marriage in Busoga and Buganda*. Saarbrücken, Germany: LAP Lambert Academic Publishing. OmniScriptum GmbH & Co., KG.

Kyomuhendo Bantebya, G., Kyoheirwe Muhanguzi, F. and Watson, C. (2013) *Adolescent Girls and Gender Justice: Understanding Key Capability Domains in Uganda*. London: Overseas Development Institute. Available online at www.odi.org/sites/odi.org.uk/files/odi-assets/publications-opinion-files/8822.pdf

Kyomuhendo Bantebya, G., Kyoheirwe Muhanguzi, F. and Watson, C. (2014) *Adolescent Girls in the Balance: Changes and Continuity in Social Norms and Practices Around Marriage and Education in Uganda*. London: Overseas Development Institute. Available online at www.odi.org/sites/odi.org.uk/files/odi-assets/publications-opinion-files/9180.pdf

Marcus, R. (2014) *Gender Justice for Adolescent Girls: Understanding Processes of Change in Gender Norms. Towards a Conceptual Framework for Phase 2*. London: Overseas Development Institute.

Mayuge District Local Government. (2010a) *Baitambogwe Sub-County Approved Three-Year Rolled Development Plan 2010/11–2012/13*, June. Mayuge: Mayuge District Local Government.

Mayuge District Local Government. (2010b) *Kityerera Sub-County: Three-Year Investment Plan for the Period 2010/11–2012/13*. Mayuge: Mayuge District Local Government.

Mayuge District Local Government. (2011) *Five-Year Development Plan (2010/11–2014/15)*. Mayuge: Mayuge District Local Government.

Mayuge District Local Government. (2012) *Mayuge District Local Government Investment Profile (2012/13–2014/15)*. Mayuge: Mayuge District Local Government.

Mayuge District Local Government. (2013) *"Education Department (2014/15)" Planning document*. Mayuge: Mayuge District Local Government.

Ministry of Education and Sports. (2012) *Dropout Study in Universal Secondary Education (USE)*. Kampala: Ministry of Education and Sports.

Ministry of Finance, Planning and Economic Development. (2014) *Poverty Status Report 2014: Structural Change and Poverty Reduction in Uganda*. Kampala: Ministry of Finance, Planning and Economic Development.

Ministry of Gender, Labour and Social Development and United Nations Children's Fund (UNICEF). (2015) *The National Strategy to End Child Marriage and Teenage Pregnancy (2014/15–2019/20)*. Kampala: Ministry of Gender, Labour and Social Development and United Nations Children's Fund.

Ministry of Health. (2004) *The National Adolescent Reproductive Health Policy*. Kampala: Ministry of Health.

Organisation for Economic Co-operation and Development (OECD)/Uganda Bureau of Statistics (UBOS). (2015) *Uganda SIGI Country Report*. Kampala: Organisation for Economic Co-operation and Development and Uganda Bureau of Statistics.

Otiso, K.M. (2006) *Culture and Customs of Uganda.* Westport, CT: Greenwood Press.

Republic of Uganda. (2015) *Second National Development Plan (NDPII) 2015/16–2019/20.* Kampala: Republic of Uganda.

Uganda Bureau of Statistics (UBOS). (2011) *Higher Local Government Statistical Abstract: Mayuge District.* Kampala: Uganda Bureau of Statistics.

Uganda Bureau of Statistics. (UBOS). (2012a) *Uganda Demographic and Health Survey 2011.* Kampala: Uganda Bureau of Statistics.

Uganda Bureau of Statistics (UBOS). (2012b) *Statistical Abstract.* Kampala: Uganda Bureau of Statistics.

United Nations Children's Fund (UNICEF). (2013) *Situation Analysis of Child Poverty and Deprivation in Uganda.* Kampala: United Nations Children's Fund.

5

FROM NATIONAL LAWS AND POLICIES TO LOCAL PROGRAMMES

Obstacles and opportunities in communications for adolescent girls' empowerment in Uganda

Grace Kyomuhendo Bantebya, Florence Kyoheirwe Muhanguzi and Carol Watson

The emerging gender-sensitive national framework

Uganda has an extensive body of national laws and policies to reduce the vulnerabilities facing adolescent girls as they make the crucial transition to adult life. The Constitution (1995) prohibits all forms of discrimination and provides for the protection and promotion of women's rights. Uganda's Vision 2040 provides for gender equality and women's empowerment for socioeconomic transformation, integrating gender analysis in policy and programme design and implementation; it also calls for the elimination of all harmful sociocultural practices that impede realisation of women's and girl's capabilities. The National Development Plan (2015/16–2019/20) prioritises gender equality and women's empowerment as well as the institutionalisation of strong gender-responsive regulatory frameworks and mechanisms. The National Gender Policy (2007) highlights the need to confront persistent cultural norms and values underlying gender discrimination and promotes gender equality and women's empowerment as an integral part of the national development process; guidelines have recently been developed for gender planning and budgeting.

Expanding educational opportunities for all has been a policy priority, with the government introducing policies on universal primary education (1997) and universal secondary education (2007), accompanied by a strategy for girls' education (2015) that highlights the national commitment to girls' empowerment and is explicit about the negative impact of discriminatory norms that constrain girls' education. Child marriage is prohibited by the Constitution, which sets the legal minimum age of marriage at 18, and a recently adopted National Strategy to End Child Marriage and Teenage Pregnancy (2015) offers a comprehensive framework which reflects the government's commitment to girls' rights to a childhood. The Adolescent Reproductive Health Policy (2004) pledged to advocate for: the review of all legal, medical and social barriers to adolescents' access to information and health services; protection of the rights of adolescents to health information and services; provision of legal and social protection for adolescents against all forms of abuse and harmful traditional practices (HTPs); and promotion of gender equality and provision of quality care for adolescent sexual and reproductive health (SRH) issues (Ministry of Gender, Labour and Social Development and UNICEF 2015). Various pieces of legislation have been enacted to protect girls and women from violence and abuse in relation to: 'defilement' (defined as sexual relations before the age of 18) (2007); female genital mutilation (FGM) (2009); and domestic violence (2010).

Against such an impressive policy backdrop, analysis of national and regional survey data reveals that many adolescents still live in poverty, deprived of full educational attainment, while many girls are impelled into child marriage or early pregnancy and subject to continuing high levels of violence and abuse (see Chapter 4). This reflects the substantial and well-recognised 'disconnect' between Uganda's positive legal and policy framework and the actual implementation of programmes (including gender-responsive programmes) on the ground. Part of the problem stems from lack of investment in the institutional structures mandated to lead on these efforts: the Ministry of Gender, Labour and Social Development has limited capacity at both central and local levels and is consistently allocated less than 1 per cent of the national budget (United Nations Development Programme (UNDP) 2015). As a result, it is difficult for government to address even the 'practical' gender needs of women and girls at local level, let alone the 'strategic' interests highlighted in policy that could lead to transformative change.

A broader problem stems from the continuing resource constraints and capacity gaps in local government overall, which hinder implementation of critical national policies for education and SRH. Most analysts of decentralisation processes in Uganda have concluded that the effects on social service delivery have been ambiguous at best (Steiner 2006; Bashaasha *et al.* 2011; Kisaame and Nampewo 2016). With its high degree of donor dependency (external donors accounted for a quarter of the national budget in 2016/2017), non-governmental organisations (NGOs) have emerged as significant actors working on both local-level programme implementation and policy advocacy. Yet they too often depend on external funding and may be constrained by uncertain funding cycles and lack of coordination – among themselves and with government partners. The recently passed revised NGO Bill is also raising concerns about potential new government restrictions on NGO activities in Uganda (Uganda National NGO Forum 2015).

In addition to the ongoing capacity gaps and complexities in programme implementation at local level, there are areas where the overall enabling environment for gender-responsive action remains uncertain. As highlighted in the preceding Chapter 4, ambiguities around the law on defilement (which criminalises sex under the age of 18) combine with limited health service provision to deny adolescents their right to SRH information and services. Meanwhile, current national debates about law reform to regulate marriage and divorce reveal deep resistance to any change to today's discriminatory practices at the household and family levels. Despite extensive mobilisation, the Marriage and Divorce Bill (2009), tabled in Parliament in 2012, was withdrawn and put on permanent hold after meeting stiff opposition from male legislators, who saw it as a threat to their gender identities and male power because it challenged the status quo of existing power relations in the family (Ministry of Gender, Labour and Social Development and UNICEF 2015). This illustrates the substantive challenges faced by all actors involved in promoting transformative change and gender empowerment in Uganda, which remains a deeply conservative and patriarchal society.

Communicating for gender norm change

Given the strong legal and policy framework but apparently recalcitrant commitment for implementation, understanding how real change for girls may happen is clearly critical to improving their well-being. Of the range of possible change catalysts, communications initiatives appear to offer potential to contribute to transformative change for girls. A recent review of such initiatives in different country contexts has indicated that they can be an effective way to challenge gender discriminatory attitudes and practices (Marcus and Page 2014).

We will here examine current efforts to promote gender equality and empowerment for adolescent girls in rural Uganda, focusing on selected communications initiatives that aim to shift discriminatory norms and practices around child marriage and adolescent pregnancy, as well as to expand community awareness of the importance of girls' education and to foster greater gender equality within the family and community. Our research is based on fieldwork conducted in communities in eastern and northern Uganda where communications initiatives are being implemented by NGOs as part of broader national efforts to promote gender equality[1] (see Figure 4.1).

Diverse programmes for adolescent girls

Our programme mapping in Uganda identified a variety of interventions underway to promote gender empowerment for girls. These include: sensitising families and communities on critical issues through a variety of communication channels; providing education (formal and non-formal) on life skills for girls; and strengthening livelihood and vocational skills. Issues of child marriage and teenage pregnancy are often addressed within broader programming around SRH and sexual and gender-based violence (SGBV) or violence against children (as a child rights issue). Given the national context, many SRH programmes focus on HIV awareness and protection, while child protection programming often focuses on orphaned and vulnerable children. Messaging on girls' education is linked to both child rights and gender empowerment, while interventions in schools often focus on creating and/or strengthening gender-sensitive learning environments and promoting access to SRH information. Many programmes adopt a twin focus on raising awareness of critical issues as a means of promoting changes in attitudes (through, for example, community dialogues, peer-based activities, information campaigns, music, dance and drama, and public events and ceremonies), while offering at least some element of improving service provision (counselling, shelter, health care, justice, education).

Project case studies

The three case study projects we selected for analysis reflect the diversity of approaches we have described. All have been designed to address specific problems related to adolescent girls' well-being and capacity development. Two are embedded in larger programmes that emphasise sexual and reproductive health rights (SRHR) and child protection; the third is a stand-alone project focused more broadly on gender equality, with specific links to SRH promotion, violence prevention and girls' education (see Box 5.1).

BOX 5.1   CASE STUDY PROJECTS

The *Unite for Body Rights* project is implemented by the Straight Talk Foundation (STF), an NGO, in the East Central region of Uganda. It is part of a larger organisation, the Sexual and Reproductive Health and Rights (SRHR) Alliance, which aims to provide good-quality education on SRHR to young people in school and out of school to empower them to make healthy and well-informed decisions and increase demand for youth-friendly SRH and maternal health services. It also implements community sensitisation, participation and mobilisation activities to create an environment that accepts and supports adolescents' rights to sexual and reproductive health. Core activities focus on individual empowerment alongside promotion of conducive and enabling conditions and policies for SRHR. Internal programme monitoring indicates significant progress over a two-year period (2011–2013) in enhancing knowledge of and positive attitudes towards SRHR as well as young people's capacity to make safe and informed decisions about their sexual and reproductive health. There appears to be less progress in imbuing the target group of adolescents with broader skills and empowerment (SRHR Alliance 2013).

The *Child Protection and Development* project is implemented by the Uganda Chapter of the African Network for the Prevention and Protection Against Child Abuse and Neglect (ANPPCAN), also in the East Central region. It is rooted in a child rights perspective and aims to provide a secure and protective environment for children. The project seeks to increase the availability of protection, psychosocial, legal, and other essential services for orphaned and vulnerable children and to strengthen advocacy for implementation of child protection laws and policies, including laws on child marriage and compulsory education. It targets child mothers, empowering them with skills and income-generating activities so that they can take care of their children while

---

also endeavouring to shift social norms that stigmatise this group. Internal programme monitoring identifies progress on 'outputs' in terms of training conducted, livelihood support provided, information disseminated and the establishment of a child hotline (ANPPCAN Uganda 2013).

The *Gender Roles, Equality and Transformations (GREAT)* project, implemented in the Mid Northern region of Uganda, is a coalition between Georgetown University's Institute for Reproductive Health (IRH), Pathfinder International and Save the Children, which works with local implementing partners. It combines a broad focus on gender equality with more specific messaging and dialogue around reproductive health, gender-based violence (GBV) and education. Under an intersectoral coordination structure, it has established community action groups composed of local leaders and service providers, while various 'platform groups' such as youth associations, church groups and school-based clubs have been trained to implement communications activities. Preliminary results of an end-line evaluation indicate significant improvements in adolescent attitudes and behaviours around gender equality, SRH and intimate partner violence, and a greater likelihood among adult participants to provide supportive advice to adolescents (IRH, Pathfinder International and Save the Children 2015).

All three projects are being undertaken in rural districts characterised by high levels of poverty and limited social service infrastructure, reflecting the severe constraints on local government capacity to implement national policies and deliver services. The districts are in turn situated in regions that display high levels of gender-based discrimination, as measured by the Social Institutions and Gender Index (SIGI) (Organisation for Economic Co-operation and Development (OECD)/Uganda Bureau of Statistics (UBOS) 2015). Baseline studies and situation analyses in the project communities identify significant challenges and constraints for adolescent girls, with high levels of child marriage, teenage pregnancy, GBV, child abuse and school dropouts.

Effecting positive changes

The power of communications

Results of our field study indicate that packaging and promoting new ideas through innovative communications and dialogue can effectively open up the debate around gender norms and behaviours as a first step towards broader social change. All of the projects have made innovative use of a variety of communications media and messaging as well as creating spaces for interaction, dialogue and role modelling around the new ideas on positive gender norms and behaviours that are being transmitted. Each uses some form of community dialogue or conversation – seen as essential in mobilising awareness in communities and popular because of its interactive, dynamic and face-to-face manner. Such dialogues are often accompanied by drama. As one community member involved in the Unite for Body Rights project explained: '*It's the drama that is so eye-catching and will attract many people – even those who wouldn't have come otherwise just for a talk*'. Participants in the GREAT project concurred: '*If you prepare a drama about early marriage, for example, and you teach the people in the community, you can make other people copy what you have done*'. One form of community dialogue employed by GREAT that is particularly appreciated builds on traditional fireside chats in which elders impart knowledge to young people, as one adult explained, '*The fireside chats are appreciated because they revive an older tradition that had fallen out of use and they bring elders together with others*'.

Mass media – in the form of radio dramas and talk shows in local languages used in all of the projects – seemed to work best when combined with collective listening groups to share and discuss the issues or 'call-ins' for questions and answers. Interactive, 'bottom–up' communications channels such as suggestion boxes in schools and a toll-free 'hotline' promoted by ANPPCAN served as effective links for reporting and follow-up on cases of child abuse, including early marriage. Peer-to-peer education and information exchange has been effectively promoted by both STF and GREAT; in the latter, this is conducted through youth 'platforms' that implement gender norm change activities. Role plays seem to be an especially powerful means of 'modelling' the behavioural changes promoted by the projects. In the GREAT project, adolescent participants act out stereotype-breaking gender roles within the household that occasion much laughter and discussion. Written and/or pictorial materials have been developed by STF, in its flagship *Young Talk* and *Straight Talk* newsletters that actively engage adolescents, and by GREAT in interactive games and learning materials that are eagerly sought after by participants.

The projects focused their activities on individuals and groups at the different levels at which change needs to occur; this is seen as a means of helping to ensure broad acceptance of the new ideas and information that is being promoted. All three projects targeted adolescents of different age groups as primary beneficiaries: as one study participant noted:

> *This is a time when socialisation is happening, when people are learning their roles. Because to transform gender norms, when you go to an older person, it's a bit hard but when you start early, then you are able to catch somebody at an early age and begin to influence their thinking early enough.*

GREAT has developed tailored materials and activities to address the specific interests and information needs of different age groups of adolescents; ANPPCAN focuses its activities on child mothers but within its wider programme for orphaned and vulnerable children; and Unite for Body Rights includes activities for both in-school and out-of-school adolescents.

At the same time, the projects implement specific communications activities designed to sensitise adults who play a significant role in the lives of adolescents, conceptualised variously as 'influencers', 'gatekeepers' and 'enablers': '*We also do not forget the adults*', noted one project manager, '*because these adolescents are also influenced by other people around them like their parents, their teachers, religious leaders, and general people in the community*'. ANPPCAN includes positive parenting activities as a way of combating norms around early marriage and underinvestment in girls' education; indeed, it credits its community conversations on these topics with significant attitudinal and behavioural change, including an increase in the reporting of early marriages and other forms of abuse as an indicator of greater awareness and willingness to take action on the part of the adults it reaches. GREAT includes cultural leaders in its project coordination framework. Teachers, health workers and child protection officers receive new knowledge and skills to help them address discriminatory norms through the different projects.

Complementing communications interventions with service strengthening and support for institutional development at local level is also an effective strategy employed by the projects to address barriers to change that may stem from the wider socioeconomic context. The Unite for Body Rights project has embedded its communications activities within the wider service provision interventions of the SRHR Alliance. It trains teachers to support young people in school and helps set up school clubs that transmit SRH information to girls. It also promotes practical activities such as teaching girls to make reusable sanitary pads out of local materials, thus addressing menstrual hygiene issues, which have been identified as a key limiting factor in adolescent girls' school attendance. The ANPPCAN model has explicitly combined service delivery and empowerment with communications *per se:* its community case workers actively intervene in cases of child abuse, linking victims to legal recourse and providing counselling; orphaned and vulnerable children receive scholastic materials and adolescent girls are given sanitary pads to enable them to stay in school; while the child mothers component provides vocational skills training for income generation and livelihood support. GREAT also found that it was not enough to raise awareness of SRH issues without some attention to strengthening services; an additional project component was added early on, focusing on training existing village health team volunteers to provide support with referrals.

Multiple changes at different levels

The projects reported achieving significant positive changes at different levels. Adolescents reported increased skills and knowledge, particularly about SRH, with the projects filling an important information gap in this regard. Attitudinal changes were also apparent, particularly around early marriage and pregnancy, as well as the value of girls' education. Perhaps one of the most striking instances of individual change reported was the heightened self-confidence and sense of agency that participating in project activities brought to adolescent boys and girls, along with new found skills in leadership and public speaking, which contributed to a sense of empowerment. Changes in household relations and expectations included more egalitarian household roles, more open communication between parents and children and among siblings, and parents placing greater value on girls' education. Such changes are significant, given the household's seminal role in primary socialisation processes around gender roles and normative behaviours.

At a broader community level, the projects have strengthened or stimulated development of local institutional structures such as the village health teams, community child protection committees, peer education fora and community platforms for adolescents. These have led to improved service provision, stronger community engagement around issues of child protection (including child marriage), and strengthened peer relations and leadership roles for young people, as well as greater awareness of their capabilities. Table 5.1 illustrates some of these changes in participants' own words.

TABLE 5.1 Reported changes at individual, household and community levels

Level at which changes reported	Nature of the changes reported
Individual new knowledge changed attitudes economic empowerment enhanced confidence	• *'The programme has provided children with information that most parents were too shy to talk about'* (parents, STF). • *'We have learned about child spacing and I am now practising it'* (**newly married adolescents, GREAT**). • *'We have learned that one should get married at about 18 years and above – after finishing school, when you have a house and a job'* (**adolescent girls, STF**). • *'I have learned that boys and girls can do the same types of activities and chores'* (**adolescent girl, GREAT**). • *'I am now able to provide for the needs of my children as opposed to before, when I was hopeless'* (**adolescent mother, ANPPCAN**). • *'I didn't know we had a right to bark at boys who try to force us. I now know I can say no without fear'* (**adolescent girl, STF**). • *'This programme has helped me become bold. I'm no longer as shy as I was before. I can now stand before my peers and speak without fear'* (**adolescent mother, ANPPCAN**).
Household more egalitarian gender roles more open communication greater parental value on girls' education	• *'I used to think cooking was just for women; now I cook with my sisters at home and am sometimes even better than them!'* (**adolescent boy, GREAT**). • *'The silence that used to exist between girl children and their parents has been broken. Straight Talk lessons gave us a starting point to educate our children'* (**parents, STF**).

(Continued)

TABLE 5.1 (Continued)

Level at which changes reported	Nature of the changes reported
	• *'We have since understood that childbearing does not mean an end to our daughters' education'* (parents, ANPPCAN).
	• *'Before, I thought girls' education was useless, but now I am struggling to pay for my daughter's schooling at senior level'* (father, GREAT).

School and community
reduced violence
enhanced school attendance
enhanced SRH services
improved learning
  environment
strengthened esteem and
  visibility for adolescents
  in community
	• *'Violence has reduced in both homes and the community because of what we have learned and have taught others'* (adolescent girls, ANPPCAN).

	• *'The intervention of Straight Talk has indeed improved the rate of self-awareness among pupils on sexuality, increased school attendance, and led to more assertive girls'* (education official, STF).
	• *'Before GREAT, we didn't know how to talk freely with young people and their parents, and young people did not talk to us freely. We have gained counselling experience'* (village health team, GREAT).
	• *'Before GREAT, as a teacher, I used to ignore problems of school dropout and would not say anything if I saw boys teasing girls in school, as I did not consider that my role; now, after GREAT training, we have stronger interactions with the community following up on dropouts and have also gained counselling skills in the classroom'* (teacher, GREAT).
	• *'Adolescents involved in the STF project later go back to their villages where they act as ambassadors of change to the others they find there'* (adults, STF).
	• *'We have become popular in society – people make reference to us in admiration of our work. We have made friends out of the work we do'* (adolescent mothers, ANPPCAN).
	• *'The community sees us with respect because of the training we have had'* (adolescents, GREAT).

Significant constraints

In spite of these positive effects, all of the projects encountered numerous challenges and constraints. These were linked to the wider structural setting of entrenched gender discriminatory norms, pervasive poverty and weak local government capacity for service provision, but also to the time and resource restrictions that limit the scope and coverage of project activities, coupled with certain weaknesses in their institutional arrangements and coordination.

We adapt for our analysis here the political economy model derived from what Rosendorff (2005) has set out as the 'Three I's', namely: *institutions* (e.g. national and local governments, cultural and religious institutions, and the institutional frameworks established by projects) and the opportunities or constraints they present for gender and girls' empowerment; *interests* of key actors at different levels (e.g. government, donors and civil society champions/programme implementers, cultural and religious leaders, parents, adolescents) and their relative power; and *ideas*, whether conveyed through the communications projects as an expression of national policy thrusts on gender equality, or the ideas held by local officials, community members and parents who may act as 'gatekeepers'.

We apply this model to the analysis of constraints encountered in achieving planned project outcomes and in generalising such outcomes beyond the project framework. In this way, our analysis follows on from the previous chapter on Uganda, which identified NGOs operating in the country and the projects they implement as 'mediating institutions' that have the potential to create positive impacts at a local level but within a broader sociopolitical, economic and cultural context that presents significant constraints to transformational changes.

Institutional constraints and complexities

Institutional constraints arise, in the first instance, from the inherent limitations and complexities of an externally financed 'project approach' to development led by non-governmental actors and, in the second instance, from resource and capacity gaps in local government service structures and institutions.

The short-term funding arrangements and project cycles of most NGO activities significantly limit their scope and coverage. All three projects were implemented within a clear timeframe of between three and five years and were dependent on external funding sources that were not foreseen to extend beyond that period. Yet norm change – entailing as it does both changes in individual attitudes and behaviours and changes in the enabling environment – is a long-term process. Indeed, 'directed' change of the type promoted through our case study projects, which seeks to transform gender roles, expectations and relations, requires continued, long-term support and encouragement to enable it to take root in communities and flourish. As one of our study participants noted: '*This is not the work of a day*'. Moreover, local communities do not exist in isolation, so the critical mass needed to embed such changes in local practice would require continued efforts to expand beyond the geographically limited project areas – all of which calls for sustained, committed support beyond the project cycle.

Some project managers felt that their communications activities were raising expectations that may not be met. As one key informant attested about the SRHR Alliance activities: '*Most projects are short-lived – they expire before they even have time to make an impact. The resources are too scarce to meet the demands of the community*'. ANPP-CAN programme managers observed that:

> It is a bit challenging because projects in most cases are implemented within one to three years, whereas programmes take a longer period. For example, this project which is so good in supporting child mothers to gain regular income is ending this year, but if it was a programme, you could see that many more people would benefit from it.

The geographic limitations of project activities were stark, and were largely attributed to the institutionally defined limits of human and financial resources, which
in turn limited impact on a wider scale. For instance, the STF project was active
in only ten schools in the district, excluding most schools and particularly those in
more remote rural areas. An ANPPCAN programme staff member also lamented
that:

> When you look at the whole of Eastern region, it is basically ANPPCAN that is
> doing work on child protection cases. We receive cases from as far away as Mayuge and
> Namutumbe, so coverage is also a big challenge. Resources will never be enough. Com-
> munities will not be reached because of inadequate resources.

Although the NGO and civil society organisation (CSO) actors all demonstrated
commitment to addressing discriminatory norms, the organisational structures
established for programme implementation could at times be unwieldy. For example, the SRHR Alliance works through partner organisations (of which STF is one)
at various levels, aiming to create positive synergies and achieve holistic responses to
complex issues by drawing on different skill sets and outreach potential that would
be beyond any one organisation. This strategy was also reported to present some
challenges, however, when partners with different approaches and ways of working are asked to collaborate to deliver a joint activity. As one key informant noted:
'*Partner organisations also have different capacities and capacity gaps, so it is sometimes difficult to ensure that everyone is moving forward at the same pace*'. In practice, this results in
cases where SRH information activities undertaken in schools by one partner in a
particular district are out of sync with complementary SRH service strengthening
within local health centres, leading to a critical gap between heightened demand
and available supply. An ANPPCAN programme manager also mentioned coordination as an issue: '*There are several NGOs doing projects which are related. You find three
NGOs in different hotels conducting trainings on similar issues. There is a lot of duplication
and if we could work together we could do much more*'.

The decentralised governance structure in Uganda offers potential for local government leadership and initiative in district development processes and the partners
who support these. All three projects recognised this and included local government structures as key partners in project implementation and follow-up so as to
foster ownership and promote sustainability. STF coordinates its activities through
the district management committees; ANPPCAN draws in district departments
most closely involved in child protection activities, including the police and proba-
tion officers; and GREAT established a reference group at district level, involving
the health, education and gender and community development sectors.

However, district governments have limited human, financial and logistical
resources with which to undertake the additional activities proposed by projects,
so unless adequate resources are built into the government's district development
plans, with sufficient funding made available, they will never really be able to
assume the 'ownership' of externally financed projects currently run by NGOs.

Accordingly, concerns about sustainability of interventions were voiced in relation to all three projects. There was considerable uncertainty surrounding the future of the GREAT project, which was designed as a pilot to be taken over and scaled up by other organisations active in the community, coordinated by the community development department at district level at the end of the project's three- to four-year period. But local government officials expressed doubts:

> *Local government will face challenges especially in terms of budgets – the local government budget is mostly set aside for capital development, not such sensitisation activities. GREAT should be integrated into local government structures and sectors, but this needs to be approved by the council.*

Project managers from ANPPCAN also contend that while local government is supposed to monitor project activities as part of its functions, '*Sometimes you go an entire quarter without seeing anyone coming*' because of lack of capacity.

The weakness of government institutions and overall service provision at district and local levels also leads to an imbalance between the supply of certain services and the demand generated by NGO communications initiatives. This was clearly seen at local level in all of the project districts. As GREAT project managers pointed out, for example, '*Even when adolescents have information on SRH services, providers are often not there*'. In that case, it led to a programme redesign decision to begin training village health teams. ANPPCAN programme managers note that local child protection services are so weak in their project districts that in the face of increased reporting of child abuse stimulated by the project sensitisation activities, it is assumed that ANPPCAN itself will take on the case management. '*For instance, if someone is defiled [sex with a minor], the case should be handled by the police, but instead, the police come to ANPPCAN for facilitation, fuel . . . .*' This means that NGOs that would perhaps have liked to focus specifically on norm change activities in their projects find that they need to invest in service strengthening as well if they hope to address – at least in a small way – some of the key supply barriers to the behavioural changes that new norms intend to promote.

Differential interests in project implementation

Following on in part from the differential resourcing levels of the various institutional actors, it can be expected that – in terms of financial motivation at least – those actors who are directly paid by the project will have the greatest interest in project implementation processes. Beyond the question of payment, however, there are more nebulous issues of 'ownership' and 'internalisation' of project activities, which relate as much to patterns of authority and decision-making and clear incentives within government as to payment *per se*.

All projects were in line with key national legal frameworks and policy thrusts around gender empowerment, education, child protection and adolescent health. All also strove to translate these into practice at the community level, working – as we have seen – through the district authorities and community structures. How-ever, the national policy thrusts themselves were not always clearly developed into national programmes of action, translating into budgeted district development plans with specific activities linked to the project and clear directives for action on the part of local government and service providers. So introduction of an NGO-supported school-based project (providing school clubs, SRH education materi-als, or training teachers in counselling, for instance), though perhaps welcomed by some teachers, in practice makes additional demands on teachers' time. This in turn may not be fully covered by ministerial directives, let alone pay increases. So teachers' interest in carrying out these activities – particularly after the project ends – may be minimal.

The sustainability of relying on volunteers for social mobilisation around norm change also needs careful assessment. All three projects, in one way or another, drew on the voluntary work of community members, organised in existing or newly formed groups such as child protection committees, 'platforms' (youth groups or women's groups) and social mobilisers. They also linked up with the village health teams, who form one of the key voluntary service structures in Uganda and provide a vital link between communities and the government's health services. Though the ethos behind such extensive use of volunteer community workers may be laudable (denoting clear community commitment to project goals), there are questions as to whether this presents a viable model for sustainability once the project ends.

Already, for example, village health teams are complaining of lack of equipment and logistical support to carry out their activities, while some of the community child rights networks involved in ANPPCAN's project are expressing 'volunteer fatigue': '*We are effecting change and we are willing to work even harder if we are supported. But we are about to abandon the job since we do not benefit in any way*'. Stakeholders involved in all of the projects acknowledge that further thought is needed on the best strategies to both elicit and retain community mobilisation around social norm change.

The interests of individual community members in participating in project activities may sometimes be motivated less by the value they see in the information and communications thrusts *per se* and more by a hope for at least some kind of direct material gain. This is largely a reflection of pervasive poverty in the project sites. Such was the case, for example, with girls counselled by the GREAT project against dropping out of school who said they needed '*knickers and sanitary pads*' in order to attend school regularly and manage their menstrual hygiene. Groups sometimes have expectations for refreshments when they are called together, as is the practice of other organisations working on various projects, and a number of GREAT 'platform leaders' also reported that community members would some-times refuse to come to project meetings unless they were paid for attendance: '*They do not like getting the knowledge without money*', explained one teacher in a group discussion.

These findings highlight the kinds of constraints that may be encountered when a communications and dialogue approach aiming to promote 'strategic' gender interests through long-term attitudinal change is not directly accompanied by material benefits for participants who are living in poverty, and therefore does not coalesce with the immediate 'practical' interests of individuals and groups. From this perspective, the skills training and livelihood support provided to child mothers by the ANPPCAN project were among the most valued interventions, as beneficiaries perceived it to be an immediate source of empowerment.

Resistance to new ideas

Our previous chapter on Uganda showed that introducing new ideas through the vehicles of national laws and policies around gender empowerment, child rights and protection, and adolescent SRH rights is not a smooth process and in fact meets concerted resistance at different levels. This was clearly the case with some of the gender norm changes our case study projects were trying to promote.

Project managers and government service providers tended to situate the bulk of this resistance at the community level, and feedback from a number of community members indeed confirmed such resistance. For example, the STF project, providing education for young people on SRH issues, faced objections from the start from different parts of the community, believing that sex is 'sacred' or socially taboo and should not be talked about openly in public, and certainly not in schools to young people.

There was also evidence of resistance within local government and service structures, reflecting a common feeling that teaching young girls about SRH issues is improper and will merely encourage them to experiment with sex, with negative consequences. In the context of Uganda's defilement laws, this brought up a number of ambiguities: 'The programme was considered rather contradictory in schools', explained one person in a group of male teachers and parents, 'as those who are under 18 should be abstaining from sex, but Straight Talk preaches condom use, so girls are more exposed and so can end up defiled as they explore condom use'. These sentiments were compounded by ambiguous national guidelines and programmes around adolescent SRH, and limited capacities to deliver services at local levels.

The issue was further complicated for the GREAT project's SRH activities in northern Uganda, which met with resistance to family planning information and services. As one project manager explained:

> Some say, 'We have been depleted by war and need to replenish'. Clan leaders in particular want to expand the clan. Others say that it brings disorder, encourages children to have sex, and is only for 'city people'. Others, such as fundamentalist Christians, are against it in principle.

There are also strong community norms around early marriage, which, as an ANPPCAN project manager noted, is seen as 'part of culture. There is a general feeling that when a girl develops breasts, she is ready for marriage'. Such norms, as we have seen in Chapter 4, are very resistant to change. The idea that physical maturation does not automatically mean that girls have become adults, and that the definition of a child includes someone up to the age of 18, remains largely incompatible with local ideas and customs, making it difficult to enforce the national law on minimum age at marriage.

Moreover, the very idea of 'child rights' – injected as it is into more traditional age hierarchies within the family and household – is quite negatively received by some communities, who translate it as '*edembe*', or '*freedom to do what they like*'; this therefore fuels resistance to the activities and messages of child rights organisations, such as ANPPCAN, who are seen to be '*spoiling*' children, according to one ANPPCAN programme manager. This was also the case in the initial phases of the GREAT project implementation, where, as a member of a village health team explained, '*Sometimes when we go to homes to speak to young people, the parents ask, "Why are you here?"*'

Negative reactions from peers within the community can also discourage people from adopting new behaviours based on new ideas of gender equality. As an older adolescent boy participating in the GREAT project observed, '*When I go with my sister to collect firewood, others around me take this badly and their negative reactions discourage me*'. Another confided that: '*When I help my sisters prepare food at home, some of my friends laugh at me*'. In some settings, men were identified as most resistant to change around gender norms, as they perceive themselves to have most to lose, prompting a female cultural leader to suggest that: '*We might have to work harder to get men more fully involved – often they will not sit for two hours for discussions of this sort*'.

Conclusions and implications for gender empowerment

Our field study showed that the institutional context for fostering change harbours considerable constraints inherent in the structures of governance and community. Many of these constraints arise from the embedded discriminatory norms held by actors themselves, or interpreted through the institutional structures such as education or government systems. More practical constraints are inherent in the models of development and small project initiatives that may not be easily scaled up; these are not, of course, unique to the Ugandan context.

Nevertheless, the communications-based initiatives we looked at are opening up multiple spaces for discussion and dialogue around gender discriminatory norms, attitudes and practices that are negatively impacting adolescent girls as they transition to adulthood. Key design features that seem to contribute to positive changes include using a variety of communications methodologies and approaches, targeting of individuals at different levels, and combining 'demand-side' stimulation for change through communications with 'supply-side' strengthening of local social services and institutions.

The case study projects were found to be bringing about positive effects at individual, household and community levels in the areas of project implementation. At individual level, adolescent boys and girls reported improved knowledge and skills, changed attitudes, broader aspirations, and enhanced self-confidence and sense of 'agency'. Within the household, participants reported more gender-equitable roles and responsibilities, improved communication between parents and children, and greater parental value on girls' education. In the broader community, participants noted improved educational quality and school attendance, stronger community engagement around issues of child protection (including child marriage), and strengthened peer relations and leadership roles for young people.

Significant constraints and challenges remain in longer-term efforts to definitively shift gender discriminatory norms and to create an enabling environment conducive to changed behaviours. Institutional capacity gaps and coordination issues were apparent; interests in effective programme implementation were not always fully matched up; and significant resistance was encountered to the ideas around gender empowerment conveyed by the projects. It is difficult, within the short time span and limited geographic reach of a particular project, to create a critical mass of people adopting new ideas that could provide the 'tipping point' needed to ensure sustainable and transformative change. The analysis suggests that overall, communications projects alone cannot fully address the long-term challenges or constraints posed by discriminatory gender norms; they need to be backed up by significant investment in social service provision, enforcement of gender-responsive laws, and consistent implementation of national policies, including those aimed at poverty reduction.

It has been observed elsewhere in this book that change is not a linear process, implying the need for concerted and continuous action on all fronts to address persistent discriminatory gender norms and their negative effects at all levels. It is clear overall that bringing about norm change requires significant investment of time and resources, close coordination among multi-sector partners working to promote change, and complementary efforts to address the context-specific structural barriers of gender inequality and discrimination. Programmes that aim to transform discriminatory norms that affect adolescent girls must not only be embedded in clear national policy guidelines and frameworks, but they must also be supported through explicit links from national to local levels, with appropriate investment in local government and community-based structures and ongoing poverty reduction measures. Though NGO projects can serve as intermediary institutions that can spark imaginations and demonstrate how different programme models can effect positive changes at the local level, national uptake of such models is needed to extend programmes nationwide and to institutionalise them within the national policy framework.

Note

1   The study was conducted by researchers at Makerere University and the Overseas Development Institute in 2014 and 2015 and included documentary review, key informant interviews (43) at national and subnational levels, focus group discussions (22) and individual interviews (43) involving a total of 244 participants. These included programme beneficiaries (adolescent girls, boys, parents), community members, programme planners

and implementers, local government officials and representatives of civil society. Full results are reported in Kyomuhendo Bantebya *et al.* 2015 and summarised in Watson *et al.* 2015.

Bibliography

ANPPCAN Uganda. (2013) *Protecting Children from Abuse and Promoting Their Rights: Annual Report 2013*. Kampala: African Network for the Prevention and Protection Against Child Abuse and Neglect. Available online at www.anppcanug.org/wp-content/uploads/annual_reports/ANP_annual_Rpt_2013.pdf

Bashaasha, B., Najjingo Mangheni, M. and Nkonya, E. (2011) *Decentralization and Rural Service Delivery in Uganda*. IFPRI Discussion Paper 01063, Washington, DC: International Food Policy Research Institute. Available online at www.ifpri.org/publication/decentralization-and-rural-service-delivery-uganda

Institute for Reproductive Health, Georgetown University. (2014) *Transforming Gender Norms Using a Research-to-Action Lens*. PowerPoint presentation, Jhpiego Gender Workshop, December.

Institute for Reproductive Health, Pathfinder International and Save the Children. (2015) *The GREAT Project, GREAT Results Brief.* Available online at http://irh.org/resource-library/brief-great-project-results/

Kisaame, E. and Nampewo, S. (2016) *Pro-poor Orientation of Budgets: The Case of Uganda*. Development Initiatives Briefing. Available online at http://devinit.org/wp-content/uploads/2016/07/Pro-poor-orientation-of-budgets-The-case-of-Uganda.pdf

Kyomuhendo Bantebya, G., Kyoheirwe Muhanguzi, F. and Watson, C. (2015) *'This Is Not the Work of a Day': Communications for Social Norm Change Around Early Marriage and Education for Adolescent Girls in Uganda*. London: Overseas Development Institute. Available online at www.odi.org/sites/odi.org.uk/files/odi-assets/publications-opinion-files/9895.pdf

Marcus, R. and Page, E. (2014) *Changing Discriminatory Norms Affecting Adolescent Girls Through Communication Activities: A Review of Evidence*. London: Overseas Development Institute. Available online at www.odi.org/sites/odi.org.uk/files/odi-assets/publications-opinion-files/9042.pdf

Ministry of Gender, Labour and Social Development and UNICEF. (2015) *The National Strategy to End Child Marriage and Teenage Pregnancy 2014/2015–2019/2020*. Kampala: Government of Uganda.

Ministry of Gender, Labour and Social Development. (2007) *The Uganda Gender Policy (2007)*. Kampala: Ministry of Gender, Labour and Social Development.

Organisation for Economic Co-operation and Development (OECD)/Uganda Bureau of Statistics (UBOS). (2015) *Uganda SIGI Country Report*. Kampala: Organisation for Economic Co-operation and Development/Uganda Bureau of Statistics.

Rosendorff, B. (2005) *Ideas, Interests, Institutions and Information: Jagdish Bhagwati and the Political Economy of Trade Policy*. Conference in Honour of Jagdish Bhagwati on his 70th Birthday. New York, 5–6 August.

Sexual and Reproductive Health and Rights (SRHR) Alliance. (2013) *Annual Report 2013*. Kampala: Sexual and Reproductive Health and Rights Alliance. Available online at http://srhralliance.org/wp-content/blogs.dir/7/files/sites/7/2014/08/ANNUAL-REPORT-SRHR-ALLIANCE-2013.pdf

Steiner, S. (2006) *Decentralisation in Uganda: Exploring the Constraints for Poverty Reduction*. Hamburg: GIGA Research Programme: Transformation in the Process of Globalisation No 31, German Institute of Global and Area Studies.

Uganda National NGO Forum. (2015) *A Position Paper and Clause by Clause Analysis of the NGO Bill 2015*. Available online at http://chapterfouruganda.com/sites/default/files/downloads/CSO-Position-Paper-on-the-NGO-Bill-2015.pdf

United Nations Development Programme (UNDP). (2015) *Uganda Country Gender Assessment*. Kampala: United Nations Development Programme.

Watson, C., Kyomuhendo Bantebya, G. and Kyoheirwe Muhanguzi, F. (2015) *Communications for Social Norm Change Around Adolescent Girls: Case Studies from Uganda*. London: Overseas Development Institute. Available online at www.odi.org/sites/odi.org.uk/files/odi-assets/publications-opinion-files/9883.pdf

PART 3
Viet Nam

6

INTERSECTING INEQUALITIES

The impact of gender norms on Hmong adolescent girls' education, marriage and work in Viet Nam

Nicola Jones, Elizabeth Presler-Marshall and Tran Thi Van Anh

Introduction

Viet Nam has made tremendous progress towards its development goals in recent years, slashing its poverty rate and achieving a number of Millennium Development Goals (MDGs) early (Government of Viet Nam 2015). Future progress, however, will depend not just on more growth, but on whether that growth can be made to include the ethnic minorities[1] who, after generations of exclusion, are effectively falling further behind the Kinh majority. Minorities currently account for only one-eighth of Viet Nam's population, yet they account for half of its poor, three-fifths of its food-insecure, and two-thirds of its extreme poor (World Bank 2012; Baulch *et al.* 2012; Truong 2011). The Hmong in particular have been left behind on many socioeconomic development indicators – largely due to their geographic isolation in Viet Nam's remote northern mountains. The fifth largest of Viet Nam's 53 ethnic minority groups,[2] the Hmong continue to have the country's highest poverty rate and lowest age at marriage, and are the only ethnic group in which the most recent census (2009) found to have a double-digit primary school gender gap and an upper-secondary (9th–12th grade) enrolment rate in single digits (World Bank 2012; Baulch and Dat 2012; United Nations Population Fund (UNFPA) 2011). This chapter addresses the neglected nexus of ethnicity, gender and age and examines the social norms that constrain Hmong adolescent girls' educational opportunities and limit their social value to marriage and motherhood.

The context for girls: understanding the mismatch between national-level statistics and Hmong girls' lived realities

In the two decades since Viet Nam's communist government opened its economy, it has seen nearly unprecedented development progress. Not only has the poverty rate at the national poverty line plunged, from more than 60 per cent in the early 1990s to just more than 17 per cent in 2012, but children's access to education has burgeoned (World Bank 2016). Viet Nam has achieved universal primary education, for girls and boys, and is closing in on universal lower-secondary education (for children aged 10–14) (Ministry of Education and Training 2015). Indeed, girls are now more likely than boys to move on to upper-secondary school and into tertiary education (General Statistics Office (GSO) and UNICEF 2015). Furthermore, on a national level, Vietnamese girls have not been especially vulnerable to child marriage for decades. The 2009 census found that women's average age at first marriage was nearly 23 years[3] and the 2014 Multiple Indicator Cluster Survey (MICS) found that less than 1 per cent of women aged 15–49 had been married before the age of 15 and 'only' one in ten girls aged 15–19 were currently married or in a union. A legacy of Viet Nam's era of tight central planning, the country's girls and women also have good access to the labour market. Of those aged 15–64, 73 per cent are in paid employment (compared to a 2014 global average of 50.3 per cent) (World Bank 2016) – albeit with a significant wage penalty (International Labour Organization (ILO) 2013) and the caveat that they remain almost single-handedly responsible for domestic and care work as well (Teerawichitchainan *et al.* 2008).

National-level statistics, however, hide the fact that Hmong girls' realities are markedly different from those of their non-Hmong peers (see Box 6.1). This is partly because Hmong families' day-to-day lives continue to be shaped by agrarian poverty. Largely untouched by the country's broader economic transformation,

---

BOX 6.1 THE HMONG AT A GLANCE

The Hmong are few and geographically isolated

- According to the 2009 census,[6] there are approximately 1 million Hmong out of a total Vietnamese population of 90 million (UNFPA 2011).
- Nearly all of Viet Nam's Hmong live in the highest regions of the northern mountains; the 2009 census found they were extremely unlikely to migrate internally[7] (ibid.).

Despite hard work, the Hmong remain very poor

- Nearly 99 per cent of the Hmong are self-employed in agriculture (GSO 2012b), but unlike other highland minorities, who tend to live in valley bottoms, the Hmong live at elevations that make all but subsistence farming difficult (Baulch *et al.* 2012).
- According to the 2009 census, nearly 96 per cent of Hmong households fall into the poorest quintile and more than 99 per cent fall into the lowest two quintiles (UNFPA 2011).

The Hmong are the least educated of Viet Nam's minorities[8]

- Less than 38 per cent of Hmong men and only 20 per cent of Hmong women are literate (ibid.).
- In 2012, the gross enrolment rate for Hmong lower-secondary school students was 64.1 per cent – up from 56.3 per cent in 2006 but far below the 94.5 per cent for Kinh (ethnic majority) students. Notably, lower-secondary enrolment for the Hmong also lags significantly behind the Tay (93.9 per cent), the Thai (92.3 per cent), the Muong (92.9 per cent) and the Khmer (77 per cent) (GSO 2012a).
- In 2012, the gross enrolment rate for Hmong upper-secondary school students was 20.4 per cent – up from 15.1 per cent in 2006 but far below the 78.1 per cent for Kinh students. Hmong enrolment also lags behind that of the Tay (79.4 per cent), the Muong (60.2 per cent), the Thai (45.7 per cent) and the Khmer (29.5 per cent) (ibid.).
- Hmong girls remain significantly disadvantaged compared to their male peers, especially at higher levels of education. Though the 2009 census found a high school net enrolment rate (NER) of only 9.7 per cent for Hmong boys, only 3.4 per cent of Hmong girls were enrolled (UNFPA 2011).
- Low levels of education have made it impossible for the government to ensure that all Hmong children are taught by Hmong teachers, despite the fact that policy[9] prioritises hiring minority teaching staff. Though nearly half of teachers in Ha Giang province are ethnic minorities,[10] there are not enough Hmong teachers for all schools in all communes (GSO 2015).

The Hmong marry early and have more children at younger ages

- The Hmong have the lowest age at first marriage in Viet Nam – 18.8 years for women, compared to over 23 years for their Kinh (ethnic majority) counterparts (UNFPA 2011).
- The rate of child marriage is not available by ethnicity. However, while nationally 10.3 per cent of girls aged 15–19 were already married in 2014, 22.6 per cent of girls that age in the Northern Midlands and Mountains (the region with the highest Hmong population) had already formed a union (GSO and UNICEF 2015).
- The adolescent birth rate is not available by ethnicity. However, while the 2014 national rate was 45 per 1,000, the Northern Midlands and Mountains had a rate of 107 per 1,000 (ibid.).
- The 2009 total fertility rate (TFR) for the Hmong is 4.96, down from 9.3 in 1989 but far above the Kinh TFR of 1.95 (UNFPA 2011).

nearly all families are dependent on onerous manual labour, which, according to local norms, still benefits from early marriage[4] and large families. Isolation from broader Vietnamese society, born of a strong cultural identity, is also key to understanding Hmong girls' lives. Located in extremely rugged mountains, the most remote Hmong communities still lack access to roads and electricity[5] and have only recently obtained access to schools. Equally important, and as will be discussed in greater detail in Chapter 7, after generations of marginalisation that culminated in government policy which labelled their traditions as 'backwards', the Hmong have a cautious approach to national goals and tend to be 'tactically selective' about how they engage with the increasingly modern world around them (Michaud 2011: 2; see also Turner and Michaud 2009; Turner 2012a, 2012b). Finally, the impact of son preference on Hmong girls' lives cannot be overstated. Whereas throughout Viet Nam sons are seen as crucial to continue the family line and to provide support in old age (Guilmoto 2012; Nanda *et al.* 2012; GSO 2011), in the Hmong community girls are seen as 'other people's women' from the moment they are born (Lee and Tapp 2010: 153; see also Long 2008).

Locating our research

Our primary research took place in Ta Lung commune, in the Meo Vac district of Ha Giang province, near Viet Nam's border with China (see Figure 6.1). Ha Giang is among Viet Nam's poorest provinces, ranked 61st out of 63. Meo Vac, which is best characterised as a mountain desert given its extreme lack of rainfall, is recognised as the country's Hmong homeland and is one of the poorest areas in Ha Giang. Ta Lung commune has eight villages, some quite central and relatively more developed, whereas others are extremely remote.

Co-designed by researchers from the Overseas Development Institute (ODI) and the Institute for Family and Gender Studies, our research involved community timelines, focus group discussions and individual interviews with nearly 275 community-level respondents (just under 150 Hmong adolescent girls and about 125 of their family members), as well as 65 key informants (Jones *et al.* 2013a, 2014, 2015).

The non-linear nature of change

Our primary research with Hmong girls found that they are located in a unique nexus in terms of norm stability and change (see Figure 6.2). On the one hand, as noted earlier, they are growing up in an isolated environment in which their ethnic identity is central to their daily lives and access to non-farm employment is rare. This works to maintain social norms. On the other hand, in addition to the transmission of ideas following improvements in infrastructure – especially new school, roads, cellular networks and television – the comparative uniqueness of the Vietnamese government is working to support change. As a one-party state with strong influence over social messaging, especially in remote rural areas, there is considerable scope for top-down change that has the potential to shift practices, if

Ta Lung commune,
Meo Vac district,
Ha Giang province

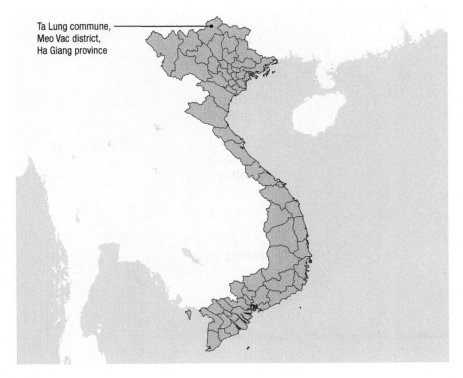

FIGURE 6.1   Ha Giang map

not attitudes, within a very short time frame. This combination has resulted in significant, uneven and sometimes surprising shifts. Indeed, in some cases, the development of new norms appears to be supporting the reinforcement of older ones.

Schooling: a sea change with a ceiling

By far the biggest change in the past decade in Hmong girls' lives has been in regard to education. In only one generation, nationally driven policy and messaging and strict local enforcement – spearheaded by Hmong officials – have altered not only what girls do (descriptive norms) but also what their communities and families believe they *ought* to do (injunctive norms). The national government has, for example, invested heavily in educational infrastructure, bringing satellite schools for the youngest primary students to even the most remote communities and recently allowing more rural upper-primary and lower-secondary students to 'semi-board' during the school week (see Box 6.2). It also provides subsidies for Hmong students, covering even the costs of school supplies. Local governments in turn engage in door-to-door mobilisation and strictly enforce fines[11] for truancy through 9th grade. These efforts, explained a local informant, have convinced parents to '*invest a*

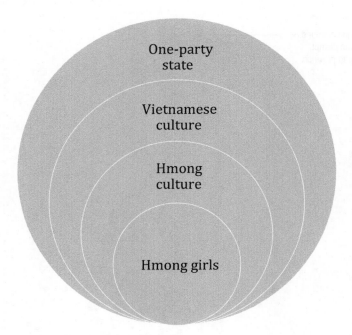

One-party
state

Vietnamese
culture

Hmong
culture

Hmong girls

FIGURE 6.2 Hmong girls are uniquely situated

BOX 6.2 THE ADVANTAGES OF BOARDING SCHOOL

Beginning in 2010, and gaining traction over time, weekly boarding schools have opened for Hmong students living in Meo Vac's most remote hamlets. They save children two dangerous walks a day by allowing them to spend the school week living at school, and then return home to live as part of their families and help their parents on the weekend. These have proven enormously popular with children. As one 14-year-old girl reported:

> *I like boarding better than home. The school meals have meat, rice and fish. At home we only have steamed ground corn. In the evening we often play blind man's bluff. I like that I can go out while I stay here; at home I have to work all the time. I like hanging out with my friends, playing, singing and dancing together with my friends.*

---

lot of time in their children's education', despite the fact that given the limitations of local labour markets, education is comparatively unlikely to lead to paid employment.

With very few exceptions – largely the poorest households who cannot afford to give up their children's and especially their daughters' agricultural labour – parents are genuinely committed to the notion of schooling for all their children, at least through to the end of lower-secondary school. Many of the adults we interviewed made similar comments: as one father in a community mapping exercise noted, '*I do not discriminate between son and daughter. I will let her to go to school*'. Parents believe that both literacy and fluency in Vietnamese are crucial, primarily so that they will not be cheated when doing business or '*looked down on by other ethnic people*' (father). They also increasingly understand that education is useful in day-to-day life. It helps improve techniques for both '*corn growing*' and '*child raising*' and offers some potential to translate into the paid employment (usually civil service or tourism in Ha Giang) that would allow their children to escape the onerous agricultural labour that is becoming more tenuous with continued soil degradation. Poorer families also send their daughters to school; however, they are often still motivated by fines rather than genuine commitment to education.

In part because the commune has invested considerable effort in helping children to believe that education is their surest route out of poverty, many girls are fiercely committed to their schooling and very aware of how different their lives are from those of their mothers. One older adolescent, planning to go to university with the full support of her parents, exclaimed '*Now I can't imagine what I would have become without going to school*'. She continued, '*(m)y mother didn't want us to have to work as hard as them. My father always says "You have to try to study. In the future we don't need you to support us, what we need is that you can take care of yourself"*'. Indeed, whereas just a few years ago girls were regularly denied the opportunity to attend school at all, now they are regularly outperforming their male peers because they '*try harder*' (boy) and are '*less playful*' (mother).

However, while girls' education enjoys broad support through the end of 9th grade, lower-secondary school remains the limit of what the vast majority of parents are willing to consider for their daughters, regardless of their academic success, because '*according to Hmong people, 9th and 12th grade are the same, they don't need an education level, they just need a person who is hard working to marry*' (mother). Most out-of-school girls we interviewed very much wanted to be in school. They missed the social opportunities that school afforded and, given that upper-secondary school requires full-time boarding in town, they had been looking forward to experiencing life outside the village. They also understood that school-leaving limited their futures to subsistence agriculture. However, as '*their parents don't let them, they have to accept it*' (teacher) (see Box 6.3). Officials told us that no girls in the most remote hamlets had yet managed to complete upper-secondary school, and only a few were even enrolled.

The ceiling on girls' education is largely driven by practical realities. Upper-secondary school is expensive because it involves longer-term boarding. Though many of the 'real' costs, for rent and food, are covered by government scholarships aimed at driving up Hmong enrolment rates, the opportunity costs remain unbearable to poorer families who are forced to forego their children's labour for weeks or months at a time. It is also the case that because local labour markets are still dependent on subsistence agriculture, most Hmong adolescents do not *need*

BOX 6.3 A 'GOOD DAUGHTER' LISTENS TO HER PARENTS

Thong Thi Mai is a 16-year-old girl who wanted to become a teacher. Though she knows that she is luckier than her oldest sister – who was never allowed to go to school and was married by the age of 16 – she is still sad, two years after leaving school, that her dreams have been thwarted by being a dutiful daughter.

Mai liked school for multiple reasons – better food, the opportunity to learn Vietnamese and to understand more about how the world worked. As we discuss in greater detail in Chapter 7 and reflecting internalised discrimination against ethnic minorities, '*People kept saying that Hmong people were unknowledgeable and couldn't speak Kinh language*'. Mai is committed to studying '*further to become more knowledgeable, to know more things*'.

When she finished 9th grade, however, Mai was told to come home and work with her mother. Unlike her peers who were faced with similar family pressures, she asked to stay – twice. '*The first time I asked, my parents said I was a girl so they wouldn't let me go to school*'. Undaunted, Mai tried to elicit help from a teacher. However, her '*teacher only advised me that if I succeeded in convincing my parents to let me continue my studies, I should go; if not, let it be*'.

'*After I stayed home for a while, my friends told me to prepare an application to study; I asked my parents one more time, but they didn't allow me*'. At that point even her friends advised her to give up and do as her parents asked.

Mai's days are now dedicated to constant labour. '*Each morning I go collecting twigs twice to help my mother, and go to gather cow grass in the afternoon*'.

Mai is wistful that '*If I had completed the 12th grade, it would have been different in the way that I would have known more, I would have known how to behave towards the others in a more cultured way*'. In other words, she has picked up the strong association between education and the 'civility' that is a core theme in the national education curriculum. On the other hand, however, she knows that by staying home she has demonstrated to both her parents and her Hmong neighbours that she is a model child. '*My listening to my parents proved that I was a good child. I stayed home to help my parents, and did heavy work, and shared my parents' work; such is a good child.*'

education beyond the 9th grade. Practical reality, however, is not the only reason that Hmong girls remain highly unlikely to complete their schooling; social norms also truncate their trajectories. Parents admitted that *if* they were to send a child to secondary school, it would be a boy, as '*the daughter will get married and can't make money for their parents. The sons can make money for their parents after graduating*' (mother). This son preference is certainly borne out by enrolment statistics.

Furthermore, there are some exceptions to even universal primary education – especially for the largest families with the highest need for childcare and agricultural support. Even in families that clearly value education and have supported some offspring (including daughters) through higher education, it is sometimes the case that another daughter is deprived of her rights to an education, in order to help at home – irrespective of fines. For example, one family allowed all of its children to graduate from high school except one – a daughter, who was chosen to leave school after only 5th grade. Her brother explained, '*My parents have so many children . . . no one is there to help my parents except her*'.

Marriage: gradual progress on some fronts

Hmong marriages are now increasingly based on 'free choice' (rather than parental arrangement) and undertaken in very early adulthood (rather than early and middle adolescence), in line with national law, which is heavily messaged at school and through the Women's Union, the Youth Union, and the Fatherland Front.[12] Nonetheless, marriage practices continue to place a disproportionate burden on girls. Under a strictly patriarchal, patrilocal clan system, Hmong girls have less choice over marriage partners than do boys and are often still expected to have as many children as necessary in order to give their husband's family a son. Many experience alcohol-fuelled gender-based violence (GBV) and none have the cultural option of divorce, despite the fact that, like equitable inheritance rights, it is legally provided for.

As Lemoine (2012) reports, and as grandparents in our research sample confirmed, as recently as two generations ago most Hmong girls were typically married even before puberty, often to cousins, to meet family needs. Today, marriage by arrangement has been nearly abandoned and child marriage is increasingly less common. Most Hmong girls appear to marry soon after they turn 18. While child marriage is not yet rare, and some girls continue to be married against their will as early as age 13[13] (see Box 6.4), even young women of 20 are increasingly single.

Ironically, given that marriage is central to Hmong girls' lives, in many ways shaping them from early childhood, the one area in which adolescent girls appear to make their 'own' choices (rather than following parental instructions) is partner selection. '*Children choose (partners) themselves*', explained one girl, '*My parents couldn't force me*'. Besides, added another, '*If my parents arrange my marriage, in the future the husband may not like me, he will blame my parents, saying that he doesn't want to marry me and telling me to go*'.

Also showing that norms can shift in non-linear ways – and surprising given the statistical relationship seen between education and declining child marriage levels on a global level (Klugman *et al.* 2014; Brown 2012) – some respondents are concerned that child marriage may be becoming more common in the community now that nearly all children are attending lower-secondary school (until about the age of 15). They believe that the prolonged, daily contact between boys and girls may be encouraging some to marry as soon as they leave 9th grade and

BOX 6.4 BRIDE KIDNAPPING

Bride kidnapping – a long-standing Hmong tradition on which the media has tended to focus because it emphasises the Hmong's 'cultural distance from the Kinh' (Nguyen *et al.* 2011: S202) – appears to be more common in remote villages than the more recent literature (including our own, Jones *et al.* 2013a) has suggested. While most adolescents reported that the vast majority of today's 'abductions' are in fact arranged between partners, rather than genuinely by force as was common in the past, girls also told us that it was not uncommon[14] for them to be attacked, often by a whole group of boys, and '*dragged*' to a boy's home for marriage (Jones *et al.* 2014, 2015).

Younger girls, with fewer emotional resources, are especially susceptible, because they lack the wherewithal to simply leave the home of their kidnapper's parents once they have been presented to their future in-laws. Furthermore, there is some evidence that as girls begin to travel further afield (primarily to the Meo Vac market), they are increasingly likely to be kidnapped by boys from other communes whom they have never met before.

Because Hmong tradition stipulates that once a girl has spent three days in a boy's home then they are married, few girls see an escape route. '*I thought that as a girl, if I entered his house and didn't get married with him, the neighbours would say some bad things about me, so I didn't dare to return home*', explained one 18-year-old married girl who had been kidnapped against her will at the age of 15.

are propelled into the relatively solitary, comparatively tedious lives of subsistence farmers. For example, one mother reported, '*Now the children . . . go to school and then meet each other in class, and then they get married*'. A health worker added, '*When a girl goes to school and sees a handsome boy, she will marry him*'. While it would be easy to dismiss these statements as the generalised concerns of adults who see their way of life changing, particularly given statistical changes in the average age at first marriage, at least one adolescent thought their concerns might have some credence. An 18-year-old boy explained, '*In grade 9, a girl makes friend with a boy and after finishing grade 9, they will get married. One month after grade 9, boys and girls get married*'. A Women's Union key informant, however, noted that this is hardly a surprising choice, especially in more remote areas that completely lack access to non-agricultural employment: '*After leaving school, they have only one option: that is to get married*', she explained.

Despite the fact that Hmong marriages are no longer arranged by parents, girls' agency in regard to partner selection, like that of their Kinh peers, remains far more limited than the boys' agency. First, it remains unacceptable in the Hmong community for a girl to show any interest in a boy until he has actively pursued her for some time. *'As a girl, I don't have the right to like them first'*, explained one girl. Second, while boys primarily approach mate selection from the perspective of maximising their gains, all too often girls are left to try to minimise their losses. Boys, for example, look for *'beautiful'* girls who do not *'speak loudly'*, are *'skilful'*, *'diligent'* and *'able to cut a big tree'*. Indeed, one 18-year-old confessed that he *'must choose the one who's uglier but good at farm work'*. Girls, on the other hand, who well understand what boys are looking for in a wife, often evaluate boys on the basis of their potential for vice. They want to marry boys who fall asleep when drunk, rather than *'beat his wife'*, or those who do not *'gamble so much his neighbours have to criticise'*. Unfortunately, most adolescents in our research indicated that *'such men are very rare'*.

Hmong girls and women, especially those in more rural villages, also continue to bear a heavy burden in terms of reproduction. Entering marriage with limited information about reproductive biology, they are expected to produce a child within *'one or two years after marriage'* (father). Moreover, despite the provision of free contraceptives to married women (though not unmarried women) and heavy messaging and fines aimed at reducing population growth, girls are all too often expected to continue having children until they have produced the son required for ancestral rites. Although Hmong fertility rates are falling, and most girls in our research well understand the economic benefits of having only two children for whom they could provide *'full care'*, many girls remain concerned that if they *'give birth to two daughters only, no son, my husband won't love me very much'*. Furthermore, due to custom as well as geography, Hmong mothers in the villages in which we worked were unlikely to receive either regular prenatal care or skilled delivery.

Alcohol-fuelled GBV – fed by social norms that reserve power for men and require neighbourly sociability (particularly, though not exclusively, for men) – remains endemic among the Hmong communities in which we worked, with grave repercussions for girls and women (see Box 6.5). *'Along this circular rocky mountain range, it [domestic violence] is normal'*, explained one young wife.

Although child abuse appears rare in Hmong families, young girls are very much affected by the abuse meted out by their fathers to their mothers. They not only try to physically shelter their mothers, telling them to *'run away'* while pulling *'his hands back not to beat her'*, but their sympathy for their mothers' plight encourages them to prioritise their mothers' needs over their own, even when that means ignoring schoolwork for chores. Upon marriage, when girls go to live with their husbands' families, most expect to become *'beaten and tortured by their husbands'* (adult woman). *'Afraid of an alcoholic husband'*, and alcoholic in-laws, some girls deliberately delay marriage because they *'want to stay with my mother for a long time'*. Others plan ahead to have small families because *'If I have too many children, when my husband beats me, I won't know where to hide'*.

Hmong girls and women have little recourse when victimised by their marital families. Though Viet Nam has national laws on domestic violence and women's right to an equitable divorce, implementation in remote Hmong communities is all but non-existent, with Hmong women rarely targeted for programming aimed at raising their awareness of legal possibilities. Indeed, patriarchal social norms

---

BOX 6.5   WHEN ONE'S BEST IS NOT ENOUGH

Ly Thi My is a 27-year-old married mother of one whose life demonstrates what resilience and hard work can and cannot do for a young Hmong woman. My's adolescence was much like that of her peers. She left school at the end of 9th grade and was shortly thereafter kidnapped by her husband. She *'didn't dare to return home'* as she knew that her neighbours would see her as already married – and thus unmarriageable – if she left.

Eventually, because she was judged to be clever and good with the Kinh language, My was invited by the commune to finish 12th grade at the Continuing Education Centre. Now employed in several official capacities, some elected and others appointed, she has an enviable income of her own. She has used that income to put her husband – who also left school after lower-secondary – through upper-secondary school and now college. *'I calculated that 700,000 dong was enough for me and the child to eat. I allocated my monthly salary for him to study.'* Her husband, however, is not as focused on his studies as she had envisioned. *'He took many photographs with his girlfriends.'*

On the one hand, My's story is one of a positive outlier. When her husband scolded her for working late, she told him, *'I couldn't go home when I hadn't fulfilled my task, because I was elected by people. Did they elect me so that I evaded my duty? I would be a waste of public money'.* On the other hand, My has also experienced the domestic violence so common in her community. *'Frankly, if he raises his hand intending to beat, it is my fault when I am inattentive and speak too much.'*

My is still full of dreams, but she keeps them to herself. She told our research team, *'You are the first one who I told my dream, I haven't told anyone else. Unsympathetic people may say that "The kind of people like you dares to dream, you are swimming upstream". I will feel humiliated, so I don't want to tell anybody.'*

---

continue to restrict Hmong women's agency so thoroughly that divorce is inconceivable even when abuse is constant – because *'according to Hmong tradition, once you stepped out of the door, you could never look back'* (mother). This is largely because Hmong girls' souls become part of their husbands' families at marriage, which means that if a wife tried to return home then she might anger her natal family's ancestors to the point of risking her own death. Non-spiritual practicalities also preclude exit options. Not only do Hmong women have extremely limited access to livelihoods, but because their children belong solely to their fathers' clans, leaving their husbands is tantamount to leaving their children.

Agricultural and care economy work: never ending and unchanging

Regardless of whether they are still children living in their natal homes or young wives living in their husbands' homes, Hmong girls continue to be unfairly burdened with domestic and agricultural labour. This not only affects their education, it also often leaves them socially isolated and with no time for rest or recreation.

That Hmong girls would work harder than their brothers is something most do not even think to question. As one noted, '*That is how work is divided. For adults, the wife does more than the husband, so the daughter has to do more than the son*'. Indeed, many girls did not mind that their brothers were allowed time off to play, noting on occasion that their *older* brothers were '*just young*'. A mother added that, in part, a girl's burden is greater simply because she will tolerate it. '*In general, in the Hmong ethnic group, the boys do less than the girls. It is because daughters are nicer. When I give orders to my daughter she is more active.*'

Many of the girls we interviewed (but none of their brothers) mentioned having to rise at 4am in order to cook breakfast for their family. After a morning of classes, they then come home to help their mother with agricultural and care work before they can focus on their homework. '*Chores are a problem as it means I don't have enough time to study and get the knowledge that my friends have*', explained one girl. This is particularly problematic, as one key informant observed, for families in remote villages that do not have electricity at home, because girls are often engaged in domestic and agricultural work up until nightfall and are then forced to do schoolwork by firelight.

Girls' school-leaving is primarily driven by the opportunity cost of sending them to secondary school: parents need their labour. Children can contribute some work to family endeavours while they are in elementary and lower-secondary school, because those schools are usually local and only half-day, but upper-secondary school typically entails boarding elsewhere, which limits the extent to which children can help make ends meet. The 'need' for adolescent *girls'* labour, as opposed to boys', is particularly strong because most (statistically speaking) will have only three or four years between finishing lower-secondary school and marriage. Knowing that their biggest contribution to their parents' well-being is their own short-term labour, and constrained by broader norms of filial piety, girls in our research – almost without exception – left school for the fields when they were told to do so. Boys, secure in the knowledge that '*in the future they will inherit everything*' (commune-level informant), appear to be far less malleable to parents' wishes. Though many do leave school in order to come home and work alongside their parents, the fact that their own longer-term interests more closely align with those of their parents means they rarely have to choose between their individual and family futures.

Unsurprisingly, given that boys overwhelmingly said they plan to choose their wife on the basis of how hard she can work, marriage most often means that a girl must work harder yet – to be a 'good wife' who caters to the needs of her husband and in-laws. Many girls feel under considerable psychological pressure to meet these gender role expectations. Girls told us that '*it was difficult to take a rest*' and admitted that they worry their in-laws will be angry if they are not '*able to do all the work they give me to do*'. As one married girl concluded, '*I am a daughter-in-law, so I have to bear hardship and unhappiness*'. Indeed, the only way 'out', according to most girls, is to eat '*heartbreak grass*' – a fatally poisonous plant that grows locally. One married girl told us that three of her sisters-in-law had killed themselves in this way in order to escape their mother-in-law, who was verbally abusive.

Indeed, acquiring a wife's labour is often a primary driver of marriage itself. Adolescent boys in our research at times flatly admitted that they wanted to marry just '*so that she could work to help my parents*' – with one telling his new wife, '*I don't work, the wife has to do it*'. Adolescent girls added that at times, boys' families were so desperate for labour that they encouraged boys to kidnap hard-working girls. One, now 18 and married against her will at 15, explained, '*The sister and brother wanted me to be their sister-in-law, so they told their younger brother to kidnap me. They liked me because I was an orphan; I worked harder than other friends who have parents*'.

Conclusions

Discriminatory gender norms continue to place severe restrictions on the lives of Hmong girls. Though girls have seen transformative change in their access to formal education in just the past few years, and most parents are now genuinely committed to girls' education through the end of 9th grade, in the absence of norm change initiatives very few girls have the opportunity to attend secondary school, even when they are motivated to succeed. There is also scant evidence that schooling is resulting in significant shifts to the daily contours of girls' lives or improving their access to agency and voice.

Hmong marriage customs, although shifting, also continue to disadvantage girls. Most are married young to boys they barely know and some are still kidnapped into child marriage by strangers. Deeply held beliefs about the allocation of their souls prevent these girls from returning home, even when they suffer abuse by their marital families or are expected to bear offspring until they produce the requisite son.

The domestic workload that Hmong girls are expected to shoulder – both before and after marriage – appears to be unchanging. Supported by gender norms that value them for what they can produce, rather than who they are, and comparatively immune to top-down policy directives because it takes place in private spaces and lacks even the public sanction implicit in birth or marriage registration, the allocation of domestic and agricultural labour deeply disadvantages Hmong girls. In their natal homes, most spend their childhoods effectively working to repay their parents (especially their mothers) for the privilege of life. As the least privileged members of their marital families – by dint of their gender, age and exogenous clan status – the most tedious work is often theirs alone.

As discussed in greater detail in Chapter 7, both top-down, policy-driven investment and local initiative are bringing significant change to Viet Nam's Hmong community. However, with only rare exceptions, they are not yet addressing the triple disadvantage – ethnicity, gender and age – facing Hmong girls. For example, policies aimed at increasing the number of Hmong children enrolled in secondary school do not offer special incentives to female students in order to offset patriarchal gender norms and son preference. Similarly, the policies that have supported girls and women to join the workforce and participate in political life have, as yet, seen little application in the Hmong community, where literacy rates are low, women are unlikely to be fluent in Vietnamese and opportunities for non-agricultural employment are scarce. Deeply held Confucian notions of filial piety mean that Hmong girls are also limited by their age. Even as their aspirations – for their own futures and the future of their broader community – have begun to grow with greater access to education, their agency remains limited by their parents' hold over their options. Our research suggests that in order to help Hmong girls achieve the futures they are beginning to imagine for themselves, it is necessary to focus attention on that neglected nexus and the ways in which social norms work to entwine femininity with cultural identity.

Notes

1 Ethnic minorities are not, as noted by the World Bank (2012), a homogeneous group. Though only the Hoa (Chinese) have poverty rates similar to those of the Kinh, there are a handful of groups, including the Khmer and Cham, who have seen significant recent reductions in poverty (see also Baulch *et al.* 2012; Baulch and Dat 2012). Our own work on Khmer communities in Kien Giang province also found significant differences in the opportunities available to adolescent girls to realise their full human capabilities compared to the opportunity structures faced by Hmong adolescents (see Jones *et al.* 2013b).

2 The 2009 census found that the four largest minority groups were the Tay and the Thai, with approximately 1.6 million people each, and the Khmer and the Muong, with approximately 1.3 million people each.

3 The most recent Demographic and Health Survey (DHS) in Viet Nam, published in 2003, found the average age at first marriage to be a stable 21 years across cohorts. The proportions of women married by 15 and 18 were also relatively stable – hovering around 1 per cent and 12 per cent respectively.

4 Many respondents believed that by the age of 35 they would be too 'old' for heavy labour, and that by having children while still in their teens they would then be assured of having their own adolescent children to take on the heaviest work when they became 'old'.

5 In 2010, 97 per cent of Vietnamese households had access to electricity. The fact that the villages in which we worked did not indicates how remote they are.

6 The census is one of the very few instruments designed to capture differences between ethnic groups. The vast majority of Vietnamese data can be disaggregated only by region.

7 There is, on the other hand, a large diaspora – primarily in the United States.

8 At the time of writing (February 2016), these remain the most up-to-date figures available.

9 Decree of ethnic minority work number 05/2011.

10 As of 2014, of the 11,462 teachers in Ha Giang, 5,757 were ethnic minorities. Teachers were less likely to be ethnic minorities at the upper-secondary level (35.3 per cent). There are no data regarding the specific ethnicity of these teachers, though given the low educational attainment of the Hmong, it is unlikely that they are especially well represented among existent teachers.

11 Fines are set on a village basis, to maximise enforcement. In Ta Lung, where villages are almost exclusively run by Hmong officials who understand the depth of local poverty, fines can be paid with public labour rather than with cash.

12 See Chapter 7 for an explanation of Viet Nam's mass organisations.

13 It is difficult to gauge how frequently the youngest girls are married. Because it is illegal, related information is presented in a highly anecdotal manner. Based on our fieldwork and discussions with local leaders and community members, perhaps as many as 30 per cent of girls in the more remote villages appear to be married at age 16.

14 Again, since this is illegal it tends to be presented anecdotally. However, of the girls we interviewed in one rural village, three had been kidnapped into marriage against their will. All had stories about friends or sisters or cousins who were also kidnapped.

Bibliography

Baulch, B. and Dat,V. (2012) *Exploring the Ethnic Dimensions of Poverty in Vietnam.* Background paper for the 2012 Vietnam poverty assessment.

Baulch, B., Pham, H. and Reilly, B. (2012) 'Decomposing the Ethnic Gap in Rural Vietnam, 1993–2004' *Oxford Development Studies* 40(1): 87–117.

Boudet, A., Petesch, P., Turk, C. and Thumala, A. (2012) *On Norms and Agency: Conversations About Gender Equality with Women and Men in 20 Countries.* Washington, DC: World Bank.

Brown, G. (2012) *Out of Wedlock, into School: Combating Child Marriage Through Education.* London: The Office of Gordon and Sarah Brown.

General Statistics Office (GSO). (2011) *Sex Ratio at Birth in Viet Nam: New Evidence on Patterns, Trends and Differentials.* Ha Noi: General Statistics Office.

General Statistics Office (GSO). (2012a) *Data Results of the Viet Nam Household Living Standards Survey 2012.* General Statistics Office. Available online at www.gso.gov.vn/default_en.aspx?tabid=483&idmid=4&ItemID=14844

General Statistics Office (GSO). (2012b) *Poverty and Migration Profile 2012.* General Statistics Office. Available online at www.gso.gov.vn/default_en.aspx?tabid=483&idmid=4&ItemID=13888

General Statistics Office (GSO). (2015) *Education.* Available online at https://gso.gov.vn/default_en.aspx?tabid=782

General Statistics Office (GSO) and UNICEF. (2015) *Viet Nam Multiple Indicator Cluster Survey 2014, Final Report.* Ha Noi. Available online at www.unicef.org/vietnam/resources_24623.html

Government of Viet Nam. (2015) *Country Report: 15 Years Achieving the Viet Nam Millennium Development Goals.* Available online at www.vn.undp.org/content/dam/vietnam/docs/Publications/Bao%20cao%20TIENG%20ANH%20-%20MDG%202015_trinh%20TTCP.pdf

Guilmoto, C. (2012) 'Son Preference, Sex Selection, and Kinship in Vietnam' *Population and Development Review* 38(1): 31–54.

International Labour Organization (ILO). (2013) *Despite High Labour Force Participation Rate for Women, Gender Pay Gap on the Rise.* Press release, 7 March. Available online at www.ilo.org/hanoi/Informationresources/Publicinformation/Pressreleases/WCMS_206104/lang – en/index.htm

Jones, N., Presler-Marshall, E. and Tran, T.V.A. (2013a) *Double Jeopardy: How Gendered Social Norms and Ethnicity Intersect to Shape the Lives of Adolescent Hmong Girls in Viet Nam.* London: Overseas Development Institute. Available online at www.odi.org/sites/odi.org.uk/files/odi-assets/publications-opinion-files/8823.pdf

Jones, N., Presler-Marshall, E. and Tran, T.V.A. (2013b) *Expanding Capabilities: How Adolescent Khmer Girls in Viet Nam Are Learning to Juggle Filial Piety, Educational Ambition (and Facebook).* London: Overseas Development Institute. Available online at www.odi.org/sites/odi.org.uk/files/odi-assets/publications-opinion-files/8824.pdf

Jones, N., Presler-Marshall, E. and Tran, T.V.A. (2014) *Early Marriage Among Viet Nam's Hmong: How Unevenly Changing Gender Norms Limit Hmong Adolescent Girls' Options in Marriage and Life.* London: Overseas Development Institute. Available online at www.odi.org/sites/odi.org.uk/files/odi-assets/publications-opinion-files/9182.pdf

Jones, N., Presler-Marshall, E., Tran, T.V.A., Dang, T., Dau, L. and Nguyen, T. (2015) *'You Must Be Bold Enough to Tell Your Own Story': Programming to Empower Viet Nam's Hmong Girls*. London: Overseas Development Institute. Available online at www.odi.org/publications/9923-adolescent-girls-gender-justice-country-reports-year-3

Klugman, J., Hanmer, L., Twigg, S., Hasan, T., McCleary-Sills, J. and Santamaria, J. (2014) *Voice and Agency: Empowering Women and Girls for Shared Prosperity*. Washington, DC: World Bank Group.

Lee, G. and Tapp, N. (2010) *Culture and Customs of the Hmong*. Santa Barbara, CA: Greenwood.

Lemoine, J. (2012) 'Commentary: Gender-based Violence Among the (H)mong' *Hmong Studies Journal* 13: 1–27.

Long, L. (2008) 'Contemporary Women's Roles Through Hmong, Vietnamese, and American Eyes' *Frontiers: A Journal of Women Studies* 29(1): 1–36.

Michaud, J. (2011) 'Hmong Infrapolitics: A View from Vietnam' *Ethnic and Racial Studies* 35(11): 1853–1873.

Ministry of Education and Training. (2015) *Viet Nam: Education for All 2015 National Review*. Hanoi. Available online at http://unesdoc.unesco.org/images/0023/002327/232770e.pdf

Nanda, P., Abhishek, G., Ravi, V., Thu, H.K., Mahesh, P., Giang, L.T., Jyotsna, T. and Prabhat, L. (2012) *Study on Gender, Masculinity and Son Preference in Nepal and Vietnam*. New Delhi: International Center for Research on Women.

Nguyen, T.H., Oosterhoof, P. and White, J. (2011) 'Aspirations and Realities of Love, Marriage and Education Among Hmong Women' *Culture, Health and Sexuality* 12(S2): S201–S215.

Teerawichitchainan, B., Knodel, J., Loi, V.M. and Huy, V.T. (2008) *Gender Division of Household Labor in Vietnam: Cohort Trends and Regional Variations*. Available online at www.psc.isr.umich.edu/pubs/pdf/rr08-658.pdf

Truong, H.C. (2011) *Eliminating Inter-Ethnic Inequalities? Assessing Impacts of Education Policies on Ethnic Minority Children in Vietnam*. Working Paper No. 69, Oxford Young Lives. Available online at http://younglives.qeh.ox.ac.uk/publications/WP/eliminating-inter-ethnic-inequalities-education-vietnam

Turner, S. (2012a) 'Forever Hmong: Ethnic Minority Livelihoods and Agrarian Transition in Upland Northern Vietnam' *The Professional Geographer* 64(4): 540–553.

Turner, S. (2012b) 'Making a Living the Hmong Way: An Actor-Oriented Livelihoods Approach to Everyday Politics and Resistance in Upland Vietnam' *Annals of the Association of American Geographers* 102(2): 403–422.

Turner, S. and Michaud, J. (2009) 'Weapons of the Week: Selective Resistance and Agency among the Hmong in Northern Vietnam' in D. Caouette and S. Turner (eds.) *Agrarian Angst and Rural Resistance in Contemporary Southeast Asia*. London: Routledge, 45–60.

United Nations Population Fund (UNFPA). (2011) *Ethnic Groups in Viet Nam: Evidence from the 2009 Census*. Factsheet, Ha Noi: United Nations Population Fund.

World Bank. (2012) *Well Begun, Not Yet Done: Vietnam's Remarkable Progress on Poverty Reduction and the Emerging Challenges*. Ha Noi: World Bank. Available online at https://openknowledge.worldbank.org/handle/10986/12326

World Bank. (2016) *Vietnam*. Available online at http://data.worldbank.org/country/vietnam

7

TRIPLE INVISIBILITY

The neglect of ethnic minority adolescent girls in Viet Nam

Nicola Jones, Elizabeth Presler-Marshall and Tran Thi Van Anh

Introduction

The focus of this chapter is on the under-explored nexus of gender, ethnicity and age in Viet Nam. Although the country is a regional leader in terms of policies aimed at fostering gender equality – especially in the public sphere – and has long devoted considerable resources to reducing ethnic minority poverty, until recently it has paid scant attention to the way in which gender, ethnicity and age work in tandem to constrain ethnic minority adolescent girls. As a result of this neglect, policies aimed at improving the political participation and economic engagement of girls and women have almost entirely ignored the diverse needs of ethnic minority girls and women (see also discussion in Box 7.1), while policies and programmes to improve the educational uptake and economic well-being of ethnic minorities have seen better outcomes for boys and men. These policy blind spots have been created – and reinforced – by a lack of gender- and ethnicity-disaggregated data. Moreover, the specific and diverse needs of ethnic minority adolescent girls have been largely ignored even by the international non-governmental organisations (NGOs) ostensibly working to serve them.

After presenting a brief overview of the unique features of the Vietnamese context, this chapter focuses on adolescent girls within the Hmong community, and how policies and programmes are simultaneously supporting and preventing change for them. Our analysis draws on three years of research, primarily conducted in Ta Lung commune in the Meo Vac district of Ha Giang province on Viet Nam's mountainous northern border (see Figure 6.1 for location map), as well as insights from an assessment of three 'good practice' programmes aimed at Hmong girls and boys (see Box 7.1). The analysis of these change initiatives – which are instructive largely because they demonstrate how low the bar is set in terms of good practice programming for Hmong children – serves as a useful window through

BOX 7.1   VIETNAMESE CASE STUDY EXAMPLES

Identifying good practice examples of communication approaches aimed at changing gender norms among Viet Nam's Hmong community proved a challenging task because the Hmong are a relatively small population clustered in a relatively small geographic location.

We were able to identify only one programme aimed specifically at helping Hmong adolescent girls delay their marriages and improve their capabilities – Plan's *Because I Am a Girl* (BIAAG) in Ha Giang province. Plan's programming recognises that Hmong girls are deeply constrained by both their gender and their age. It aims to provide safe spaces and gender rights education for girls, but also to develop their communities more generally through infrastructure improvements.

Throwing the net a bit wider, we included Oxfam's *My Rights, My Voice* (MRMV) in Lao Cai province. Oxfam's programming is aimed at improving Hmong children's access to their rights by fostering accountability in the education sector. It empowers children to understand and express their needs, builds local capacity to implement child-centred teaching and fosters cooperation between parents and educational actors.

For our third case study we examined the extra-curricular/life-skills programming offered by the government-run Meo Vac High School, also in our original study site location in Ha Giang province. This programming, which is run by classroom teachers on an ad hoc basis, is primarily focused on teaching children about the marriage and family law and the health consequences of child and consanguineous marriage.

which to explore some of the complex inter-linkages between policies and their implementation, programming and social norm change processes. The chapter then highlights some reasons for optimism that social norm change processes in Viet Nam's Hmong community can be facilitated through strategic interventions. It concludes by reflecting on future policy and programming implications.

The Vietnamese context

Governance structure

The Socialist Republic of Viet Nam is a one-party state, led by the Communist Party, which retains national control over a wide variety of policy areas – including 'social evils' (see Box 7.2) (Fritzen 2006). There are four layers of government: central, provincial, district and commune (Nguyen-Hoang and Schroeder 2010). There are 63 provinces and more than 10,000 communes, each comprising several villages.

BOX 7.2 THE NOTION OF 'SOCIAL EVIL'

Viet Nam's increased integration into the global market economy has entailed rapid and dynamic changes and has fostered new ways of acting, interacting and thinking. It has also increased the potential for 'social evils' such as drug use and video game addiction. In response, in 1999 the government created the Department for Social Vices Prevention under the Ministry of Labour, Invalids and Social Affairs, which invested in widespread public education campaigns and legal reforms. This approach has served to slow social norm change – particularly around gender and sexuality – because of its focus on the 'global and poisonous culture', while situating the government as the guarantor of 'appropriate morality' (Rydstrøm 2006: 283).

Viet Nam's citizens are represented *de jure*, if not *de facto*, by a plethora of state-sponsored mass organisations such as the Women's Union and the Youth Union, established in the late 1920s and early 1930s by the Communist Party as 'the people's front' in the pursuit of independence from French colonisation. In recent years, these organisations have implemented many development-oriented activities to improve the health, economic and social well-being of their members. However, their reach in remote highland communities is somewhat limited.

Also important, given the nature of our research, is the tension between continued centralisation and increasing decentralisation. On the one hand, policy tends to be top-down and, once enacted, 'actors involved are then expected to be bound by it' (Harris *et al.* 2011: viii). This not only tends to leave lower-level authorities in a holding pattern, waiting for proclamations from above, but also stifles local innovation and targeted responses, particularly in areas where language and cultural barriers make it difficult for locals to make their needs known (Jones *et al.* 2012). On the other hand, the elaborate system of tax sharing to which recent decentralisation is tied is ultimately more beneficial to wealthier southern provinces[1] (Beresford 2008; Bjornestad 2009; Fritzen 2006; Nguyen-Hoang and Schroeder 2010).

Ethnicity

As noted in Chapter 6, Viet Nam's ethnic minority populations are falling behind the Kinh majority in terms of development. For example, whereas ethnic minorities were only 1.6 times more likely to be poor in 1993, by 2010 they were 5.1 times more likely to be poor than the Kinh – albeit with highly significant differences between ethnic minority groups (see Box 7.3). However, despite the widening outcome gap between the Kinh and ethnic minorities, Viet Nam has a strong platform of policy and programming aimed at improving living conditions in ethnic minority areas (World Bank 2012). Based on rights enshrined in the Constitution – which specifically calls for the government to prioritise ethnic minority peoples, especially

---

BOX 7.3   'ONE OF THESE THINGS IS NOT LIKE THE OTHER'

Viet Nam's ethnic minority groups are far from homogenous, as evidenced by the gap between the Hmong and the Khmer.[3] The Khmer, who live in the Mekong Delta, have a poverty rate[4] of 'only' 43.2 per cent, compared to 93.3 per cent for the Hmong (World Bank 2012). Furthermore, poor Khmer families are significantly less poor than poor Hmong families. The poverty gap for the former is 11.6 per cent compared to 45.3 per cent for the latter (ibid.).

Geography plays an important role in differences between the Khmer and the Hmong. Land in the delta is more productive and access to markets is easier. However, as the World Bank (2012: 71) notes, geography is not destiny. Even within a given location, poverty rates between ethnic minorities and the Kinh 'average between four and seven times higher'. A key reason why Khmer households are less poor than Hmong households is that they have more diversified incomes. They are not only moving into commercial rather than semi-subsistence production, and developing formal and informal cooperative groups to help support their agricultural efforts, but they are also moving into non-agricultural sectors. Indeed, the Khmer, unlike the Hmong, are very likely to migrate to Viet Nam's cities, where they are heavily involved in both trading and industrial work (ibid.).

---

those living in the mountains and other 'extremely difficult socioeconomic conditions'[2] – programmes (such as Programme 135) target communities with large minority populations for improvements in transportation, health, education, sanitation and power infrastructure. They also work to increase agricultural production and develop local capacity (e.g. by providing Hmong students with educational stipends). While this geographical targeting frequently misses the poorest minorities, who tend to live in the most remote areas and have little access to services clustered in commune centres, the sharp decline in ethnic minority poverty – from 75.2 per cent in 1998 to 50.3 per cent in 2008 – suggests that policy and programming is having a significant although insufficient impact (World Bank 2012).

On the other hand, the 'selective cultural preservation policy' adopted by the Vietnamese government after the Viet Nam–American war has helped foster a widespread belief that some ethnic minority groups – especially those living in the highlands such as the Hmong – are particularly 'backwards' (Michaud 2010: 32; see also Turner 2012a, 2012b). That policy, while encouraging the ethnic dress, dance and music which makes Ha Giang a popular tourist destination, calls for the eradication of minority cultural practices believed to endanger socialist progress (ibid.). This not only situated the Hmong as 'others' in the eyes of the Kinh, especially given their geographic isolation, it has also largely precluded exposure to recent modernisation, and fostered an especially strong sense of ethnic identity among the Hmong.

Gender

The Vietnamese government has a long-standing commitment to gender equality, with documents dating to the 1930s proclaiming it a key party objective (Abjorensen 2010; Knodel *et al.* 2004). The country's gender machinery is relatively strong and it has a solid regional track record in terms of women's political and economic participation (Jones *et al.* 2012; Schuler *et al.* 2006). However, although its gender policy infrastructure is comprehensive, there is 'considerable disconnect between these policy frameworks and their implementation at the provincial, district and commune levels' (Jones *et al.* 2012: 13). Many institutions – particularly at the commune level – are unable to fully integrate gender into programming. This leads to tokenistic, generic interventions that, for example, inadvertently exclude Hmong women because they lack the Vietnamese language skills of Hmong men (ibid.). Furthermore, the repeated policy emphasis on the family as the 'key space to maintain and promote good cultural traditions'[5] has inadvertently reinforced women's domestic responsibilities, despite calling for gender equality in the household (Abjorensen 2010; Schuler *et al.* 2006). This is also echoed in the Domestic Violence Law, which has a strong focus on family reconciliation and tasks People's Committees (the lowest level of government) and the Fatherland Front (an alliance of political organisations) with resolving domestic disputes at the local level. Critically, and as will be discussed in greater detail on page 147, because gender equality and ethnic-related concerns have both largely been seen as policy 'add-ons' rather than central objectives, there has been little attempt to coordinate across domains.

Changes for Hmong girls

The lives of Ta Lung's Hmong girls are in some ways changing rapidly but in other ways continuing to mirror those of older generations. On the one hand, today's adolescent Hmong girls are the first to have had the opportunity to attend school, and most now complete 9th grade. On the other hand, continued son preference – in the context of the extreme poverty which accompanies subsistence farming in a hostile, arid environment – means that beyond access to school, most girls are experiencing only incremental change compared to the lived realities of their mothers and grandmothers. Marriage practices are shifting slowly, with some girls still subject to child marriage and marriage by abduction. Meanwhile the allocation of domestic and agricultural work continues to leave most girls socially isolated and with no time for rest or recreation.

What drives change?

Top-down change

Changes in Hmong girls' lives are primarily the result of macro-level change, especially top-down, policy-driven programming that has improved their access to education, provided them with the first Hmong role models, and built the infrastructure that links them to the outside world.

The impact of policy is clearest in regard to shifts in the social norms that govern girls' education. As noted in Chapter 6, there have been very recent and significant changes not only in what girls do (descriptive norms) but also in what their families and communities believe they *ought* to do (injunctive norms).This remarkable transition is largely due to national-level policy, which has prioritised building schools in ethnic minority communities, provided Hmong students with educational stipends and committed to achieving universal lower-secondary schooling. All eight of Ta Lung's villages now have their own schools for children aged 5–9 and the commune centre has its own lower-secondary school. Children from the more distant villages are allowed to board throughout the school week, which girls universally appreciated because it saves them a difficult daily commute, affords them '*beans and meat . . . meals better than at home*', and – most importantly – means they can '*hang out with my friends*' after school instead of '*working all the time like at home*'.

Affirmative action policies within the civil service are also leading some Hmong girls to imagine new futures and invest in their own capabilities.While there are not enough Hmong teachers to serve every commune, much less every classroom, the national government has worked hard to provide minority students with minority teachers.[6] These teachers, as well as Hmong commune officials, are serving as role models to girls, who see that they have '*stable jobs*' and a '*salary at the end of every month*'. Nearly all of the girls involved in our research were interested in becoming teachers and contributing '*my part to society*'.

Policies aimed at reducing ethnic minority poverty have also helped shift norms. Reductions in food insecurity[7] have allowed parents to send their children to school. Similarly, improved infrastructure has exposed Hmong girls and the rest of their community to the wider world.Though many of the more remote villages remain inaccessible to vehicles, most now have improved paths which make getting to school easier, facilitate participation in the cash economy, and encourage girls' independent travel to local markets. Many villages also have access to mobile phone services, which allow adolescents to listen to downloaded music and, in some cases, text one another. Some of the less remote villages have electricity, which reduces girls' workloads and means '*there's light for girls to study in the evening*' (health worker).

Local initiative

Local initiative is also key to understanding recent changes in Hmong girls' lives. Again, the clearest evidence is on education. In Ta Lung, Hmong village leaders have paired shame-inducing fines with savvy messaging that encourages families to invest in their children's education. Teachers have convinced children to invest in their own studies by juxtaposing for them the poverty of their parents with the potential salaries of commune officials. Girls, even more than boys, have enthusiastically embraced the notion that schooling is key to a future where the sun '*shines bright always*' because '*they don't have to work hard on the field*'. Their parents, initially motivated by fines of up to 50,000 Vietnamese Dong (VND)/day[8] – payable through public labour for the poorest households – are now rarely in need of a reminder to send their children to school, at least through the end of 9th grade (now compulsory). These policies have not only served to reduce truancy but have also (according to teachers) begun to have a significant impact on learning outcomes.

Local leadership has been crucial to recent progress in other areas. In some cases, commune-level officials have single-handedly altered the trajectories of individual girls' lives. An 11th-grade girl at Meo Vac High School, for example, told us that she was inspired to continue her education by a Hmong commune official who intrigued her with tales of travel (see Box 7.4). In other cases, officials have rapidly scaled up successful interventions – without waiting for higher-level permission. For instance, in Man Than commune in Lao Cai province, where Oxfam has been implementing its programming for children, local leaders were so impressed by the way in which anonymous access to comment 'mail boxes'[9] improved students' communication with their teachers (about academic and non-academic issues) that they took the idea to scale almost immediately. A key informant at the provincial-level Department of Education reported that nearly every classroom in Lao Cai province is now using the technique.

NGO programming and demonstration models

NGO programming, while reaching only a handful of girls, is also helping to drive change. Both Plan and Oxfam have demonstrated that hands-on, participatory

---

BOX 7.4 HELPING GIRLS TO DREAM

Chu Thi Vang is 18 years old and in the 11th grade. She is a year behind her classmates because she sat out a year after 9th grade – before being inspired by a Hmong commune official with stories of successful Hmong girls and the larger world. Although her parents initially refused to allow her to go to school, she insisted, and won.

Because '*I am the youngest child*,'[10] Vang explained, '*my parents always said that they would let me continue my education*'. When the time came for her to apply to high school, however, they refused and told her she must stay and work in the fields with them. After '*one year at home*', she added, working and talking with '*my cousin and a friend living in the same hamlet*', they all decided to go back to school. '*One day, we went to the commune office and asked the man if the school still had quota to enrol students or not.*'

He told them many things. '*He told me about two girls in other hamlets. After finishing the school, one is an officer and one is a teacher. He told me to try to study and find a job.*' He told them '*that girls don't have to get married early*'. Most amazingly, from Vang's perspective, he told them that when they had graduated, and found jobs of their own, they would have money and could travel. Ultimately, she concluded, '*I want to see all of my country*'.

programming helps girls become stronger and more confident, able to dream of futures beyond early marriage and motherhood. Given that filial piety[11] has traditionally dictated near-total subservience and silence in the younger generation, particularly for girls, the fact that programming is helping girls become '*more confident*' and '*no longer afraid of other children, teachers, parents, aunts, uncles and elder brothers or sisters*' – and become '*bold enough to tell your own story*' (13-year-old girl) – is nothing short of remarkable. Indeed, nearly all of the participant girls we interviewed were committed to attending upper-secondary school and having careers of their own, although it should be noted that because few had yet reached 9th grade, they had yet to encounter the 'ceiling' that parents typically put on girls' education (see Chapter 6).

Specific programming elements also show great promise, albeit on a small scale thus far. For example, while key informants in most villages have been clear that they cannot prevent child marriage because by the time they notice that a girl is living with a boy it is too late (and she may already be pregnant), Plan's Child Protection Board offers a potential solution.[12] Comprising villagers, the board intervenes immediately whenever it hears of a child marriage. Board members go directly to the groom's home and cancel the marriage by sending the girl home to her parents. The board '*invites*' the boy's parents to '*sign on a commitment paper to keep our son from marrying too young*' (mother of a boy who kidnapped a 16-year-old girl).

Oxfam's work demonstrates that with longer-term investments, which build local capacity and institutionalise NGO–government linkages, programming begins to have spillover impacts that far exceed intervention targets. Oxfam has worked in Lao Cai province for more than a decade and in Viet Nam for more than 30 years. The result of this partnership is a strong base of local teachers – about a third of whom (on a provincial basis) are ethnic minorities – willing to champion children's rights to their peers, as well as a group of committed parents able to mobilise other parents by modelling investment in education. With trust already established, new ideas are far more easily taken on board.

What slows change down?

Policy and leadership blind spots

A primary reason that the lives of Hmong girls continue to mirror those of their mothers and grandmothers is that they are largely invisible to policymakers. Situated in a nexus of disadvantage – constrained by their gender, ethnicity and age – policy and programming rarely targets their unique needs. For example, while the 2014 Law on Marriage and the Family[13] raises the minimum age for girls' marriage to 18,[14] it addresses ethnic difference only to the extent that it mandates promoting 'good tradition . . . embodying the identity of each nationality' and calls on the state to 'mobilize people to abolish backward marriage and family customs'. It does not, for example, provide guidance as to the additional support that will be needed in Hmong communities to raise parents' awareness about the importance of girls' schooling and the longer-term individual and familial payoffs of avoiding child marriage.

Similarly, while ethnic minority policy has prioritised education for Hmong children, it takes no account of the ways in which Hmong girls are especially disadvantaged. Our primary research has indicated that adolescent girls would find it highly beneficial if they were, for example, exempted from more types of educational fees or provided with free school meals. An informant at the Ministry of Education, however, admitted that '*despite traditions and customs that don't allow girls to go to school and force them to get married early, policies have not mentioned female, only refer to supporting children in general*'. Informants from the Committee for Ethnic Minority Affairs (CEMA) noted that one reason why ethnic minority girls and women have received so little attention within CEMA is the relative dearth of women's voices within the organisation. Efforts are only now being scaled up to ensure that ethnic minority women are well represented in committee leadership.

This acute siloing of policy – further reflected in a lack of coordination between the various ministries and departments tasked with providing programming that may be relevant to ethnic minority girls – is reinforced by the way in which responsibilities and budgets are distributed. CEMA, for example, does not extend below the provincial level, which means that it '*misses opportunity for across-sector coordination*' (United Nations Population Fund (UNFPA) informant). Furthermore, its budget is very small[15] and disbursements are often delayed by the national government. Similarly, neither the Youth Union nor the Women's Union has any mandate to address issues facing adolescent girls. The Youth Union (for young people aged 16–30) is largely political and appears to have no real presence in Hmong communities outside of a chapter at the Meo Vac High School. The Women's Union is almost exclusively for married women aged 18 and older, and while national key informants reported that they were keen to serve younger and unmarried adolescents, they lacked the resources and support to do so. Indeed, as Plan and Oxfam discovered in the course of rolling out programming, leaders of the Women's Union '*at the grassroots level*' tend to have '*such a big workload*' that for them to do so would be almost impossible (United Nations Children's Fund (UNICEF) informant). This is especially the case in poorer provinces, such as Ha Giang, which have extremely limited resources with which to supplement nationally allocated budgets. According to a Ministry of Justice informant, this has meant that laws aimed at ethnic minorities and women '*are not implemented evenly*'. Minority girls and women are almost totally ignored as those tasked with ethnic minority activities overlook gender dimensions, and those tasked with gender-related activities overlook ethnic diversity and the role it plays in shaping specific patterns of gendered disadvantage (CEMA informant).

Hmong girls' near-total invisibility is highlighted by the data which the government does *not* collect (see also Box 7.5). Statistics are rarely disaggregated by ethnicity (with most including the Hmong as one of many 'other Northern upland minorities'), are often reported only by province (meaning that differences between the Hmong and the Kinh must be inferred by comparing Ha Giang with other provinces) and – with the exception of school enrolment statistics – are almost never available by both gender and ethnicity. A CEMA informant explained that even drafting new minority policies '*faces many challenges due to inadequacy of statistics*'. Indeed, even the government does not know how prevalent child marriage is among the Hmong community. Recent attempts by CEMA to find out have not worked, as the new surveys which are gathering '*data on the factual social economic situation of 53 ethnic minorities*' have been unable to collect '*sensitive information on child marriage*', in part because '*reports from grassroots levels stress more on achievements and don't fully reflect child marriage in reality*'.

Finally, despite the growing consensus that tackling social norms is key to changing girls' trajectories in the longer term, because Vietnamese policy and programming focuses on top-down propaganda that attempts to disseminate goals without any attempt to engage in the genuine dialogues that research suggests are needed to facilitate sustainable norm change, there is only limited penetration into '*people's thoughts, minds and hearts*' (Ministry of Justice informant). Indeed, a Women's Union informant explained that '*the approach to policies is not suitable to ethnic minority conditions and culture*'.

This was evident across our research sites – especially the most remote villages – in attempts to eradicate child marriage. Vietnamese law prohibits both child marriage and bride kidnapping, and calls for perpetrators to be fined. However, because

---

BOX 7.5 DATA LACUNAE

Jump-started by the World Bank's 2012 poverty assessment, it is only in the past five years that significant national and international attention has been directed at differences between Viet Nam's ethnic minority populations and its Kinh majority. As a result, much of the data typically used to track progress among vulnerable populations sheds little light on ethnic minority experiences.

For example, UNICEF's Multiple Indicator Cluster Surveys (MICS) are often used to compare rates of child marriage over time and across countries. However, due to its sample size, the MICS is unable to illuminate the incidence of child marriage among Viet Nam's Hmong community.

MICS5 (2015), for example, reports that nationally, 10.3 per cent of girls aged 15–19 years were currently married or in a union. In the 'Northern Midlands and Mountains', that figure rose to 22.6 per cent. These numbers are especially alarming given that MICS4 (2012) found only 8.4 per cent and 16.5 per cent respectively.

However, the MICS5 included only 1,374 girls aged 15–19 in the entire country (MICS4 sampled 1,707). Of those girls, only 185 were from the northern areas. Such a sample size is not adequate for generating valid child marriage rates among ethnic minority groups, thus hindering appropriately tailored programming.

Hmong marriages are accomplished by the simple expedient of moving in with one another; when marriages between legal minors take place, families simply do not register them until the couple is old enough to legally marry. Furthermore, when child marriages do become visible, officials tend to look the other way – even when they are the result of kidnapping – because of Hmong beliefs about girls' souls belonging to their husbands' families upon marriage (see Chapter 6). A Women's Union informant noted that the *'fine makes no sense'* for already poor families, especially since it would effectively penalise the kidnapped bride, and that health care providers – concerned that young mothers might choose to forgo health care – simply *'forget'* to write down the age of the mother when she is clearly too young to be legally married. Similarly, one village headman admitted that unlike fines for educational truancy, he would never enforce a marriage fine, because he wanted his people to respect him and feared that such messages would undermine his social standing.

NGO programme shortcomings

Although our research suggests that hands-on NGO programming can be trans-formative for participant girls, only a fraction of Hmong girls have access to any sort of programming. This was brought into stark relief by the fact that we were only able to locate one NGO programme specifically aimed at Hmong girls and two others aimed at Hmong children. Unlike countries in sub-Saharan Africa and South Asia, Viet Nam does not have a national-level problem with girls' school enrolment (even at secondary and tertiary levels) or child marriage. This has blinded many NGOs to the reality of Hmong girls' lives. UN Women, for example, primar-ily focuses on economic empowerment and has no mandate to address the issues facing adolescent girls, which are – according to our key informants – given to UNICEF and UNFPA. However, whereas UNFPA focuses more generally on sex-ual and reproductive health (SRH) and UNICEF focuses on child protection issues such as trafficking and mother-tongue education, neither are directly addressing the broader vulnerabilities facing Hmong children and other ethnic minority children, such as child marriage. As a CEMA informant noted, '*UNICEF or UNFPA seem to pay little attention to addressing child marriage at its roots. They don't support CEMA.*' While within the UN context, the social exclusion of minority populations falls under the purview of the United Nations Development Programme (UNDP), none of our informants mentioned any activity aimed at minority adolescent girls. Very recently, the importance of tailored interventions with marginalised ethnic minority communities has risen up the policy agenda for governments and devel-opment partners as the discourse has shifted from an emphasis on national-level targets towards a focus on equity and supporting the hardest-to-reach populations.

The two NGO programmes serving Hmong children that we examined also have a number of design and implementation shortcomings. Plan's project, for example, bundles hands-on programming for girls with broader community-level infrastructure investments (primarily in schools and safe water) aimed both at improving local life and securing community buy-in. Positive results for participant girls notwithstanding, our research found that in Meo Vac, girls have been effectively lost within this community development strategy. With only two girls' clubs serving just 60 girls, no messaging aimed at the boys who instigate child marriage (see Box 7.6), no apparent girl-focused education for parents, and little reported interface with the local power structure regarding the needs of adolescent girls, Plan's work is unlikely to transform Hmong girls' lives at scale. Similarly, while the child-centred methods of Oxfam's programme appear to have been genuinely transformational, we found that the rights-based messaging has often failed to resonate – largely because it appears to have been insufficiently contextualised to local

BOX 7.6 LESSONS FROM MEO VAC HIGH SCHOOL

Meo Vac High School has had a range of programming aimed at preventing child marriage. Sensitive to cultural concerns about showing '*the ways for the deer to run*' (encouraging sexual experimentation through education), these classes primarily teach children about the Marriage and Family Law and the health consequences of child and consanguineous marriage. They include only the biological basics of reproductive health and tend to make 'young people feel embarrassed' (Women's Global Network for Reproductive Rights 2012; see also Hong *et al.* 2009). Furthermore, because the high school is growing so quickly that it is running out of space and teachers, current programming is more ad hoc than systematic. We found that while students understand the higher-level messages, they want graphic and detailed information about reproductive biology and help in managing the conflicting emotions that adolescence brings – mainly so that they know how to live and study with the opposite sex without becoming distracted from their studies. Teachers – who found the material as embarrassing as their students did – wanted outside professionals to handle delivery.

Our research at the high school led to two other important findings. First, it was evident in our interviews with Hmong girls that today's high school students – many of whom have fought hard to overcome the long odds stacked against them – have tremendous potential to serve as role models for their younger peers. Second, ending child marriage among Viet Nam's Hmong population will require programming that targets boys and their parents too. While earlier rounds of research found that boys sometimes initiate child marriage because they believe themselves to be in love or because they want girls to work for their families, students at the high school – who were especially forthcoming – explained that boys as young as 13 were quite often '*forced by their parents to get married*' so that they would gain a daughter-in-law to '*do housework for them, picking vegetables on the mountain*'.

realities. Girls are not, for example, taught that child marriage and kidnapping violates their rights or that they have a right to live free from violence.[16] Plan and Oxfam's programming impacts are further limited by the way in which participants are selected. Rather than choosing the girls most in need of support, both rely on a peer-influencing approach, which, in practice, effectively reinforces Vietnamese schools' meritocracy and means that clubs are mainly open to girls who are classroom leaders or academic success stories.

Hmong isolation

Hmong isolation is also crucial to understanding norm stasis. While our research found that geographic remoteness and agrarian reality slows change, evidence from the Hmong diaspora suggests that Hmong cultural norms have remained remarkably 'sticky' even in the context of broader opportunities[17] (Long 2008; Vang and Bogenschutz 2011; Thao 2010; MB 2013; Khang 2010; Lee *et al.* 2009).

In the communities in which we worked, highland agrarian life plays an important role in maintaining Hmong gender norms and marriage practices. As noted in Chapter 6, Hmong villages continue to be comparatively isolated not just from broader Vietnamese culture but from the influx of agro-processing and textile jobs that have transformed the national economy so rapidly. Indeed, private sector jobs are nearly non-existent in the highlands – especially for girls and women who, even if they '*completed the 12th grade, would come back home and work in the fields anyway*'. Moreover, because today's Hmong families farm in the same way that they always have, given that rocky soil and sparse rainfall restrict agricultural change, farming continues to be very hard work, best left to the young and requiring as many hands as possible. A 16-year-old father, for example, explained, '*I thought that I would get married early, to have children early*'.

Hmong ethnic identity, however, continues to be the strongest factor reinforcing the status quo, slowing norm change even in the face of top-down policy. For example, the importance of son preference cannot be overstated. Hmong traditions – which assign girls' spirits to their husbands' families at the time of marriage and place gender roles at the heart of culture, freighting them with 'extraordinary importance' – serve to limit girls' lives from birth (Long 2008: 20). Expected throughout childhood to work for their parents, simultaneously mastering the skills required to be a good daughter-in-law and effectively reimbursing their parents for the costs incurred by their lives – girls know they are not as important as boys. They understand that they are not '*allowed to worship the ancestors*', lest they affect the '*soul of the next generation*', and hold out little hope that their parents will commit scarce family resources for a high school education that is largely meaningless '*because after finishing grade 9 or grade 12, they only get married*'.

Critical also to understanding the resistance of the Hmong community to norm change is the fact that their cultural identity has long been focused on ethnic independence and identity survival, resulting in 'a vexed relationship to Vietnamese national identity and ideology' (Long 2008: 20; see also Turner and Michaud 2009;

Michaud 2010, 2011; Turner 2012a, 2012b). With a clear understanding of their social marginalisation – made worse in recent years by widespread belief that those who have not benefited from Viet Nam's economic progress are simply 'unwilling to develop themselves' – many adults involved in our research appear to have drawn lines around what is Hmong and what is not Hmong (World Bank 2012: 131). In most cases, this line delineates what is possible for Hmong people and what is not, serving as a rational way to manage their own and their children's expectations. In other cases, our Hmong study participants had internalised negative stereotypes about subsistence farmers in general (Nguyen and Locke 2014) and the Hmong in particular. They repeatedly referred to their ethnic group as *'silly'*, *'backwards'*, *'ignorant'*, *'unknowledgeable'*, unable to *'learn anything'*, *'superstitious'* and *'unable to listen'*. While these response types differ in that one emphasises the external and the other the internal, they both result in the construction of a 'self-image of inferiority . . . which further disempowers them to attempt social and educational transformations' (Luong and Nieke 2013: 30).

As a result of the monolithic impact of cultural identity, Hmong girls – unlike their peers in other countries – have little access to the broader capabilities they need to secure the futures they are beginning to want for themselves (see Chapter 3 on Ethiopia). Most critically, Hmong girls are rarely able to express their thoughts and aspirations. Faced with violence at home, a typical girl feels obliged to *'keep things in my heart'* because *'we don't like to share about family problems'* – even with *'friends'*. Aspiring to attend high school, most girls immediately shelve their dreams when their *'parents don't allow me'* and do not even *'try to persuade'*. Kidnapped into a 'marriage' they do not want, or trapped in a marriage that threatens their wellbeing, Hmong girls silently and piously fulfil the roles expected of them. One consequence of this silence is that girls also have very few 'champions'. Teachers and officials, some of whom would be glad to help, only rarely understand girls' vulnerability until it is too late, while girls' mothers – who usually do understand their daughters' vulnerabilities – are trapped by the same rules. As one noted, *'the mother is sorry for her daughter, but she has to accept it, she can't do anything'*.

Reasons for optimism

Despite the forces working to slow change for Viet Nam's Hmong girls, there are some promising trends. At the policy level, 2015 was a watershed year: not only did the government create a new programme[18] to eliminate child marriage among ethnic minority populations, but – due to a growing understanding that national progress towards the Sustainable Development Goals (SDGs) depends on the progress made by its most vulnerable ethnic minority groups – it also called for the collection of disaggregated data and specific SDG targets for ethnic minorities.[19] Furthermore, the child marriage scheme directly acknowledges, for the first time, that *'for ethnic minority people, prohibition or punishment are not enough, the law is required to convince them, help them to understand and then to follow'* (CEMA informant). The government has also begun to draft a new law on ethnic minorities to help them access their constitutional rights by streamlining existing policy. Draft inputs call for mother-tongue education, improving educational outcomes, and more thoroughly addressing the nexus of ethnicity and gender. A World Bank informant reported that the government hopes to have passed the law by 2017, and a CEMA informant told us that some resources are already being allocated.

The comparative uniqueness of the Vietnamese government, which controls not only the law but social messaging, also suggests that Viet Nam's Hmong girls are better positioned to see rapid change than their peers in other environments. Highly successful investment in education indicates that thorough change is possible in a very short time frame if it is prioritised – and adequately funded.

Conclusions and policy recommendations

Very recent policy shifts notwithstanding, the gender norms constraining most Hmong girls' lives continue to be largely ignored in policy and programming, even though evidence suggests these norms are key to perpetuating girls' and women's disadvantage. Siloed government policy, poor intersectoral coordination and minimal investments in local capacity mean that beyond recent improvements in schooling, government policy has not translated into significant shifts in the contours of Hmong girls' lives. Partly due to the relative invisibility of ethnic minority populations in Viet Nam until very recently, NGOs have paid very little attention to the vulnerabilities and needs of Hmong adolescent girls despite their pronounced disadvantage. Programming is rare, often poorly tailored and, because of Viet Nam's meritocratic traditions, almost exclusively available to the least vulnerable girls.

Given that previous interventions targeted at the Hmong community have tended to emphasise cultural difference and reinforce inferiority, our research suggests that future efforts should aim for dialogue which simultaneously respects cultural identity and encourages investment in the capabilities of all children. To foster sustainable impacts, those efforts will need to focus not only on establishing new norms, such as academic excellence, but on eliminating the negative norms that hold adolescent girls back from maximising their own futures and helping improve the development of the broader Hmong community. For example, our findings from the three small-scale participatory programmes we reviewed (including girls' clubs, peer-to-peer mentoring, and student-teacher-parent dialogues) show that they can be pivotal in helping Hmong girls identify and voice their own aspirations – especially where they offer girls a glimpse of the world beyond the confines of their villages. Moreover, given that Hmong adolescent boys are often key decision-makers in the marriage process, our research highlighted that Hmong boys should be prioritised for programming aimed at eliminating child marriage and establishing new masculinities. Similarly, the dividends of supporting Hmong parents to develop more lucrative, non-agricultural sources of income are likely to be significant in terms of minimising the need for adolescent girls' household labour (see also World Bank 2012). We also suggest directly incentivising parents to support their daughters' education (through conditional cash transfers or educational scholarships), and – given the success of educational fines – appropriately penalising the minority of parents who allow their children's underage marriages.

Because this is the first generation of Hmong adolescent girls to have widespread access to formal education, the government must recognise this as a critical juncture and heavily invest in genuine transformation rather than comparatively slow, linear progress. Collecting the gender- and ethnicity-disaggregated data needed to adequately monitor SDG progress would be a good start, as it would necessitate a strong focus on Hmong girls' education and employment – by the government and its development partners. Using school stipends to further encourage girls' studies and prioritising them for local jobs – including placing recent graduates in classrooms as teaching assistants to simultaneously offset the lack of Hmong-speaking teachers and provide role models for younger students – the government could capitalise on the momentum that has already been built in regard to lower-secondary education and use it to provide evidence to the broader Hmong community that investing in adolescent girls can return lasting dividends.

Notes

1 This is because subnational governments have no capacity to create or alter taxes, leaving them with user fees as the only potential source of fundraising.
2 Article 58.
3 Government statistics are reported for a single group that includes both the Khmer and the Cham. The Khmer, however, outnumber the Cham by at least 2:1.
4 The poverty rates calculated for ethnic minority populations combined data from the 2009 Population and Housing Census and the 2010 Household Living Standard Survey and used the 2010 Government–World Bank poverty line.
5 Family Development Strategy, p. 1.
6 As noted in Chapter 6, approximately half the teachers in Ha Giang are ethnic minorities. There are still, however, very few Hmong teachers.
7 Improved food security has been achieved via the supply of hybrid corn and rice seeds aimed at improving yields (Wells-Dang 2012).
8 About $2.25.
9 Traditionally schools have had only one mailbox per school, which eliminates children's anonymity because it is typically placed in a central location. Oxfam put one mailbox in each classroom.
10 In Viet Nam, the oldest child traditionally bears the highest responsibility to the family. It is common, among Kinh families too, for the oldest child to leave school well before his or her younger siblings in order to make the money needed to keep them in school. Among Hmong families, oldest children typically provide labour – not cash – for their families.
11 Filial piety is a Confucian philosophy centred around respect and obedience to older relatives, especially fathers and grandfathers.
12 In contrast to Ethiopia, as discussed elsewhere in this book, where married girls increasingly do have an opportunity to continue their schooling, our research did not find any examples of married girls in school.
13 The Law on Marriage and Family, see http://vbpl.vn/TW/Pages/vbpqen-toanvan.aspx?ItemID=10874
14 It was raised from 16. The minimum age for men is now 20 rather than 18.
15 For example, CEMA has been allocated (as of February 2016) only $270,000 to implement the new policy for eliminating child and consanguineous marriage. Half is to be

used at the national level and half is to be split among the 15 provinces with the highest rates of problematic marriage.

16 As noted in Chapter 6, we found that alcohol-fuelled gender-based violence is endemic in Ta Lung's villages.

17 For example, while Hmong-American girls attend urban public high schools and are increasingly likely to transition to college and have jobs of their own, they are often still married in mid-adolescence and expected to cater for their husbands and in-laws. Long (2008: 20) argues that 'because cultural identity is the defining feature of Hmongness ... and because kinship ties define culture and priorities ... for women (and men) to resist Hmong kinship roles and the "oppressions" they entail is for this migratory Hmong culture to disappear'.

18 Decision No. 498, entitled 'Minimizing Child Marriage and Near Blood Marriage in Ethnic Minority Regions from 2015 to 2025', was approved by the Prime Minister on 14 April 2015. Delayed funding, however, has delayed implementation.

19 Decision No. 1557/QD-TTg was issued on 10 September 2015 and has a variety of targets for a wide range of outcomes, including poverty, stunting, child and maternal mortality, and access to water and sanitation. Most importantly, it also includes some targets for ethnic minority girls and women, including literacy, upper-secondary enrolment and political representation at all levels. A UNICEF informant, while acknowledging that disaggregated targets are an important step forward, also expressed concerns that targets are not '*logical and orderly*' and are '*not accompanied with the corresponding tasks*' necessary to implementation.

Bibliography

Abjorensen, N. (2010) 'Two Faces of Gender Equity in Vietnam' *Canberra Times* 15 May.

Beresford, M. (2008) 'Doi Moi in Review: The Challenges of Building Market Socialism in Vietnam' *Journal of Contemporary Asia* 38(2): 221–243.

Bjornestad, L. (2009) *Fiscal Decentralization, Fiscal Incentives, and Pro-Poor Outcomes: Evidence from Viet Nam.* Manila: Asian Development Bank. Available online at www.adb.org/sites/default/files/publication/28387/economics-wp168.pdf. Accessed 11 November 2016.

Fritzen, S. (2006) 'Probing System Limits: Decentralisation and Local Political Accountability in Vietnam' *The Asia Pacific Journal of Public Administration* 28(1): 1–23.

General Statistics Office and UNICEF. (2011) *Viet Nam Multiple Indicator Cluster Survey 2011 Final Report.* Ha Noi, Viet Nam. Available online at https://mics-surveys-prod.s3.amazonaws.com/MICS4/East%20Asia%20and%20the%20Pacific/Viet%20Nam/2010-2011/Final/Viet%20Nam%202011%20MICS_English.pdf

General Statistics Office and UNICEF. (2015) *Viet Nam Multiple Indicator Cluster Survey 2014 Final Report.* Ha Noi, Viet Nam. Available online at https://mics-surveys-prod.s3.amazonaws.com/MICS5/East%20Asia%20and%20the%20Pacific/Viet%20Nam/2013-2014/Final/Viet%20Nam%202013-14%20MICS_English.pdf

Harris, D., Kooy, M. and Pham, Q. (2011) *Scaling Up Rural Sanitation in Vietnam: Political Economy Constraints and Opportunities.* ODI Working Paper 341. London: Overseas Development Institute. Available online at www.odi.org/sites/odi.org.uk/files/odi-assets/publications-opinion-files/7550.pdf.

Hong, K.T., Duong, L.B. and Huong, N.N. (2009) *Sexuality in Contemporary Vietnam: Easy to Joke About But Hard to Talk About.* Ha Noi: Vietnam Knowledge Publishing House.

Jones, N., Anh, T.T.V. and Malachowska, A. (2012) *The Politics of Gender and Social Protection in Viet Nam: Opportunities and Challenges for a Transformative Approach.* London: ODI Background Note, Overseas Development Institute. Available online at www.odi.org/sites/odi.org.uk/files/odi-assets/publications-opinion-files/7650.pdf.

Khang, M.S. (2010) *Hmong Traditional Marital Roles and the Pursuit of Higher Education for Married Hmong American Women*. MA Thesis, University of Wisconsin-Stout.

Knodel, J., Loi, V.M., Jayakody, R. and Huy, V.T. (2004) *Gender Roles in the Family: Change and Stability in Vietnam*. PSC Research Report No 04–559. Lansing, MI: University of Michigan Population Studies Center. Available online at www.psc.isr.umich.edu/pubs/pdf/rr04-559.pdf.

Lee, R.M., Jung, K.R., Su, J.C., Tran, A. and Bahrassa, N.F. (2009) 'The Family Life and Adjustment of Hmong American Sons and Daughters' *Sex Roles* 60: 549–558.

Long, L. (2008) 'Contemporary Women's Roles through Hmong, Vietnamese, and American Eyes' *Frontiers: A Journal of Women Studies* 29(1): 1–36.

Luong, M.P. and Nieke, W. (2013) 'Minority Status and Schooling of the Hmong in Vietnam' *Hmong Studies Journal* 14: 1–37.

MB. (2013) *A Hmong Wife's Role*. A Hmong Woman Blog, 13 October. Available online at http://ahmongwoman.com/2013/10/13/a-hmong-wifes-role/. Accessed 14 November 2016.

Michaud, J. (2010) 'Handling Mountain Minorities in China, Vietnam and Laos: From History and Current Concerns' *Asian Ethnicity* 10(1): 25–49.

Michaud, J. (2011) 'Hmong Infrapolitics: A View from Vietnam' *Ethnic and Racial Studies* 35(11): 1853–1873.

Nguyen, M. and Locke, C. (2014) 'Rural-Urban Migration and Householding: Care, Migrant Livelihoods, Patriarchy and the State in Vietnam and China' *The Journal of Peasant Studies* 41(5): 855–879.

Nguyen-Hoang, P. and Schroeder, L. (2010) 'An Analysis of Quasi Decentralized Budgeting in Vietnam' *International Journal of Public Administration* 33: 698–709.

Rydstrøm, H. (2006) 'Sexual Desires and "Social Evils": Young Women in Rural Vietnam' *Gender, Place and Culture* 13(3): 283–301.

Schuler, S., Anh, H., Ha, V., Minh, T., Mai, B. and Thein, P. (2006) 'Constructions of Gender in Vietnam: In Pursuit of the "Three Criteria"' *Culture, Health & Sexuality* 8(5): 383–394.

Thao, M. (2010) *Ntxhais Hmoob: 'Hmong Daughters' Supporting the Well-Being of Young Hmong Women*. Saint Paul, MN: Wilder Research.

Turner, S. (2012a) '"Forever Hmong": Ethnic Minority Livelihoods and Agrarian Transition in Upland Northern Vietnam' *The Professional Geographer* 64(4): 540–553.

Turner, S. (2012b) 'Making a Living the Hmong Way: An Actor-oriented Livelihoods Approach to Everyday Politics and Resistance in Upland Vietnam' *Annals of the Association of American Geographers* 102(2): 403–422.

Turner, S. and Michaud, J. (2009) '"Weapons of the Week': Selective Resistance and Agency among the Hmong in Northern Vietnam" in D. Caouette and S. Turner (eds.) *Agrarian Angst and Rural Resistance in Contemporary Southeast Asia*. London: Routledge, 45–60.

Vang, P.D. and Bogenschutz, M. (2011) 'Teenage Marriage, and the Socioeconomic Status of Hmong Women' *International Migration* 52(3): 144–159.

Wells-Dang, A. (2012) *Ethnic Minority Development in Vietnam: What Leads to Success?* Background Paper for the 2012 Programmatic Poverty Assessment.

Women's Global Network for Reproductive Rights. (2012) *Sexuality Education in Vietnam*. Available online at http://archive.wgnrr.org/blog/11/sexuality-education-vietnam) Accessed 14 November 2016.

World Bank. (2012) *Well Begun, Not Yet Done: Vietnam's Remarkable Progress on Poverty Reduction and the Emerging Challenges*. Ha Noi: World Bank. Available online at https://open knowledge.worldbank.org/handle/10986/12326. Accessed 14 November 2016.

PART 4

Nepal

PART 4

Nepal

8

SMALL BUT PERSISTENT STEPS ON THE ROAD TO GENDER EQUALITY

Marriage patterns in Far West Nepal

Fiona Samuels and Anita Ghimire

Summary

Despite impressive progress in Nepal in recent decades in promoting human rights and gender equality, adolescent girls still face discriminatory gender norms that prevent them developing their full capabilities. Norms around marriage seem particularly 'sticky', and the country has one of the highest rates of child marriage (defined as marriage before the age of 18 years) in the world – with 48.5 per cent of women aged 20–49 married before the age of 18 and 24.5 per cent of girls aged 15–19 already married (Central Bureau of Statistics (CBS) and United Nations Children's Fund (UNICEF) 2015). This chapter looks at how marriage patterns are changing for the better in the Far West region of Nepal, where parents were found to be marrying their daughters at a later age and encouraging them to go to school and complete at least primary education before marrying. Some married girls have also reported that they had a say in the choice of marriage partner, have been able to negotiate with their in-laws to stay on in school, and it is apparent that the age gap between spouses is narrowing. However, despite these positive changes, social pressures remain, with entrenched notions of how girls, boys, women and men should behave, and with family honour and girls' marriage inexorably linked. Consequently, girls' mobility remains restricted, marriage and motherhood continue to be valued over education and employment, and girls are pushed into early fertility to produce the sons needed to continue the male ancestral line. The chapter also shows how new marriage patterns, including unforeseen effects of young adolescents' growing penchant for 'love' marriage, and polygamy as a continued preference, are poised to disrupt the pattern of progress for girls and women.

Introduction

Nepal has made impressive progress in recent decades in its human development indicators. From 1990 to 2013, gross domestic product (GDP) per capita increased by 75 per cent (from $1,240 to $2,173), while expected years of schooling increased from 7.8 years to 12.4 over roughly the same period. Life expectancy at birth has increased from 54.3 years to 69.6, while infant mortality has dropped from 98.8/1,000 live births in 1990 to 32.2 in 2013 (United Nations Development Programme (UNDP) 2015). If these patterns continue, Nepal will graduate out of the ranks of least-developed countries by 2022. However, this progress has been experienced unevenly, and disparities remain, particularly among certain population groups and in certain regions. Adolescent girls[1] and young women are among those who have not benefited equally from this progress, in part because they remain subject to a range of discriminatory gendered norms that greatly hinder their capability for achieving well-being (Samuels and Ghimire 2013). Many of these norms are guided by Hindu notions of chastity and honour, which apply to women and girls more than men and boys, who are instead expected to provide financially for their families (see, for example, Shradananda *et al.* 1992). These restrictive norms translate and guide the social structures and power relations within the private boundary of the family as well as in public spaces (Ghimire *et al.* 2013). This continuing disparity is reflected in the Social Institutions and Gender Index (SIGI), which, as noted in the Introduction, rates Nepal 'high' in terms of discriminatory norms (Organisation for Economic Co-operation and Development (OECD) 2014).

Understanding the disadvantages facing Nepali girls and women requires understanding the centrality of marriage to their lives. Marriage not only determines their personal social status, but is seen as a sign of success for their families (Ghimire and Samuels 2014; Samuels and Ghimire 2013; Goonesekere 2006). Indeed, in patrilocal Nepal, the idea that girls will eventually become brides and leave not only their natal homes – but their natal families – shapes girls' lives from birth (Lundgren *et al.* 2013; Beutel and Axinn 2002). In preparation for eventually becoming a 'good' daughter-in-law, girls are expected from early childhood to be silent and submissive and to shoulder the bulk of domestic chores while their brothers play (see

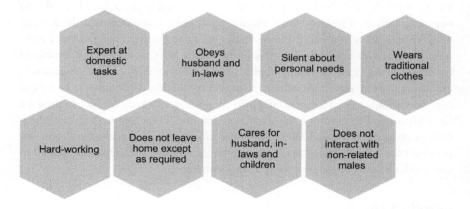

FIGURE 8.1 Characteristics of good wives and good daughters-in-law

Source: Author

Figure 8.1) (Samuels and Ghimire 2013; CARE 2015). In preparation for being a 'good' wife, they are expected to stay at home, dress modestly and avoid the contact with boys that might lead their neighbours to question their purity, doubt their family honour and restrict their marital options.

Unsurprisingly, given the importance attached to girls' marriage, Nepal continues to have one of the highest rates of child marriage in the world, with 37 per cent of young women aged 20–24 married before the age of 18 (CBS and UNICEF 2015), and girls are four times more likely to get married before the age of 18 than boys (Amin *et al.* 2014; Guragain *et al.* 2016). Because child marriage typically results in girls leaving school, impacts cascade across girls' lives, leading to a range of other capability deprivations including limited support networks and a diminution of career and employment opportunities (Ghimire *et al.* 2013; Amin *et al.* 2014; Bajracharya and Amin 2010). Norms such as child marriage are not, however, static. While gender norms tend to be among the 'stickiest' (Boudet *et al.* 2012; Samuels and Ghimire 2015; Lundgren *et al.* 2013), in Nepal there is clear evidence of change.

Study location and methods

This chapter draws on three rounds of fieldwork carried out between 2012 and 2014 in the Far West region of Nepal in the districts of Doti (Ranagaon, Salena, Wayal and Dipayal) and Kailali (Sahajpur, Geta and Chaumala), as well as one round of fieldwork in the district of Ilam in the Eastern region (Jamuna and Barbote) (see Figure 8.2).[2] These districts were chosen based on a number of criteria, including their ethnic diversity – with respondents from high-caste Brahmin and Chhetri groups as well as low-caste Dalit communities and indigenous groups (e.g. Tamang,

FIGURE 8.2   Map of Nepal showing study sites

Source: Author

Gurung, Magar) – and range of religious affiliations (with respondents following a mix of Hindu, animist and Buddhist religions). In choosing study sites we also paid attention to remoteness from district headquarters and the existence of programmes for adolescent girls.

We used a range of qualitative and participatory approaches with more than 630 respondents, including adolescent girls as well as their parents, their brothers, adolescent boys in the community, and a range of key informants at the community, district and national levels. Body-mapping, for example, helped girls show us what sorts of work they did on a regular basis (e.g. hands carry water) and what sorts of threats they face (e.g. head is not allowed to attend school). Similarly, community timelines and intergenerational trios permitted us to explore change over time, in communities as well as in individual families. In addition, outlier case studies allowed us to understand how some girls 'broke the mould' while others did as they were told, and marital networks facilitated understanding of the power dynamics between married girls and their husbands and in-laws.

Persistent but slow progress for Nepali girls

Our research found reason for optimism in Nepal. Girls are increasingly not just allowed but are actively supported to go to school, and the average age of marriage is increasing. Furthermore, girls are beginning to have some input into the decision about whom they will marry and are less likely to be significantly younger than their husbands – both of which are contributing to improved spousal communication, which is also likely to lead to lower levels of intimate partner violence (IPV) and gender-based violence (GBV).

Increasing education

Mirroring national-level data, which show Nepali girls' achieving gender parity (90.99 per cent) in primary completion (National Planning Commission (NPC) and United Nations Country Team Nepal 2013), much progress has been made in our study sites in terms of enrolment of girls in primary schools (grades 1–5). According to study respondents, whereas previously girls were sometimes not sent to school at all, now some girls are even sent to tuition classes after school and their domestic workload has been taken on by their mothers. Recent progress has a broad range of drivers. Investment in school-building, for example, has reduced the distances children have to travel to school. This has led to children enrolling 'on time', which in turn has increased the likelihood that girls can complete at least ten grades before marriage. The government's School Sector Reform Programme[3] has also contributed to progress, by supplying material incentives for school attendance and conducting mobilisation drives.

Indeed, our fieldwork found not only evidence of changing practices, but changing beliefs, with girls' education increasingly viewed as valuable – albeit especially in terms of its impact on marriage and motherhood. Respondents reported that educated girls made better mothers since they would have '*more knowledge and information to share when bringing up their children'*. Additionally, according to male study respondents, education would encourage girls to have '*broader thinking*' and be '*more accommodating*' towards their in-laws. They believed that this, in turn, would lead to greater harmony in the household.

Appreciation for girls' education has grown so markedly in recent years that even married girls – previously completely prohibited from attending school – are now, in some cases, permitted to continue their studies. Although this trend was found in all study sites, it appeared to be more common in places with active development programmes and in areas closer to the district headquarters. An obstacle to the spread of this nascent possibility is the expectation – primarily among in-laws and parents – that girls will begin childbearing soon after marriage. With very few exceptions (see Box 8.1), even where marriage does not end girls' education, motherhood does. However, we also see positive evidence of support for women and girls from strong male advocates, be they husbands, fathers or fathers-in-law, as is also shown in Box 8.1. This support from men and boys shows up in multiple cases and locations globally and is part of the vital supportive context essential for driving girls' educational equality.

Despite recent improvements, however, Nepali girls continue to be disadvantaged in terms of education, and that disadvantage tends to grow as they progress through

---

BOX 8.1 SUPPORT OF IN-LAWS AND HUSBAND IN CONTINUING EDUCATION

Radhika lives in Salena (in Doti district, in Far West Nepal) and was married when she was in grade 10. Her husband also completed secondary education and is in the police. Her parents did not negotiate with his parents about continuing her education after marriage. So after they married, she did not take her exam. However, her father-in-law very much wanted her to study. He had a shop and used to see children going to school. Upon knowing that it was exam time and that Radhika was not taking her exams, he cried in front of the children.

When Radhika heard this she was deeply moved and she took the exam. She failed twice and again thought of stopping her studies. But her husband informed her father-in-law and asked him to fill the forms so that she could sit the next exam. She failed again. Her father-in-law counselled her to continue education and she did.

After the birth of her first child, she again wanted to stop going to school. But her mother-in-law took charge of the housework and the child. Today she has two children, aged 9 and 4. She is doing her graduate degree from a college in Silgadi and works on various projects in the community.

Source: Case study with woman married in adolescence, Salena, Doti, 2014

secondary, higher secondary and graduate/tertiary education. Thus, while gender parity has been achieved in primary as well as secondary education, beyond secondary education the gap between boys and girls widens again: 6.85 per cent of boys attend higher secondary versus 5.94 per cent of girls and 3.5 per cent of boys attend graduate education compared to only 2.08 per cent of girls) (Ministry of Education 2015) – trends that were mirrored in our study sites. Furthermore, girls who are in school told us that enrolment is not a panacea; their heavy domestic work burdens make it difficult for them to focus on their studies and more likely that they will fail exams. As one adolescent explained, comparing her own life to that of her brother, '*I like to study – but where is there the time for study? There is work. I have to make food and do other work. Boys have more time for study – they eat and leave the dishes.*'

Our study also found evidence that the undervaluing of girls' education is changing shape in recent years. Specifically, even though more girls are attending school, they – unlike their brothers and male peers – almost exclusively attend lower-quality state schools rather than higher-quality, English-language, private schools. As one respondent in a focus group discussion in Doti explained,

> *The people lovingly send their sons to the boarding schools thinking that boarding are better and the girls they send to the government saying 'We do not care if you study or not' or even they do not send to school.*

In addition, because parents typically believe that husbands should be more educated than their wives, many families continue to put a 'cap' on how long girls are allowed to attend school for. Indeed, our study found that some educated girls had had difficulty finding husbands and that their struggles had only further cemented some parents' certitude that child marriage was the best route to avoiding the stigma of an unmarriageable daughter.

> *Before, education was considered for earning money only. Now, slowly, the thinking has changed. Yes, it is a means to success, and even if nothing happens you are educated. People value education.*
>
> (Focus group discussion, young adolescents, Doti)

As our discussion illustrates, norms concerning girls' rights to educational opportunities are contested terrain. On the one hand, there is significant evidence of change, with girls and parents both increasingly valuing girls' education. On the other hand, while girls value education for its own sake, parents are inclined to value it through a more instrumental lens that revolves around the traditional centre of girls' worth (marriage). Where families see education as improving girls' marriage prospects (natal parents), supporting them to become better wives and mothers (natal parents and in-laws), or potentially opening doors to the paid employment that would allow girls to contribute to improving household economics (in-laws), support is growing. Where they view education as restricting marriage prospects, however, buy-in remains minimal.

The age at marriage is increasing and the age gap between spouses is reducing

Although there are some variations according to study sites, caste/ethnic groups and household socioeconomic status, the age at which girls marry is rising. Girls in Doti, for example, reported an average age at marriage of 17.7 years, with no system of earlier betrothal. This is a dramatic departure from the practices of their mothers' and grandmothers' generations. Mothers reported betrothal between the ages of 10 and 12 and grandmothers between 5 and 6. Both generations told us that they were often sent to live with their husbands' families even before their first menstruation.

In terms of caste/ethnic variations, both high-caste (Chhetris, Brahmins) and Dalit families were found to marry their daughters at a younger age compared to indigenous groups. This may be because gender norms are more liberal for indigenous communities, with women often having more decision-making power (e.g. in choosing their spouse) as well as more freedom in terms of mobility and ability to earn an income than their peers in other communities. In terms of socioeconomic variation, parents who were poorer or had less education were more likely to marry their daughters as children than their better-off and more educated peers.

The second major positive change for girls in regard to age at marriage is a narrowing of the age gap between spouses. Grandmothers, particularly Brahmins, Chhetris and Dalits, reported that their husbands had often been as much as 30 years older. Mothers reported gaps as large as 18 years – though most were no more than eight years younger than their husbands. For today's adolescent girls, however, in most cases the age gap is less than five years (Ghimire *et al.* 2015). This closing of the age gap means that spouses are more likely to share similar life experiences and expectations. It may in some cases also increase the likelihood of improved communication and dialogue between spouses, which can in turn have a positive effect on young married women's decision-making and well-being.

So the drivers of change appear to be a complex combination of reduction in poverty, greater educational opportunities and support, and a cost-benefit analysis of educational worth within an individual's family situation. The reduction in spousal age gaps points to a weakening of a practice of betrothals in order to further kin ties, and an increase in aspects of gender equality.

Progress towards reducing child marriage – or, in this case at least, delaying child marriage – has resulted from a range of factors, including government and non-governmental organisation (NGO) awareness-raising programmes on the benefits of later marriage (and its corollary of continued education for girls, see page 164) (see also Chapter 9). The influence of positive role models, such as women teachers, health care providers and development workers, has also been important, as those women provide real-life proof to girls – and their parents – that committing to education can open doors to employment. Decreases in the spousal age gap are largely due to young people having more of a say in choice of marriage partner (see the following section).

More say for girls in decision-making about marriage partner

Traditionally, marriage across most ethnic and caste groups in Nepal was organised by parents and was essentially a relationship between two families, one largely managed by men. The boy's father would approach the girl's father and ask for her hand in marriage. The girl's father, if he agreed, would provide dowry and the marriage would take place. The bride and groom had no say in the transaction and indeed had often never even met each other. This is now changing, driven by the changing educational and economic landscape and supported by the programming that will be discussed in more detail in Chapter 9. Adolescent girl respondents in our study noted that they now have more decision-making power regarding their future spouse when compared with their mothers' and grandmothers' generations. Some girls told us that they were able to find out about their proposed groom from friends and relatives. Some (particularly those who had mutual friends) (see Box 8.2) even managed to arrange a pre-wedding meeting. Parents by and large agreed that girls' input into marriage is growing. Though most indicated that the final decision remained theirs, they also reported that it was now common to consult girls about their prospective husband and his family.

Caste again emerged as an important factor in relation to the extent of girls' decision-making, with indigenous girls from the Magar community in Wayal having more say in terms of partner choice than high-caste Chhetris and Brahmins or low-caste Dalits (Ghimire *et al.* 2013; Samuels and Ghimire 2013).

BOX 8.2   GIRLS HAVE MORE OF A SAY IN THEIR PROSPECTIVE HUSBAND: THE ROLE OF PEERS

Manashi was born in Salena and is married into Wayal. She stopped going to school when she was 6 years old. A proposal came when she was 15. The boy's *Phupu* (father's sister) was married into Manashi's village and had informed the boy's family about Manashi. The father came with the proposal to Manashi's house and Manashi's father thought it was a suitable proposal. He told Manashi about the boy and wanted her to marry him.

Manashi wanted to see the boy and decide for herself but she was afraid to say so. Instead, she told her best friend. Her friend managed to get the phone number of the boy from her boyfriend who was also from Salena. She also arranged that they could see each other at the village fair in Wayal. They did see each other, from a distance. Both of them liked each other and started to talk over the phone. A few months later they got married.

Source: Fieldwork, Doti, 2014

When asked why today's girls (and boys) have more input into marriage, respondents were unanimous and unequivocal: education. One adult in a focus group discussion in Doti explained,

> *In our days people were not educated, we knew nothing. In those days, the father of the future groom was the one who used to see the future bride. He used to decide everything. The girl would not get the chance to meet or see the boy. Later on, the girls became educated. They started to demand that they get to see their soon-to-be-husband and check if they limp, are deaf or dumb.*

Our research also suggests two other drivers of choice. The first involves the more practical side of education, which not only encourages girls to make demands on their parents, but also provides a venue for meeting and interacting with boys of the same age that are totally off limits to them within their broader community. Because of school, today's girls and boys know one another. We also found, among our adolescent respondents, a budding belief that marriage ought to be about individuals, rather than families. While few boys – and even fewer girls – were able to put words to this belief, it was clear from some respondents that the seeds of this idea were silently germinating.

Improved communication and support

Nepali girls' (and women's) relationships with their husbands exhibit some similar patterns. While the marital relationship is central to girls' financial and personal safety and security, it is often not one that includes open communication, emotional support or affection. Girls in our study reported that they are often too shy to talk to their husbands and therefore do not share problems with them. This shyness has several drivers. First, there is a widely held belief that wives must afford their husbands the utmost respect and that sharing personal concerns and worries undermines this respect. Second, because young couples typically live with the groom's family – and most young men continue to hold their parents' opinions and desires in higher esteem than those of their wives – girls are disempowered on a daily basis in terms of decision-making. For example, girls and young women told us that when their husbands migrated for work, remittances were usually sent to their in-laws, leaving girls feeling dependent and undervalued. This was particularly painful where girls and in-laws had tumultuous relationships. As one married girl in Doti explained, 'Father- and mother-in-law are not like our own mother and father, they get angrier'.

Again, however, there are recent signs of progress. Whereas girls' mothers and grandmothers told us that they had seldom talked to their husbands, at least when their children were young and their marriages comparatively recent, girls today reported more open communication. This appears driven partly by girls' growing education and partly by the reality that today's couples are closer in age and more likely to have at least tacitly approved of each other as a marriage partner.

Technology is also playing an important role; girls and young women told us that thanks to mobile phones, they often spoke directly to their husbands even when they had migrated for work. They explained that while they rarely initiated calls, and indeed were sometimes prohibited from doing so by their in-laws, on balance mobile technology had made spousal communication significantly easier.

Mobile phones also emerged as important to some girls' growing connection with their natal families. Across South Asia and East Asia, girls and women have traditionally been seen to be the responsibility of their fathers before marriage, their husbands after marriage, and their sons after widowhood. Supported by this tradition, and reinforced by patrilocal marriage patterns, Nepali girls have historically had little contact with their natal families after marriage, leaving them without the social support of those who know and love them best (Ghimire and Samuels 2014). While some married girls are able to grow new support networks in their marital families, usually relying most heavily on their sisters-in-law but also sometimes on their younger brothers-in-law, mobile phones are allowing others to stay in contact with their mothers and sisters – a hugely important source of support.

The persistence of 'sticky' gender norms

Given the centrality of marriage to girls' and women's social value and identity, and the way in which marriage is bound with Hindu notions of honour and shame, even in the face of progressive change, there is evidence of 'stickiness' and stasis. This is most evident in terms of the restrictions that girls face on their mobility and the pressure that they continue to face around producing not just children but sons. As noted earlier, it can also be seen in the ways in which families are supporting girls' education or not.

Nepali girls have little freedom of movement compared to their brothers and male peers. Furthermore, while boys tend to be given more freedom as they grow up, girls in Nepal usually see their freedom further restricted as they enter and pass through adolescence. Driven by parents' fears that they may come into contact with boys – and even fall in love, which could lead neighbours to malign their purity and thus impact their chances for a good marriage – girls have to seek permission from their parents to go out of their homes (except to carry out domestic chores such as collecting firewood and fodder). Indeed, a 15-year-old girl explained that the never-ending burden of domestic work is in itself another reason why girls' mobility is restricted:

> We don't see girls playing outside the village because parents fear they would get spoiled. Secondly, they also fear that they may flirt with boys, and thirdly, we need to study and also we have to work in our households, which boys don't have to do.
> (Outlier case study with a school-going girl, aged 15, Salena, Doti)

Girls' lives also continue to be restricted by pressure to demonstrate their fertility by becoming pregnant (and preferably having a son) soon after marriage. Though the rate of adolescent pregnancy has fallen rapidly over the past few decades, from 130.7/1,000 in 1995 to 71.3/1,000 in 2015, 19.4 per cent of girls still give birth before the age of 18 (United Nations Population Fund (UNFPA) 2013). The pressure on girls comes both from their own parents and their in-laws. Since one of the main purposes of marriage is to produce a male heir to continue the husband's lineage, girls' in-laws are anxious over what they perceive as a child for their own family. Girls' parents, on the other hand, are anxious for what they believe is the best hope for their daughter's continued security. Young brides who do not quickly become pregnant may be assumed to be infertile, and find themselves in a polygamous marriage when their husband takes another wife to cement his lineage.

In some ways unexpected, given recent improvements in girls' school enrolment and completion rates, our research found strong undercurrents that speak to a continued preference for 'cultured' brides over educated brides. Indeed, even as girls begin to surpass boys in terms of primary and lower-secondary graduation, the reasons why girls and boys drop out of school tell an important gendered story. Boys leave school to work; girls leave school to marry – or to at least ensure that they are 'honourable' enough to marry when the time comes. Adolescents themselves acknowledged this disparity. Girls in our study told us that it was important for them to marry an educated boy, as educated boys are more likely to be good providers. Boys, on the other hand, did not feel that education was a critically important trait in a wife. Instead, a combination of obedience and meekness – expressed by the local term '*sanskar*', meaning cultured – and the status of the family (in terms of *sanskar*) were considered paramount. As one village leader explained,

> *An educated boy prefers a girl who follows culture even if she is not well-educated. It depends on their way of behaving with others and her work. People also see other qualities like family name. Due to this, even if a girl is not educated, boys accept them.*
>
> *(Key informant interview, Salena)*

Nevertheless, despite this preference, the national data for Nepal suggests that the momentum and drivers for girls' education are strong, with girls' school attendance more or less equalling boys' attendance in both lower secondary and upper secondary (Ministry of Education 2015). Clearly, specific locations will differ from this national average, and suggest important internal gender inequalities which must be addressed for both boys and girls in different contexts.

Two steps forward and one step back?

As well as identifying the ways in which gender norms are changing or not, our study found evidence of surprising non-linear shifts. Specifically, we found that as arranged child marriages begin to become less common, child-chosen love matches have become more common. We also found, more than 60 years after polygamy was outlawed, evidence of a resurgence in this practice.

The dangers of 'love' matches

Elopement emerged as surprisingly common in all of our study sites. Of the 26 married girls and young women we interviewed in Wayal and Salena, 14 had eloped, as children, to marry the boy they 'loved'. On the one hand, child-chosen love matches are evidence of girls' increased decision-making. On the other hand, the risks of such relationships far outweigh any potential benefits.

Adolescents elope because they are afraid that their parents will not give them permission to marry. Many of the children involved are very young, often only 13–15 years old (the youngest we found was 12). Furthermore, most eloping couples have met each other only once or twice, though many are related through the marriage of their brothers or sisters. According to study respondents, mobile phones are enabling the spread of elopement. Girls and boys use their mobiles to communicate and, in some cases, never meet face-to-face before deciding to run away together. Attempting to understand how decisions unfold, we held informal discussion groups with girls and boys to explore their ideas about love and marriage in the context of elopement. Boys told us that they saw elopement as the 'honourable' thing to do. They explained that when an unmarried girl's name is attached to a boy, the girl's name is tarnished and the boy takes it as his fault. To avoid dishonour, couples simply chose to marry. They also told us that in some cases, girls' parents encourage couples to elope because elopement saves the cost of both a dowry and a wedding ceremony. Probing boys' responses more deeply, it seems that a lack of parent-child communication (itself an outcome of norms expecting obedience without explanation), and thus appropriate guidance and mentorship of adolescents, ultimately underpins the trend towards elopement (Ghimire *et al.* 2013).

While girls and boys both choose to elope as children, girls bear the brunt of the consequences. First, girls are usually a few years younger than boys – a critical few years, given that most are young adolescents only beginning to move towards abstract thought and longer-term planning. Second, early marriage exposes girls to pregnancy before their bodies are ready. Third, because some parents are responding to the growing risk of elopement by ensuring that their daughters are married before they are old enough to fall in love independently, elopement is poised to reverse progress not only on the incidence of child marriage but also (ironically) on the incidence of arranged marriage. Finally, because elopement is seen by parents and community members as a far less desirable form of marriage, as it becomes more common, girls are scrutinised very severely and there is considerable social pressure on them to show they are not the 'eloping type' (e.g. by being demure and obedient). This ambiguity is not uncommon in processes of change and can be seen in other countries and locations. The extent to which it stalls more progressive trends is as yet unclear.

Modern polygamy on the rise?

We also found evidence that polygamous unions are still occurring, especially among young couples in Wayal, where 5 out of 30 recent marriages were polygamous. Indeed, while polygamy has been illegal since 1962, except where the wife has severe mental health problems or is unable to bear children (see also Dahal *et al.* 2008), we identified cases where husbands took a second wife even when their first wife had given them a son. Whether this is linked to early elopements for first wives is unclear, but the banning of polygynous marriages recognises the inequality in relationships between men and women and the likelihood of this type of union representing gender unequal choice, power, voice and economic standing between men and women in the union. So continuity in, and local acceptance of, polygyny is unfortunate for progressive gender equality goals.

Those involved in polygamous relationships shared a number of characteristics. All five men in the study site, for example, were businessmen in the local market, usually owning a shop. All five men had arranged first marriages that had produced children; first wives were mostly illiterate and uniformly living with their in-laws in the ancestral home and taking care of farming. All five second wives, on the other hand, were literate and helping their husbands with the daily work of running the business.[4]

Our case studies found that this uptick in polygamy has important implications for child marriage and child brides. Specifically, despite the fact that husbands and second wives claimed that first wives and their children were being well taken care of, interviews with first wives (who had all been child brides) show that upon her husband taking a second wife, she loses her social standing, respect and identity, and has no options for reclaiming them. Abandoned wives are highly stigmatised in the community and cannot return to live with their natal families because of gendered social norms that effectively consider them marital property. Thus not only does a woman lose her networks based on marriage as a result of polygamy, but she cannot call upon her own maternal social network for support either. As one first wife put it, her life was like that of a widow and it was only '*in the children that she found solace*'. Divorce, according to our respondents, is impossible. Not only do women need to have a man's name and household association, but they and their children are economically dependent on their husbands' families.

The fact that these unions continue to exist and that women cannot exit easily from them, despite national legislation, indicates a disconnect between policy and the conditions necessary for its effective implementation. Clearly, women remain powerless to make good choices for themselves and polygynous unions are an indicator that progress in gender equality is far from smooth.

Conclusions

Findings from the three years of our research on adolescent girls in the Far West region of Nepal are well captured by the adage 'two steps forward, one step back'. On the one hand, recent progress is remarkable. Girls are staying in school longer, they are less likely to be married as young adolescents (albeit still very likely to be married in adolescence), they are more likely to be involved in choosing their own husband and there is some evidence of improved communication between husbands and wives. As we discuss in greater detail in Chapter 9, outside of broader economic and demographic change, a variety of actors have helped make this change real. The government, for example, has built schools and worked with NGOs to design and implement programming aimed at educating and empowering girls. Teachers and health care providers, typically the best-educated local women, have inspired girls to dream. Peers provide support which is critical as boundaries shift and girls need help to stand up to the discriminatory gender norms that threaten to truncate their trajectories.

However, gender norms that are embedded in deeply rooted patriarchal structures are sticky and difficult to change. Our research found that because they are part and parcel of both daily experience and identity from early childhood, many of the norms shaping Nepali girls' lives remain embedded in the belief and social structures which both guide and control everyday life and which have evolved over the long term. This historical development of gendered social relations and social stratification exists irrespective of caste/ethnic group and location of residence (urban, rural, peri-urban). Girls' mobility remains restricted, largely to protect their purity and safeguard their family honour; marriage and motherhood remain central to the value that parents and communities place on girls; and parents continue to profess to invest more heavily in boys' education – because they see boys not only as providers today but as a source of old-age security tomorrow – even if the data is beginning to contest this widely held sentiment. Indeed, we found that gender norms are so deeply rooted in the fabric of Nepali life that change can be unexpected and non-linear, and hearken more to the past than the future. This is most evident in the emergence of child-driven love marriages, which reflect some ambiguity both in revealing a newfound freedom of choice but also exhibiting characteristics of earlier traditions. The polygamous marriages apparently becoming more common in peri-urban areas similarly draw on past traditions to condone preferences that seem out of step with much of the overall direction of change. These 'new old' customs further disadvantage those who are already disadvantaged – adolescent girls and the women forced to marry as children – and possibly reflect resistance to change or confusion in relation to shifts in power relations between men and women in broader society.

Our research suggests that the fight for gender equality in Nepal will not be won in one or even two generations. Given stark differences in girls' and boys' gender roles and women's and men's gender roles, change will take time. In addition to the modern infrastructure that can reduce demands on girls' and women's time, freeing them for study and employment and opening up new job opportunities even in rural areas, it will be critical that the government and NGOs invest in supportive and long-term policy and programming, focusing not only on adolescent girls but also on others who have influence over their lives. Programming should be centred on helping people to rethink – and build consensus around – what makes a good daughter/daughter-in-law, woman or girl. It should support girls to become confident agents in their own lives. It should help parents recognise that today's girls have options unimagined a generation ago, and encourage them to embrace those options (even if for fundamentally instrumental reasons) by allowing them the time they need to successfully complete their education. Critically, programming aimed at ending child marriage and supporting girls' education must engage boys and men, who, as brothers and husbands, can support girls by helping with domestic work and the care economy and opening communication channels, and as fathers can set an example by standing up to community pressure and choosing higher education for their daughters over child marriage.

In the next chapter we explore efforts to change discriminatory gender norms through women's development programmes and girls' empowerment processes.

Notes

1 Adolescents in Nepal are defined as girls and boys aged 10–19 and comprise 24.19 per cent of the population (Central Bureau of Statistics 2011).
2 Ilam was selected in the first year of study as an area which was seen to be doing relatively well in terms of human development indicators and, as such, was to act as a form of comparator to the Far West region. However, given the focus of the study and the desire to understand why human development indicators lagged behind and gendered norms remained sticky, the study team returned to Doti in all three years, conducting research in similar/adjacent sites, while the study in Ilam was carried out in the first year only.
3 The School Sector Reform Programme was a joint initiative of the World Bank and the Government of Nepal, which ran between 2009 and 2015.
4 We also heard – second-hand – of cases where adolescent girls were effectively tricked into polygamous unions, not knowing until it was too late that they were destined to be a second wife.

Bibliography

Amin, S., Bajracharya, A., Chau, M. and Puri, M. (2014) *Highlights from the UNICEF Adolescent Development and Participation Baseline Study*. New York: Population Council.

Bajracharya, A. and Amin, S. (2010) *Poverty, Marriage Timing, and Transitions to Adulthood in Nepal: A Longitudinal Analysis Using the Nepal Living Standards Survey*. New York: Population Council. Available online at www.popcouncil.org/uploads/pdfs/wp/pgy/019.pdf

Beutel, A.M. and Axinn, W.G. (2002) 'Gender, Social Change, and Educational Attainment' *Economic Development and Cultural Change* 51(1): 109.

Boudet, A., Petesch, P., Turk, C. and Thumala, A. (2012) *On Norms and Agency: Conversations About Gender Equality with Women and Men in 20 Countries*. Washington, DC: World Bank.

CARE. (2015) *Nepal: Gender Relations in Nepal Overview*. Available online at www.care.org/sites/default/files/documents/RGA%20Overview%20Nepal_Final.pdf

Central Bureau of Statistics (CBS). (2011) *National Population and Housing Census, 2011: National Report*. Kathmandu: Central Bureau of Statistics and National Planning Commission.

Central Bureau of Statistics (CBS) and UNICEF. (2015) *Multiple Indicator Cluster Survey: 2014*. Kathmandu: Central Bureau of Statistics and UNICEF.

Dahal, G.P., Padmadas, S.S. and Hinde, P.R. (2008) 'Fertility-Limiting Behavior and Contraceptive Choice Among Men in Nepal' *International Family Planning Perspectives* 34(1): 6–14.

Ghimire, A. and Samuels, F. (2014) *Change and Continuity in Social Norms and Practices Around Marriage and Education in Nepal.* London: Overseas Development Institute. Available online at www.odi.org/sites/odi.org.uk/files/odi-assets/publications-opinion-files/9181.pdf

Ghimire, A., Samuels, F., Giri, I. and Adhikari, P. (2015) *Communication Strategies for Addressing Discriminatory Social Norms in Marriage and Education for Adolescent Girls in Nepal.* London: Overseas Development Institute. Available online at www.odi.org/sites/odi.org.uk/files/odi-assets/publications-opinion-files/9900.pdf

Ghimire, A., Samuels, F. and Wagle, S. (2013) *Understanding Key Capability Domains of Adolescent Girls and Gender Justice: Findings from Nepal.* London: Overseas Development Institute. Available online at www.odi.org/sites/odi.org.uk/files/odi-assets/publications-opinion-files/8821.pdf

Goonesekere, S. (2006) *Harmful Traditional Practices in Three Countries of South Asia: Culture, Human Rights and Violence Against Women.* Gender and Development Discussion Paper 21. Bangkok: United Nations Economic and Social Commission for Asia and the Pacific (UNESCAP).

Guragain, A.M., Paudel, B.M., Lim, A. and Choonpradub, C. (2017) 'Adolescent Marriage in Nepal: A Sub-Regional Level Analysis' *Marriage & Family Review* 53(4): 307–319.

Lundgren, R., Beckman, M., Chaurasiya, S.P., Subhedi, B. and Kerner, B. (2013) 'Whose Turn to Do the Dishes? Transforming Gender Attitudes and Behaviours Among Very Young Adolescents in Nepal' *Gender & Development* 21(1): 127–145.

Ministry of Education. (2015) *Nepal Education in Figures, 2015, at a Glance.* Kathmandu: Ministry of Education.

Ministry of Health and Population, New Era and ICF International. (2012) *Nepal Demographic and Health Survey 2011.* Kathmandu: Ministry of Health and Population, New Era and ICF International.

National Planning Commission and United Nations Country Team Nepal. (2013) *Nepal Millennium Development Goals Progress Report: 2013.* Kathmandu: National Planning Commission and United Nation Country Team Nepal.

Organisation for Economic Co-operation and Development (OECD). (2014) *Social Institutions and Gender Index: 2014 Synthesis Report.* Available online at www.genderindex.org/sites/default/files/docs/BrochureSIGI2015.pdf

Samuels, F. and Ghimire, A. (2013) *Social Norms for Adolescent Girls in Nepal: Slow but Positive Progress.* Country Briefing. London: Overseas Development Institute. Available online at www.odi.org/sites/odi.org.uk/files/odi-assets/publications-opinion-files/8654.pdf

Samuels, F. and Ghimire, A. (2015) *Girls' Clubs and Radio Programmes: Addressing Discriminatory Social Norms in Nepal Briefing.* London: Overseas Development Institute. Available online at www.odi.org/sites/odi.org.uk/files/odi-assets/publications-opinion-files/9882.pdf

Shradananda, R., Biraj, S., Sharma, T. and Tandan, G. (1992) *Character Science: Characterology.* Banepa: Rishi Kumar Panchasil.

United Nations Development Programme (UNDP). (2015) *Human Development Reports, Human Development Data.* Available online at http://hdr.undp.org/en/data.

United Nations Educational, Scientific and Cultural Organization (UNESCO). (2017) *UIS Stat.* Available online at http://data.uis.unesco.org/

United Nations Population Fund (UNFPA). (2013) *Adolescent Pregnancy: A Review of the Evidence.* New York: United Nations Population Fund.

United Nations Children's Fund (UNICEF). (2011) *The State of the World's Children 2011 Adolescence: An Age of Opportunity.* New York: United Nations Children's Fund. Available online at www.unicef.org/sowc2011/

9

CONTINUITY AND SLOW CHANGE

How embedded programmes improve the lives of adolescent girls

Fiona Samuels, Anita Ghimire and Matthew Maclure

Summary

This chapter analyses the effectiveness of two different models adopted by programmes to empower girls in Nepal: one adopted by the government, which uses the country's decentralised governance structures to reach girls at village level with empowerment activities, and another adopted by an international non-governmental organisation (NGO) that does not. We discuss what works well and what works less well in terms of shifting discriminatory gender norms and empowering adolescent girls. The government model appears relatively more effective, largely because it enjoys community ownership – supported rather than threatened by its more gradualist approach that builds on economic empowerment – as well as strong links to local services. We also note areas for improvement, the most significant being the lack of tailored programming for local and age-related needs and the failure to integrate programming for girls with that aimed at women, men and boys. We conclude that though established government structures can be an important vehicle for delivering change, not least because of their coverage and legitimacy, there nevertheless remains a tension between valuing local tradition and norms on the one hand and catalysing change for girls on the other.

Introduction

As noted in Chapter 8, despite some progress, Nepal remains one of the poorest countries in the world. Although it halved the proportion of the population living on less than $1.25 a day between 2003 and 2011 (from 53 per cent to 25 per cent) (World Bank 2015), its economy is still reliant on agriculture and its gross national income (GNI) per capita is only $730 (World Bank 2016). Disparities between urban and rural areas, regions, and ethnic groups and castes remain stark.

Rural poverty rates are estimated to be nearly twice those of urban areas, with a 46 per cent poverty rate in the Far West development region (International Fund for Agricultural Development (IFAD) n.d.). Recent progress in education notwithstanding, girls and women remain especially disadvantaged. The Social Institutions and Gender Index (SIGI) ranks Nepal 'high' in terms of discriminatory institutions Organisation for Economic Co-operation and Development (OECD) 2014), the Gender Inequality Index (GII) ranks it 108th out of 155 countries (United Nations Development Programme (UNDP) 2015a) and the Gender Development Index (GDI) places it in the 4th of 5 categories (UNDP 2015b).

Despite its poor performance on gender indices, Nepal has a surprisingly long history of investing in women's development. The Women's Development Programme was launched in 1982,[1] and since 1990, with the enactment of the Eighth

BOX 9.1 KAILALI

Kailali district is located in Nepal's Far West region, on the border with India (see Figure 9.1). Although its educational infrastructure is relatively well developed and there is high uptake of education (the net enrolment rate (NER) is 94.3 per cent for primary school and 75.4 per cent for lower secondary), its poverty rate is far above the national average (33.6 per cent versus 25.2 per cent) (DDC 2013). Furthermore, only 6 per cent of women are employed in the formal sector, compared to the national average of 19 per cent (National Planning Commission Secretariat and Central Bureau of Statistics (CBS) 2015). The district has 14 women's cooperatives and 42 adolescent girls' groups.

FIGURE 9.1 Map of Nepal showing Kailali district

Source: Author

Development Plan, the agenda for women has received attention in various policies, programmes and institutional structures. Indeed, over the decades the notion of women's development has evolved from calling for women to support the national economy by doing what they were already doing (e.g. farming) to recognising the centrality of women's empowerment (Department of Women and Children n.d.). However, while reinforcing the importance of women to the country's sustainable development, until recently, policy and programming have taken them as a homogeneous group and did not distinguish the needs of different sub-groups of women.

Whereas gender has thus been on the Nepali development agenda for decades, adolescents have only recently been conceptualised as a group with specific needs in terms of programmes and action plans. Outside of their needs for sexual and reproductive health (SRH) care, which were seen as important to efforts to reduce fertility and maternal and child mortality, adolescents were largely ignored. That changed in 2013 with the National Plan of Action for the Holistic Development of Adolescents (National Planning Commission 2013). The plan, which broadly addresses adolescents' health, education, employment prospects, skills development and civic participation, has paved the way for a wide variety of interventions to improve adolescents' well-being. This new policy and programming is significant in that it recognises that adolescents are a heterogeneous group with different needs based on their age, sex, religion, geographic location, culture, caste and ethnicity.

This chapter explores two types of programmes aimed at empowering adolescent girls living in Nepal's Kailali district (see Box 9.1). The first is implemented by the government, through the decentralised structures originally created to foster local participation in government. The second is run by an international NGO, implemented through local partners (see Box 9.2). We begin by briefly describing those decentralised structures and then move on to assess how both programmes are working to shift the gender norms that constrain adolescent girls' lives.

BOX 9.2 NGO PROGRAMMING FOR GIRLS

In addition to exploring how the Nepali government's adolescent girls' programming is working to effect change, we also assessed the girl-focused work of international and local NGOs. That work was funded by an international NGO, but implemented in different communities by local partners in different ways. The international NGO's overarching aim is to empower vulnerable children by working for the well-being of their families and the communities in which they live. Adolescents are prioritised under the theme of 'Maternal and Child Health'; programmes aim to sensitise teens to sexual and reproductive health issues and support them to spread messages throughout their communities. Specific activities, which vary depending on the implementing partner, include life-skills training and street drama.

Decentralisation and the lead-up to adolescent-focused programming

Decentralisation has been central to Nepali governance since the 1960s, with the adoption of the Panchayat political system.[2] Though the approach to decentralisation has shifted over the years, especially in 1990 when the country became a multi-party democracy, commitment to ground-level participation has remained strong (Chhetri *et al.* 2008; UNDP 2009). The Local Self-Government Act (1999), for example, not only made local bodies more responsive, accountable and transparent, it also allowed local authorities to identify – and engage with – issues that are important to local populations.

There are three tiers of local government in Nepal: wards, Village Development Committees (VDC) or municipalities, and District Development Committees (DDC) (Regmi *et al.* 2009; Mallik 2013). The lowest level of government is the ward (consisting of about 200 households); the next level up is the VDC (which consists of nine wards); and finally there are the DDCs. The VDCs are then grouped by district. The Department of Women and Children, nested at the national level within the Ministry of Women, Children and Social Welfare, has offices in each of Nepal's 75 districts. Those district-level offices then establish and work through village-level thematic committees, such as the Gender-Based Violence Monitoring Committee and the Civic Awareness Committee. They also liaise with committees formed by other ministries, such as local mothers' groups (Ministry of Health), extending their reach from exclusively women-focused programming to an overall community development engagement of women. Ultimately, Nepal's decentralised government structures ensure that gender empowerment programmes – including the Women's Development Programme – operate through VDCs and have a presence in every community.

Programming offered by the Department of Women and Children is founded on the belief that women's economic empowerment and economic independence are central to the fight for gender equality. However, it also recognises that economic empowerment is about far more than money. Consequently, the core of programming consists of a network of 1,700 women's cooperatives that operate at village level.[3] They help women learn social and economic skills in the context of participatory group activities that foster voice and agency and encourage organised activity aimed at eliminating discrimination (Department of Women and Children n.d.). These cooperatives, of which membership is voluntary, target women with low levels of education and whose families are food insecure; they are initially organised and supported by social mobilisers who receive a small stipend from the district-level Office of Women and Children. The cooperatives have largely proven to be stable and self-sustaining (Ministry of Women, Children and Social Welfare 2015). Indeed, they have been so successful that the Office of Women and Children rolls out its entire programme at village level through these cooperatives, using them to raise awareness about gender-based violence (GBV), human trafficking and child protection issues, improve reproductive health and conserve natural resources, among other things.

Men are not allowed to become members of these cooperatives. However, a few men are selected from each community to act as supporters and advisors. These are usually respected civil society members and experts in thematic areas that are relevant to cooperative programming.

The Adolescent Girl, or Kishori, programme

With the growing understanding that adolescents have particular developmental needs that can be leveraged to maximise both their own development and the development of the country, women's cooperatives provided a ready-made framework for the introduction of targeted interventions for adolescent girls. To that end, cooperatives now host adolescent girls' groups. First launched in 2005/2006 as the United Nations Population Fund (UNFPA)-funded Choose Your Future programme, since 2007/2008 this programme has received central government funding through the Department of Women and Children and is now referred to as the Kishori, or Adolescent Girl, programme. Like the women's groups on which they were modelled and under which they remain nested, adolescent girls' groups as part of the Kishori programme target individuals who have missed out on education – including those who have never been to school at all and those who do not attend regularly due to their responsibility for household chores. The groups aim to increase girls' livelihood and income earning skills, self-awareness and self-confidence.

The Kishori programme brings together groups of 15–20 girls who receive a ten-day training course run by the local Office of Women and Children. Training starts with livelihoods (e.g. farming or sewing), but also includes a life-skills curriculum that covers reproductive health, GBV and child marriage. After the training, girls are given about $45 as seed money to start their own income-generation projects and are supported to begin saving as a group. Girls who are out of school are encouraged to return to school (and given educational stipends if necessary), while girls who need health care are given funds to obtain it. Girls are encouraged to share what they have learned with their peers and, in some communities (including seven in Kailali district),[4] girls have access to adolescent information centres where they can obtain counselling and information about topics relevant to their lives.

The Kishori programme is still growing, so in terms of beneficiary headcount, remains limited. Though there were nearly 1,900 groups serving nearly 25,000 girls in 2013/2014, only 8,000 girls had completed the training and were issued with seed money, and less than 4,800 girls had started their own small business (Ghimire *et al.* 2015).

Programme impacts on girls

Overall, girls who had participated in programming were positive about their experiences. Some of those involved in cooperative-supported groups had gone back to school and others were earning money to support themselves and their families.

Previously we used to think that if we speak, people will backbite us because what we speak is silly. Now we do not think so.

We learn new things about the world that we cannot learn from books. We get knowledge about the things that help us a lot in our life. I want to encourage more girls to take part in such training.

Previously, I was scared about what others would think rather than doing what is right for me. Now I know when people do wrong and can speak out or take necessary actions or avoid such situations.

I have learnt a lot of things from this training that I had no clue about before. Things like how sexual harassment can take place anywhere. We can control such problems and take actions against such people.

We have so many new friends and know some problems are not only ours, other girls too face. We share and we are happy.

Now I think I don't have to rely on anyone for money. In future I can do something myself to earn my living.

I can ask things that I do not know. This has even made me confident that I can speak well now. It used to be difficult earlier but now it is not.

I dropped out after failing the School Leaving Certificate exam, but I have filled up my forms for the coming examination this year.

We know how to sow vegetables in a proper way and what to do when the crops are ailing.

I learnt tailoring and will now buy a machine from my own money.

FIGURE 9.2 Girls' reflections on programming

Source: Author

Some of those participating in activities supported by the international NGO were proud of their efforts to prevent child marriage. Girls identified improvements in their social networks, confidence, and voice as central to programme impacts on their lives – though they also identified training on sexual harassment, sewing and farming as important (see Figure 9.2.).

Strengths of using the decentralised system to implement girls' empowerment activities

While the adolescent girls' groups supported by women's cooperatives have certain shortcomings (discussed in more detail later in this section), our assessment found that overall, adolescent girls' programming delivered through decentralised government structures was stronger than that delivered by NGOs. This comparative strength appears to have several key drivers. Namely, the programming delivered through existing decentralised structures is trusted and locally owned – in part because it builds on already accepted programming that prioritises economic empowerment – and is well linked to local services and resources.

The parents we interviewed reported higher levels of trust and acceptance of government programming as opposed to NGO programming. The primary reason for this is that the Kishori programme is implemented by village-level women's cooperatives. This not only means that they were run by local women, but also that in most cases, girls were in groups that were tightly linked to the groups of which their own mothers were members. There were therefore no surprises. Training sessions and meetings for girls were held in the same spaces as training sessions and meetings for mothers. Furthermore, girls did not have to be entrusted to strangers and were never required to stay away overnight (which was not the case for the NGO training) – something that is critically important in an environment where norms dictate that girls are not to travel or be out late without a male relative acting as chaperone, especially given the recent rise in elopement (see Chapter 8). As one ex-beneficiary reported:

> *Here, people blame training sessions which have allowed children to roam here and there. They attend the training where they are taught about child marriage and its consequences, but those who participate in such training eloped. Here, some parents raised these issues. Even some parents do not send their children to such training because of this.*
> *(In-depth interview with ex-beneficiary girl, Sahajpur, Kailali)*

The more gradual approach to the girls' groups run by women's cooperatives has also facilitated trust and uptake. The Office of Women and Children, after decades of working with women in rural villages, understands the importance of first acknowledging local gender norms and values and then slowly working towards change. They have found that doing so both increases participation and decreases resistance. In terms of programming for girls, this has meant that rather than starting directly with a curriculum for SRH, which is deeply taboo, programming began with livelihoods training and seed money. Parents who would have been resistant to their daughters learning about child marriage and contraception – the more immediate focus of the NGO programming – were happy for them to learn about acceptable and 'useful' things, especially when their learning benefited the entire family. As one father noted, '*My daughter has been doing good, she sometimes give us Rs200, Rs400 that is helpful for us to buy oil, vegetables*'. Once trust has been established, the adolescent girls' groups have introduced more sensitive themes such as child marriage and dowry. By then, they have found, families and neighbours are used to girls taking training and '*do not complain about such things*' as girls '*getting spoilt . . . by wandering around*'.

The teaching methodology of the Kishori programme also respects local norms and values. For example, while some of the NGO-supported interventions used male teachers to lead sessions with girls about SRH, the cooperative-supported programme used female nurses from local health posts to conduct 'sensitive' sessions and only allowed male teachers to teach 'safer' subjects such as livelihoods and human trafficking, and even then only with a local woman in the building listening in to make sure girls were safe. Building on existent relationships, nurses then became counsellors at the district's adolescent information centres. Girls reported that they vastly preferred single-sex settings for learning about more sensitive subjects. They were uncomfortable when male teachers described female reproductive organs, found it impossible to comply when instructed to '*look in his eyes when answering*', and reported that after class, boys '*tease us with embarrassing things*'. Our research found that while the Kishori programme moved slowly – and did not initially tackle gender norms and harmful traditional practices (HTPs) in a forthright manner – its respect for tradition ultimately enabled it to raise those issues with real buy-in and support from the community.

The theory of change on which the government's Kishori programme is based has also contributed to its success. Similarly to the women's cooperatives on which it is modelled, it postulates that economic empowerment is a prerequisite to girls' broader well-being. As such, it has prioritised girls from marginalised and impoverished backgrounds and helped them build the financial resources they need in order to support their families – and their own education. It acknowledges that most girls are out of school because their families need their labour and are loathe to 'waste' scarce resources educating a girl who will soon leave home to join her husband's family. The programme helps girls to help themselves by also recognising their roles within households. In doing so, it brings them together in face-to-face groups that enable them to discover their shared interests, forge new friendships, and be more confident in planning their future.

> We talk about addressing GBV [gender-based violence] and empowerment of women, but never address the root cause. As long as women have to depend on the husband and his house for their daily needs and a place to stay, she will not complain about GBV. She has to return to the same house after filing the complaint, so why would she take the risk of speaking against him or his family?
>
> (Key informant from Kathmandu)

A further strength of the Kishori programme is its strong links to local services and resources, which fosters ownership and improves girls' learning opportunities. For example, meetings are held in women's cooperative buildings. This saves on rent and also means that the mothers involved in the cooperative are on hand to teach girls how to conduct and record meetings, draw up agendas, and keep financial records. Nurses from village health posts teach SRH classes and serve as counsellors; they are seen as non-threatening allies, which encourages girls' (and women's) health-seeking behaviour. Similarly, representatives from the Ministry of Agriculture run training sessions for girls and provide auxiliary services such as animal care when needed. NGO programming, on the other hand, was found to be more siloed and not able to offer girls a broader network of support.

Our research also found that girls' groups within the Kishori programme were far more sustainable than NGO programming. NGOs tend to have relatively short funding cycles; while some are able to weave together longer-term funding, in many cases they provide girls with training sessions that are effectively one-off. The Kishori programme did not have this problem. They were not only centrally funded, but because they were tied to village-level women's cooperatives, many had existed for years and even when girls 'aged out' they still had access to the same basic support they had enjoyed as younger girls. Indeed, in one of our case study sites, girls had saved so much money over the years that they were able to offer loans – using the interest as income for the group. This had been so successful that the group no longer required external funds and was thinking of expanding by offering loans to girls who were not members.

Challenges of using the decentralised model

Although the Kishori programme girls' groups have been broadly successful in terms of helping girls increase their incomes and build social networks, confidence, aspirations and voice, they are not without their challenges. Our research suggests that they are sometimes too tightly bound to women's cooperatives, depend too much on top-down programming that ignores local and age-related need, and exclude the boys and men – and even mothers – who must join dialogues and play an active role in order to shift gender norms over the long term.

As already noted, the close ties between women's cooperatives and adolescent girls' groups have been critical to the latter's success. On the other hand, those ties have also introduced a source of bias into participant selection, since most participant girls (while meeting the selection criteria) were also often the daughters or nieces of cooperative members. More importantly, our assessment also found that while the programme ostensibly targets girls from the most marginalised households, if a girl's family does not have enough savings for the mother to become a member of the local cooperative, then her daughter may lose out on the chance to participate in the girls' group. If common, this selection bias would undermine the programme's long-term objectives of empowering the most vulnerable young girls.

The way in which girls' groups have been modelled on women's cooperatives has also introduced a more practical challenge. Specifically, while adult women may have little difficulty saving a small sum each month, many girls are still in school, so may find even a minimal savings target unattainable. This leaves girls to either rely on their parents for the cash they are required to save, undermining the broader theory of change, or to drop out of the group. Our research suggests the latter is far more common than the former.

The rigidity of the state-supported decentralised structures also undermines programme success to the extent that it prioritises top-down thinking over local need. While key informants maintained that the content of training – which is determined at the national level and is similar across the whole of Nepal – is revised based on feedback from the field, we found that feedback pathways are too slow to be useful. Though districts do make suggestions, it can be years before they see them taken up by the curriculum. In Kailali, for example, we were told that while the girls' club curriculum is heavily focused on child marriage, it does not address suicide, which is currently a more pressing issue locally, as child marriage rates are falling but suicide rates are rising.

Girls also reported having too little input into the curriculum. Though they were glad to have livelihood training and modules on SRH and GBV, they also wanted classes aimed more broadly at their lived psychosocial realities. They wanted, for example, to know how to deal with being rejected by boys they liked, how to resist peer pressure, and how to talk with their parents. A key observation that emerged regarding girls' requests for changes to adolescent programming was that, as with earlier programming for women, it tends to treat adolescent girls as a homogenous population. The curriculum does not sufficiently recognise that lower-caste girls may have markedly different needs than higher-caste girls, even when both are poor, or that the needs of 11-year-old girls are very different from those of 19-year-olds. Indeed, because livelihoods training is not especially useful for the youngest adolescent girls (who are still children despite their legal designation as adolescents), adolescent girls' groups effectively excluded young adolescents.

Programming would also be more effective if it included men and boys. Our research found that male family members – whether fathers, fathers-in-law, brothers or husbands – often play important roles in promoting adolescent girls' well-being, especially when they are willing to leverage their more privileged positions and push back against the patriarchal norms that restrict the lives of their daughters, daughters-in-law, sisters and wives (Ghimire *et al.* 2015; Ghimire and Samuels 2014). However, rather than working with men and boys to empower adolescent girls, the decentralised structures in which programming is embedded isolate programming for girls and women from programming for boys and men. Indeed, most local committees are overwhelmingly male, with women largely ignored even when they are present, and gender issues are effectively sidelined, as 'women's issues' are left to the women's and girls' groups from which men are excluded. In Kailali, the isolation of girls' programming was marked. While the brother of one girl observed that '*Earlier she has no brain but these days she uses it*', fathers overwhelmingly did not know what training their daughters were taking part in.

A local leader (male) in Kailali pointed out another shortcoming of current programming: not only does it not include boys and men; it does not target mothers. The end result is that while parents continue to have almost absolute control over their daughters' lives, particularly after puberty when threats to their sexual purity and honour become more salient (see Chapter 8), they are not exposed to programming that would encourage them to see the unique opportunities and threats facing adolescents or help them better invest in their daughters as individuals rather than as future wives and mothers. He explained,

> Now we have these various programmes for adolescents but what I would like to suggest is that you involve the parent as well in these programmes and make them understand about these things as well. We should teach the parents about what behaviour of good father should be like and this is what behaviour of good mother should be like.

Finally, while reiterating that the links between girls' groups and other community-based resources are a key reason for their success, our assessment found that weak collaboration and insufficient resourcing may threaten that success. At the national level, we identified poor inter-ministerial collaboration (e.g. between the Ministry of Women, Children and Social Welfare and the ministries of Finance and Education) and low levels of human and financial resourcing as threats to programme success. For example, the former has precluded attempts to link school dropouts with more intensive vocational training, while the latter has short-circuited officials' plans to offer regular refresher classes and expand the programme to reach more girls. As one Development Officer noted, 'We are not . . . able to go to all places, we have limited resources. We can't provide adolescent classes to the entire district.' At the village level, we identified inadequate tracking of girls' outcomes as especially problematic. Mothers' groups and other children's and adolescents' groups, for example, appeared to have no role in monitoring which girls had left school and might benefit from programme participation.

Conclusions

Overall, the government's Kishori programme, which works through decentralised adolescent girls' groups, appears to be more effective at reaching vulnerable girls and effecting change in their lives than the NGO-supported programming we analysed. This was largely because the government programming was embedded in a gradual and context-appropriate process towards change. Like the GBV watch committees and the women's and children's development centres supported by VDCs, adolescent girls' groups have efficiently and sustainably opened local space for participation, strengthened social networks and improved access to information and services – all without engendering a backlash (see Asian Development Bank 2004). Girls feel the impact of these changes in their lives. Whether they were earning their own incomes, were back in school, had made more friends, felt stronger, or were enjoying their first opportunity to do something for themselves, the girls we interviewed were glad they were taking part in the programme.

Based on the programming challenges our research uncovered, it is clear that adolescent girls' programming should be linked into broader efforts to shift gender norms, and a starting point would be a more appropriate curriculum. As already noted, there is at present little effort to provide tailored programming that better meets the needs of different groups of girls – and no apparent efforts to include mothers, fathers, in-laws, brothers and husbands in dialogues about the norms that limit girls' lives. If curricula were tailored to local levels and links built between adolescent girls' groups and local children's and adolescents' committees, it would be much easier to ensure the availability of age-appropriate programming for all adolescent girls – and boys. We also suggest that empowering girls alone is unlikely to be enough to shift norms. Because their lives and trajectories are controlled by their parents and communities, broader efforts must be made to improve girls' skill sets and agency while also working to change the ways in which their gatekeepers see them.

The strengths and weaknesses of the Kishori programme girls' groups provide clues as to why Nepal's long history of gender programming has not yet borne fruit that is visible in the global indices that measure gender inequality. However, by acknowledging local norms and moving slowly to encourage trust and build local ownership, the programme has maintained a slow but steady course and encouraged buy-in. In adopting such an approach, the pace of change has been slow, but sustainable. The question remains as to whether this slow pace is acceptable, both for girls and their families locally and in respect of national development progress.

Notes

1 It was initially called the Production Credit for Rural Women Programme.
2 The Panchayat system is a political system found mainly in Bangladesh, India, Nepal and Pakistan. It is the oldest system of local government in the Indian subcontinent. The word 'Panchayat' means 'assembly' (*ayat*) of five (*panch*). Traditionally, Panchayats consisted of wise and respected elders chosen by the local community. However, there were varying forms of such assemblies. In Nepal, the King would be the head of the system, appointing ministers directly, and under the ministers, zonal heads.
3 Technically, cooperatives operate at the Village Development Committee level, with most women organised into groups that are formed at the ward level. For the purposes of this discussion, however, this technicality is irrelevant. What is central is that women's programming is available to all women in all communities.
4 There are currently 399 centres across Nepal.

Bibliography

Asian Development Bank. (2004) *Gender and Governance Issues in Local Government*. Manila: Asian Development Bank.
Chhetri, R., Timsina, N., Luintel, H., Regmi, R., Bhattarai, B. and Magar, R. (2008) *Decentralization and Promotion of Women's Rights in Nepal: Exploring Constraints, Opportunities and Intervention Avenues*. Kathmandu: Forest Resources Studies and Action Team.

District Development Office. (2013) *District Development Profile: Kailali District*. Kailali: District Development Office.

Department of Women and Children. (n.d.) *Approach to Empowerment*. Available online at http://dwd.gov.np/en/page/18/21

Ghimire, A. and Samuels, F. (2014) *Change and Continuity in Social Norms and Practices Around Marriage and Education in Nepal*. London: Overseas Development Institute. Available online at www.odi.org/sites/odi.org.uk/files/odi-assets/publications-opinion-files/9181.pdf

Ghimire, A., Samuels, F., Giri, I. and Adhikari, P. (2015) *Communication Strategies for Addressing Discriminatory Social Norms in Marriage and Education for Adolescent Girls in Nepal*. London: Overseas Development Institute. Available online at www.odi.org/sites/odi.org.uk/files/odi-assets/publications-opinion-files/9900.pdf

International Fund for Agricultural Development (IFAD). (n.d.) *Rural Poverty Portal*. Rural poverty in Nepal. Available online at www.ruralpovertyportal.org/country/home/tags/nepal

Mallik, V. (2013) *Local and Community Governance for Peace and Development in Nepal*. Bonn: German Development Institute.

Ministry of Women, Children and Social Welfare. (2015) *Women's Development Program Managerial Guideline*. Kathmandu: Government of Nepal, Ministry of Women, Children and Social Welfare, Department of Women and Children.

National Planning Commission. (2013) *National Plan of Action on Holistic Development of Adolescents*. Kathmandu: National Planning Commission Secretariat.

National Planning Commission Secretariat (NPCS) and Central Bureau of Statistics (CBS). (2015) *Nepal in Figures 2015*. Kathmandu: National Planning Commission Secretariat and Central Bureau of Statistics.

Organisation for Economic Co-operation and Development (OECD). (2014) *Social Institutions and Gender Index: 2014 Synthesis Report*. Available online at www.genderindex.org/sites/default/files/docs/BrochureSIGI2015.pdf

Regmi, K., Naidoo, J., Pilkington, P. and Greer, A. (2009) 'Decentralization and District Health Services in Nepal: Understanding the Views of Service Users and Service Providers' *Journal of Public Health* 32(3): 406–417.

United Nations Development Programme (UNDP). (2009) *Nepal Human Development Report 2009: State Transformation and Human Development*. Kathmandu: United Nations Development Programme. Available online at http://hdr.undp.org/sites/default/files/nepal_nhdr_2009.pdf

United Nations Development Programme (UNDP). (2015a) *Gender Inequality Index*. Available online at http://hdr.undp.org/en/composite/GII

United Nations Development Programme (UNDP). (2015b) *Gender Development Index*. Available online at http://hdr.undp.org/en/composite/GDI

World Bank. (2015) *Nepal Country Snapshot*. Washington, DC: World Bank.

World Bank. (2016) *Nepal*. Available online at www.worldbank.org/en/country/nepal

CONCLUSION

Pushing the boundaries of social order: adolescent girls and norm change

Caroline Harper and Rachel Marcus

Norms change – even those that are deeply entrenched, long-experienced and seem firmly enforced. All the contexts explored in this volume illustrate contested and changing gender norms, with girls subject to some improved and some mixed outcomes for their well-being. But norms do not always change in predicted directions, and the manner in which change comes about is highly varied. The Uganda chapters, for example, note that the age at marriage or first sexual union has fallen over time, from 16 years as reported by grandmothers to 12 or 13 years nowadays – a pattern ascribed to looser controls on adolescent sexual activity and temporary unions. In Nepal, the rise of elopement-based marriages and adolescent access to social media were said to explain some similar patterns. At the same time, among other girls in both countries, a rising age at marriage was equated with increased education, with respondents in Nepal observing that the most common age at marriage had risen from 13 to 18 years over three generations. By contrast, both in these countries (fieldwork sites) and in Viet Nam and Ethiopia, some norms seem stuck or sticky, not changing, or changing slowly, only to be replaced by other norms replicating similar outcomes for girls. This, as Chapter 1 notes, is ascribed to what Bourdieu (1990) termed '*doxa*', a gradual socialisation of people into gendered norms through everyday practice, such that certain practices are beyond questioning, and certain outcomes of these practices – such as women and girls' domestic servitude, the importance of maintaining purity or the favouring of sons over daughters – are the norm.

Despite very different contexts, there are some striking similarities in girls' experiences of gender norms, reflecting some common underpinning factors across all countries. These highly varied contexts and outcomes, coupled with the sensitivity and politically charged nature of norm-related issues, make this complicated territory for development actors whose intention is to improve the lives of adolescent girls and young women. As a result, and as noted in the Introduction, tackling discriminatory and harmful norms has only recently been an acceptable 'development' undertaking and, even so, is frequently contested by governments, communities and individuals.

Why this is so is in part related to the fundamentally influential system of patriarchy in many parts of the world and common to all our research sites, acutely reflected in the patterning of girls' lives. Male grip on political leadership, moral authority, social privilege, and control of property and assets is a primary factor in how girls experience their lives. This male grip limits girls' voice, efficacy and control, and is embedded not just in the lives of individual girls but extends upwards throughout society, making change and challenge to the norm a political act. Flowing from this authority and combined with other societal preferences are norms of patrilocal residence, notions of purity, taboos around menstruation (to the extent that many girls interviewed in all countries had virtually no understanding of menses at their onset) and multiple choices made regarding girls' educational and work opportunities, marriage and bodily integrity.

Common to all our four study countries, social expectations within the prevailing patriarchal system view marriage and motherhood as fundamental for social stability, and as key markers of adult femininity, with a continuing strong emphasis on initiation into these adult roles soon after girls reach puberty. While this is changing due to some political leadership and strong policy (in Viet Nam, for example), the pressure to marry young and before the end of secondary school is persistent in many countries. Young girls from Uganda explained that *'young girls get married as soon as they grow breasts – even at age 12; at 15 years old it is already too late'* (this volume, Chapter 4); indeed, 'cultural taboos' against shedding menstrual blood in the father's home are still quite strong in Uganda and reinforce the urgency of early marriage. Likewise, as noted in Chapter 2 (Ethiopia), *'if a girl's leg touches the ground when she sits on a chair, she is ready for marriage'*. This urgency to marry girls is maintained by notions of purity and shame, a theme long recognised in anthropological enquiry (Douglas 1966), and notions which are reinforced through world views related to religion or valued cultural traditions. Bourdieu (1984) described this process as 'habitus' – importantly not individual learning but patterns of behaviour created over time by an interplay between individual and group structures, and creating world views which then come to guide individuals as to appropriate behaviours. For example, in Viet Nam, the Hmong world view, or habitus, determines norms for girls' marriage, among which is the perception that a Hmong girl who marries or is abducted must not return to her parental home for fear of upsetting ancestral spirits.

In Nepal, strong norms of premarital purity persist and in Ethiopia, where the average age at marriage is rising and girls have increasing, although variable, say in partner choice, norms around sexual purity remain strong, creating a tension with trends for later marriage, which are forcing some girls out of school prematurely and shaping their expectations. As noted in Chapter 2 (Ethiopia), *'girls' reputations are central to their families' social status'*. Norms around purity are reinforced by religious ideologies, to the extent that religious leaders seek child brides themselves, because it is seen as particularly important for representatives of the church to marry virgins.

While theorists have differing explanations, there is a long-established tradition deriving from the eminent sociologist, Émile Durkheim, that religion and belief are expressions of social structure (Durkheim 1912). Thus the interpretation of male moral authority in notions of purity and shame (common in all our studies and, indeed, known to be common throughout societies) is often further fixed into religious or moral world views. There is also the suggestion that social structure can be represented in the human body (Douglas 1966). These world views are argued to emanate from a common and strong imperative to construct patterns of order to combat disorder and to build models and categories to explain and contain a complex world. This search for order and explanation is played out both through control of girls' bodies and concurrently in the ideational sphere.

The previously described notions of girls' purity, their potential pollution if menstruating within parental homes, the transfer of a girl's spirit from her father's household to her husband's, and the pressure to produce sons for ancestral continuity can all be seen as an embodiment of social structure, literally in girls' bodies and reproductive potential. If the body represents society and its boundaries are dangerous, then the body margins themselves are also vulnerable points, ripe with power and danger too. Pollution rules are generally seen to be unequivocal and clear (Douglas 1966) – i.e. what is clean and dirty is strongly known in most societies. Thus pollution rules around menstruation, and virginity and sex, can be seen as protective of the social structure, precisely because they are strong rules and an ordered set of rites and practices can banish polluting threats and restore order. Indeed, for Hmong communities in Viet Nam, they report that divorce is not an option because '*according to Hmong tradition, once you stepped out of the door you could never look back*' – the ancestors would not allow it and you would be spiritually bereft with no prospect of an afterlife. Returning to a natal home could anger the ancestors of a girl's natal parents to the point of risking the death of family members. Furthermore, her children belong solely to the father's clan. Stricter boundary rules to maintain social order are hard to imagine. This illustrates how deep and powerful norms related to purity and danger, virginity and sexual initiation, reproduction and continuity of patriarchal authority can be.

Many may suggest this explanation sits better within anthropological texts. However, what this crystallises for us here is an explanation of the ambiguities we encountered time and again. Our Uganda team identified the paradoxical nature of change processes underway and the often ambiguous effects. They refer to a 'cultural unravelling' – the 'sense of chaos', with which the leaders, the guardians of ethnic and religious values in the ideational sphere, are struggling, in the face of larger forces of socioeconomic and cultural change, their authority challenged as cultural control and the power of sanctions are lost. But as Douglas wrote, 'Perhaps all social systems are built on contradiction, in some sense *at war with themselves*' (1966: 140). She identified that 'The final paradox of the search for purity is that it is an attempt to force experience into logical categories of non-contradiction. But experience is not amenable and those who make the attempt find themselves led into contradiction' (ibid.: 162). In this way, paradoxical change (rather than order and continuity) is actually the prevailing experience. It just happens to be an experience which sits uncomfortably with societies' tendency to try and construct order and patterns of the familiar and to build models and categories to explain things and construct boundaries to hold back potential dangers. The flux, however, always provides challenges, as Douglas wrote:

> There are several ways of treating anomalies. Negatively, we can ignore, just not perceive them, or perceiving we can condemn. Positively we can deliberately confront the anomaly and try to create a new pattern of reality in which it has a place.
>
> *(1966: 38)*

All of these reactions we noted in our work – change and stasis, acceptance, modification and backlash. Change causes fractures in social relations and in the embodiment of those relations, which takes time to be absorbed, and resistance can be strong. As noted in Chapter 1 in this volume, giving up power and privilege is challenging for individuals and groups, where one party perceives that they gain considerably from the status quo. Thus, while embedded in the ideational sphere, there is also an undeniable practical interest in the maintenance of norms that confer power and authority to particular individuals and groups. In Uganda, as in all our four countries and in many other places, it is suggested (Chapter 4) that customary marriages are arranged between clans as a practical means of cementing social structure. Furthermore, there is an undeniable economic interest in bride wealth payments. Nowadays this is often demanded as compensation payment, after the fact of marriage, and in recognition of the loss of bride price expected through traditional institutional arrangements between families and entire clans and represented through marriage. Similarly, the gains for families in acquiring a compliant daughter-in-law, able to undertake considerable labour, should not be underestimated, and congruently this explains the lack of investment in daughters, who are expected to leave the parental home and not therefore contribute economically over the longer term, unlike sons.

Thus another interpretation of these binding norms is as a functional and pragmatic preference – preferences which are then reinforced in the ideational sphere, as a reflection of preferred social structure and as according to Durkheim's interpretation. Whatever constellation of factors is locally more important, resistance to change, to letting go of authority and economic gain, can be strong. In the pursuit of power and authority and moral privilege, maintaining girls' lesser power – including ignorance of their own bodies and reproductive potential (an alarming finding across all our country studies), alongside limiting girls' autonomy – is one way to ensure maintenance of a preferred social system in the face of potential change.

Do gender norms help explain girls' capability constraints?

So, how useful is a gender norms lens in explaining the constraints adolescent girls face and the changing landscape of opportunities to live lives they value?

A sociologically informed approach to social norms as described earlier highlights how gender norms can become naturalised and beyond question, as with the Ugandan men described in Chapter 1 who considered it unthinkable that a man could do 'women's work' if a woman was around or vice versa. Such naturalised norms can be understood as the translation of practice into the ideational sphere and, conversely, the translation of gender ideologies and broader world views into day-to-day practice. Rather than something that people choose to comply with, norms are often – until questioned – part of the fabric of society that people adhere to because 'that is how we do it here'.

Digging further into explanations of norm *maintenance*, apart from the idea that this is '*doxa*' and beyond questioning, analysts (such as Heise and Manji 2015) have identified sanctions that reinforce the norm, effectively punishing those that dare to question or push boundaries. These analysts argue that the fear of social disapproval, gossip or ostracism and, conversely, the expectation of social reward, serve to maintain norms and hold them in place, as can be seen in Nepal and Viet Nam, for example, with fears that educating a girl 'too much' will mean she is unable to find a suitable husband. Within the realm of behavioural science, as discussed in Chapter 1 of this volume, programmes for change seek to open up alternative views by exploring whether an identified norm is actually as 'normal' as claimed. This approach has especially been utilised in addressing practices such as female genital mutilation/cutting (FGM/C). In other words, while individuals may think that FGM/C is what everyone expects of them or their daughters, when deeply questioned, it is revealed that many people want the practice to stop but dare not say so (United Nations Children's Fund (UNICEF) 2013). Exposing these views, it is argued, leads to changed practice.

With this knowledge in hand, any activities that challenge gender norms – such as incentives to adopt new practices or communication initiatives – can actively engage with the idea of '*doxa*' to try to move these norms held within the realm of naturalised '*doxa*' to a realm of contestation where people can discuss, advocate and try to convince others of the value of changing beliefs and practices. This operates largely at an individual or community level but can be extended to powerful institutions such as religious bodies. Some theorists, as discussed in Chapter 1, suggest that the primary mechanism for achieving change is community-level deliberation, leading ultimately to coordinated agreements to change (Cislaghi *et al.* 2014; Bicchieri and Mercier 2014; Cloward 2015). Attempts to change gender norms have become more nuanced in recent years, with stronger emphasis on engaging 'gatekeepers' (people in key positions of influence and decision-making authority) and people who have the potential to be champions of norm change, such as community and religious leaders. Such approaches recognise the power these groups have to influence others. This is all well and good if those leaders are amenable to change and to persuading others to adopt new norms and practices. However, norm change approaches tend to rest on the assumption that people who have the power to make decisions about others will be guided by principles of gender equality, and will be willing both to act against their own interests and guide others to do so. As we saw in Ethiopia, with the case of priests who were negotiating to marry young brides themselves, this assumption may be erroneous.

The challenge, of course, is that many practices are rooted in patriarchal power, and changing this requires action on multiple fronts at the same time. Separating norms that are closely connected to gendered ideologies from those that are considered more as rules for everyday behaviour and more easily within the realm of contestation can also help actors make choices about approaches to norm change. It can also help identify circumstances where backlash may be a serious problem – as with the promotion of girls' education (much more generally accepted) than, for example, broader change in support of women's or children's rights.

However, the maintenance of patriarchal power is not the only fault line that helps illuminate why some norms persist but others change; nor is it the only perspective on whether such change can be accommodated within existing frames of reference and without making it necessary to change one's world view. A focus on norms as naturalised in world views cannot substitute for, and must not obscure the economic and institutional factors that underlie particular practices and constellations of gender inequality, and which, together, undermine girls' capability development. An exclusive norms focus at the individual or community level rather than the institutional level can also lead to insufficient consideration of the power and interests that uphold gender discriminatory practices and thus undermine girls' capability development, as discussed in Chapter 1 and Marcus and Harper (2015).

As we saw in the Hmong villages of northern Viet Nam, government exhortations and financial support had led to the creation of a new norm of sending boys and girls to school up to the end of grade 9. But the very limited livelihood options in these mountainous rural communities meant that most parents considered it a better use of time to stop their children's schooling after grade 9 so they could hone their domestic and farming skills rather than allow them to stay in school. Similarly, as revealed most clearly in the Uganda chapters, efforts to communicate new norms can seem only partially relevant to disadvantaged people's lives if they do not take into account the grinding material poverty and lack of services and infrastructure. Thus the girls interviewed considered that the information and awareness-raising sessions they had attended had been interesting, even transformative in some ways, but the associated practical activities (e.g. training in how to make sanitary pads) were considered more immediately useful. Furthermore, there was a disconnect between norm change campaigns urging school attendance and the financial obstacles that many girls face. Though discriminatory gender norms can affect adolescents of all social classes, it is essential to recognise that it is the combination of those norms and poverty that together limits most girls' opportunities for capability development, and that enhancing livelihoods and access to good-quality services remains essential. Indeed, programmes that tackle these structural constraints are likely to have greater purchase on norm change, because they are seen as achieving tangible change and not 'just' talk (Kyomuhendo Bantebya et al. 2015).

Finally, because of the short time frames of many projects, insufficient attention is often given to the length of time needed to change norms. Although norms can change quickly when driven by an external impetus such as rising or declining economic opportunities, deliberate efforts to change norms often take rather longer. This is particularly the case if it is only a relatively small and often powerless constituency (adolescent girls and their supporters) that is arguing for change, if others have strong interests in maintaining the status quo, or if change is perceived to be imposed by external agencies. As we saw in our study area in Ethiopia, for example, once people perceived that the official spotlight on early marriage had receded, and the risk of fines or arrest had reduced, the rate of early marriage rose again.

What is transformational change for girls and young women and how is it brought about?

Given both the ideational and practical realities that maintain girls' limited power and agency, what does transformational change for girls look like and how can it be achieved? Clearly, individuals have their own visions of what transformative change would mean for them. However, a number of broad elements can be outlined. Returning to the framework we outlined in Chapter 1, we argued that realising gender justice would require both personal empowerment and transformation of unjust social arrangements, requiring change in the political, economic and social arenas. In support of this we suggest that the international human rights framework (which, of course, includes specific attention to women's and children's rights) gives countries and individuals a legitimate framework for action – one that permits the questioning of norms without reverting to the notion that this is simply 'our culture'.

Starting with personal empowerment, as our case studies and the wider literature have shown, development of individuals' agency – self-confidence, resilience and a sense of oneself as having a right to an opinion and aspirations – underpins the development of capabilities. Increasingly shown to reinforce learning and educational outcomes, effective agency also increases girls' opportunities for developing viable livelihoods, the likelihood of them having more egalitarian marital relationships, and the effective exercise of voice (Calder and Marcus 2014). Our case studies show a combination of formal education, informal girls' and adolescents' clubs, and radio phone-ins that provided access to a wider set of knowledge and experiences, and enabled girls to re-conceptualise themselves as well as their potential futures. In Nepal, in particular, increased access to mobile phones also played an important role, as they enabled girls to communicate with each other and with boys without adults' knowledge, and thus were seen as contributing to girls' empowerment.[1] Our Uganda and Nepal case studies highlighted how girls felt very strongly that they were deprived of information, and how empowering they found basic knowledge about their bodies and rights, without which girls are profoundly disempowered. Our lead Ugandan researcher, for example, recounts meeting a 13-year-old with a baby, who asked her: '*I know I have this baby but can you tell me how I came to have him?*' In some contexts, exposure to new information, growing self-confidence and practice in communication skills led to increased aspirations and broader horizons (Ethiopia, Viet Nam and Uganda), while in others, it led to girls coming together to challenge discriminatory practices (such as the girls' clubs in Nepal that started doing outdoor theatre to educate others on the risks of child marriage) (Samuels and Ghimire 2015).

The personally transformative nature of education emerges strongly from the country case studies and from wider literature on education and women's empowerment (Marcus and Page 2016; Unterhalter *et al.* 2014; Murphy–Graham 2012). As one of the young women we interviewed in Viet Nam put it, '*Now I can't imagine what I would have become without going to school*'. The current generation is the first in which significant numbers of girls from poor backgrounds in the case study countries are receiving secondary education;[2] this has the potential to underpin a step-change towards gender justice. However, this will only be achieved in politically, economically and socially supportive environments.

Supportive social, political and economic environments for change

Political commitment to gender equality, to enhancing opportunities for all young people, and to ending harmful practices is often a key driver of sustainable change in gender norms. In Ethiopia, gender equality is enshrined in the Constitution. In Viet Nam, the government has a long-standing commitment to gender equality, with documents dating back to the 1930s proclaiming it a key objective. Indeed, all of our four country examples have governmental commitments to international conventions on the rights of the child and women's equality, and have stated equality policy frameworks. Three of our country case studies illustrate the contribution of high-level political commitment that has been translated to the local level through state structures: for example, in Viet Nam and Ethiopia, local-level officials have – with varying degrees of commitment – enforced anti-early marriage laws. In Nepal, government women's development agents have played an important role in convincing parents to send their daughters to school. As the country case studies make clear, these local officials and leaders are not immune to social norms that favour early marriage or undervalue girls' education, and there is a constant tension between progressive high-level policies and locally dominant social norms.

At the same time, we know that positive high-level commitments often remain unimplemented for lack of resources – officials moonlighting because their salaries are insufficient, they lack transport to reach outlying villages, or there are insufficient funds to make schooling effectively free or incentivise attendance. This is a salutary reminder of the importance of public finance for building a positive environment for girls' capability development and thus for gender justice. Equally, increasing economic opportunities often underpin a degree of change – or at least of relaxation – in gender norms, as with the massive migration of young women to factory employment in East and South-East Asia and Bangladesh (Hossain 2011; Kabeer 2012). By contrast, the localities where our research took place were largely poor, rural and isolated, and had seen no significant increase in economic opportunities. In Ethiopia, opportunities for female migration existed (though were somewhat curtailed during the period of our research), but the reconfiguration of gender relations associated with these changes was complex. It involved exploitation of girls' labour and demands for control over the resources they generate as well as contradictory measures to marry in advance of migration (to safeguard girls' reputations) but also to then divorce so that the resources generated could flow to girls' parents rather than to their husbands and in-laws. There was, overall, little evidence of progressive norm change related to these specific economic opportunities.

An equally important element of a transformative political environment for girls' empowerment and gender justice is the presence of engaged social movements. For example, women's movements have been instrumental in changing perceptions of gender-based violence (GBV) (Htun and Weldon 2012) and in pushing for legal change. They also play a vital role in holding governments to account – for example, publicising cases of GBV and arguing for criminal prosecution, as with the women's and anti-rape movements in India. Such social movements must also make space to support and nurture young activists who are starting to find their civic and political voice.

Effective, impartial legal systems have the potential to back up political commitments to gender equality such as laws against early marriage and there are examples, from our focus countries and others, where judges have ruled to uphold the law even where it conflicted with local social norms – sometimes at significant personal risk. However, in most low-income contexts, access to justice is both physically remote and financially unaffordable, and the legal system is seen as open to corruption, limiting its transformative potential (Marcus and Brodbeck 2015).

Technological change also has the potential to propel change in gender norms. In our field research, this was most apparent through the spread of mobile phones (in Nepal and, to a lesser extent, Viet Nam) and through increased (though still patchy) access to mass media, in particular radio. Access to broader knowledge and a wider set of possibilities through mass media and social media have been shown to be important drivers of change in gender norms in contexts as diverse as Afghanistan, India and Brazil (Jensen and Oster 2007; Kabeer et al. 2011; La Ferrera et al. 2008), though organisations with conservative agendas are increasingly making use of technological developments to promote traditional gender norms (Balchin 2011). Beyond communications technology, little is known about how far other technological changes (e.g. the introduction of labour-saving technology) has contributed to shifts in gender norms, though some evidence from high-income countries suggests that it is essentially incorporated within the gender division of labour (Ridgeway 2009). That said, the kinds of labour-saving technologies that are starting to be more available in our research communities – such as corn-grinding or rice-hulling mills, piped water and improved cook stoves – could reduce demands on girls' labour, potentially reducing the obstacles to girls' education and reducing demand for young daughters-in-law to augment household labour power.

Change, harm and danger

Supportive contexts can do much to facilitate positive norm change, but change in highly contested domains usually comes with considerable backlash, friction and pain.

It is clear from many studies that change can be dangerous and painful, and simultaneously positive and negative for girls. In many countries, girls attending secondary school, for example – while commonly seen as a fundamentally important transition – nevertheless report alarmingly high levels of sexual harassment and rape (Leach *et al*. 2014) in the school environment, with teachers securing sexual favours and boys harassing girls. Despite this, girls regularly report a huge desire to continue to attend school, not least because of the social opportunities school affords. In Ethiopia, respondents agreed that men do not want to marry an illiterate girl and educated wives are better able to contribute to the family income. If families want an educated son-in-law, they increasingly have to educate their daughters. However, these forces for change are met with often equally powerful forces for stasis, which can be reinforced by the previously mentioned lack of post-school opportunities, poverty or lack of legal frameworks, among other missing elements. The results, as with other issues of empowerment, are therefore mixed, with some girls attending school and delaying marriage, others leaving school for marriage, and many finding post-school that opportunities for productive work outside the household are limited.

Where girls do seek new opportunities, the safeguards they may have found within their communities are often non-existent. The Uganda chapters reveal the challenges for girls seeking liaisons with older men, tempted by the excitement and change, and ultimately left as unsupported single parents. In Ethiopia, too, the temptation to migrate to undertake domestic work often leaves girls exceptionally vulnerable, both within Ethiopia and in destination countries (Jones *et al*. 2014).

Economic autonomy and political voice are exceptionally rare, and few girls or women mentioned these aspirations, which are in fact foundational for empowerment. And it is not just poverty that makes girls more vulnerable; in Ethiopia, girls from better-off families are seen as more desirable marriage prospects because of their families' assets, and are often betrothed at a younger age because of this.

Norm change can also result from serious crises that lead to fundamental changes in social order, often arising from forces beyond local or sometimes national control, such as a global economic crisis forcing a recession; conflict as a result of ethnic, religious or territorial war; and health challenges such as HIV/AIDS or Ebola. The resulting population loss, significant structural changes in livelihoods (for example) or population movement can all reshape gender relations and norms. Never desirable routes for change, these nevertheless can prove revolutionary in terms of changes in the social order, although trauma of this kind can equally create its own paralysis for positive change (Le Masson 2016).

Conclusion

There remains much to be done to improve the lives of women and girls, but much change has already taken place. At a broader, global level, we can see that change is happening in some positive ways, with figures showing that child marriage is declining and girls' secondary school attendance is increasing (United Nations Educational, Scientific and Cultural Organization (UNESCO) 2016).

However, in 2015, the Beijing Platform for Action 20-year review reported 'uneven progress towards gender equality'. In some cases progress has been unacceptably slow, with stagnation and even regress in some contexts, and change has 'not been deep enough; nor has it been irreversible'. Of particular significance for girls is lack of progress regarding the care economy, job opportunities, the gender gap in wages and property ownership, and the fact that women's contributions have led to economic growth but not to gender equality. An emphasis on empowering women and girls as drivers of economic growth is misplaced (Chant 2016). It is very clear that women and girls can support economic growth; but economic transformation requires that women and girls also gain from growth on an equal footing with men.

These global findings reflect back to specific country contexts where policy commitments may not be the issue. At the core of norm change – and specifically norms that keep girls from achieving their potential capabilities – lie powerful structures of patriarchy, which change slowly. They cannot just be shifted through policy, systems adaptation, programmes or individual changes of mind – all of which, while essential, are also insufficient. Rather, policy combinations, policy implementation and genuine commitment to transformation, with strong political leadership at multiple levels, are vital to support all the other potentially transformational initiatives. Momentum for change may be painful and slow, but ultimately any action must be complemented through the empowerment of women and girls and, at every level – personal, institutional and political – a commitment to gender equality.

Notes

1 Phones were, however, perceived by adults as facilitating elopement and contributing to a locally reduced age at marriage.
2 With the exception of Uganda, where the proportion of girls enrolled in secondary education is notably lower, at 46.6 per cent, than for the other countries (see Chapter 4).

Bibliography

Balchin, C. (2011) *Towards a Future Without Fundamentalisms: Analyzing Religious Fundamentalist Strategies and Feminist Responses*. Toronto: Association for Women's Rights in Development (AWID).
Bicchieri, C. and Mercier, H. (2014) 'Norms and Beliefs: How Change Occurs', in B. Edmonds (ed.) *The Dynamic View of Norms*. Cambridge: Cambridge University Press, 37–54.
Bourdieu, P. (1984) *Distinction: A Social Critique of the Judgement of Taste*. London: Routledge.
Bourdieu, P. (1990) 'Structures, Habitus, Practices', in P. Bourdieu (ed.) *The Logic of Practice*. Stanford, CA: Stanford University Press.
Calder, R. and Marcus, R. (2014) *Girl Effect. Theory of Change Evidence Paper*. London: Girl Effect.
Chant, S. (2016) 'Women, Girls and World Poverty: Empowerment, Equality or Essentialism?' *International Development Planning Review* 38(1): 1–24.
Cislaghi, B., Gillespie, D. and Mackie, G. (2014) *Values Deliberations and Collective Action in Rural Senegal: How Participants Respond in the Human Rights Sessions of the Tostan Community Empowerment Program*. Report for Wallace Global Fund and the United Nations Children's Fund (UNICEF).

Cloward, K. (2015) 'Elites, Exit Options, and Social Barriers to Norm Change: The Complex Case of Female Genital Mutilation' *Studies in Comparative International Development* 50(3): 378–407.

Douglas, M. (1966) *Purity and Danger: An Analysis of the Concepts of Pollution and Taboo*. London: Routledge and Kegan Paul Ltd.

Durkheim, E. (1912) *The Elementary Forms of Religious Life (Oxford World's Classics)*. Oxford: Oxford University Press.

Heise, L. and Manji, K. (2015) *Introduction to Social Norms*. Briefing note for DFID. London: Department for International Development.

Hossain, N. (2011) *Exports, Equity, and Empowerment: The Effects of Readymade Garments Manufacturing Employment on Gender Equality in Bangladesh*. Background Paper for the World Development Report 2012.

Htun, M. and Weldon, S.L. (2012) 'The Civic Origins of Progressive Policy Change: Combating Violence Against Women in Global Perspective, 1975–2005' *American Political Science Review* 106(3): 548–569.

Jensen, R. and Oster, E. (2007) *The Power of TV: Cable Television and Women's Status in India*. NBER Working Paper No. 13305. Cambridge, MA: National Bureau of Economic Research. Available online at www.nber.org/papers/w13305.pdf

Jones, N., Presler-Marshall, E. and Tefera, B. (2014) *Rethinking the 'Maid Trade': Experiences of Ethiopian Adolescent Domestic Workers in the Middle East*. London: Overseas Development Institute.

Kabeer, N. (2012) *Women's Economic Empowerment and Inclusive Growth: Labour Markets and Enterprise Development*. SIG Working Paper 2012/1, Ottawa: International Development Research Centre (IDRC).

Kabeer, N., Khan, A. and Adlparvar, N. (2011) *Afghan Values or Women's Rights? Gendered Narratives About Continuity and Change in Urban Afghanistan*. IDS Working Paper No. 387. Brighton: Institute of Development Studies.

Kyomuhendo Bantebya, G., Kyoheirwe Muhanguzi, F. and Watson, C. (2015) *'This Is Not the Work of a Day': Communications for Social Norm Change around Early Marriage and Education for Adolescent Girls in Uganda*. London: Overseas Development Institute.

La Ferrera, E., Chong, A. and Duryea, S. (2008) *Soap Operas and Fertility: Evidence from Brazil*. Working Paper 172. Berkeley, CA: Bureau for Research and Economic Analysis of Development.

Le Masson, V. (2016) *Gender and Resilience: From Theory to Practice*. London: Overseas Development Institute. Available online at www.odi.org/sites/odi.org.uk/files/odi-assets/publications-opinion-files/10224.pdf

Leach, F., Dunne, M. and Salvi, F. (2014) *School-Related Gender-Based Violence: A Global Review of Current Issues and Approaches in Policy, Programming and Implementation Responses to School-Related Gender-Based Violence (SRGBV) for the Education Sector*. Paris: United Nations Educational, Scientific and Cultural Organization (UNESCO).

Marcus, R. and Brodbeck, S. (2015) *Girls' Clubs and Empowerment Programmes*. Research and Practice Note, Knowledge to Action Resource Series. Available online at www.odi.org/sites/odi.org.uk/files/odi-assets/publications-opinion-files/9810.pdf

Marcus, R. and Harper, C. (2015) *Social Norms, Gender Norms and Adolescent Girls: A Brief Guide*. Knowledge to Action Resource Series. London: Overseas Development Institute.

Marcus, R. and Page, E. (2016) *An Evidence Review of School Environments, Pedagogy, Girls' Learning and Future Wellbeing Outcomes*. Available online at www.ungei.org

Murphy-Graham, E. (2012) *Opening Minds, Improving Lives: Education and Women's Empowerment in Honduras*. Nashville, Tennessee: Vanderbilt University Press.

Ridgeway, C. (2009) 'Framed Before We Know It: How Gender Shapes Social Relations' *Gender & Society* 23(2): 145–160.

Samuels, F. and Ghimire, A. (2015) *Girls' Clubs and Radio Programmes: Addressing Discriminatory Social Norms in Nepal.* Available online at www.odi.org/sites/odi.org.uk/files/odi-assets/publications-opinion-files/9882.pdf

United Nations Children's Fund (UNICEF). (2013) *Female Genital Mutilation/Cutting: A Statistical Overview and Exploration of the Dynamics of Change.* New York: United Nations Children's Fund.

United Nations Educational, Scientific and Cultural Organization (UNESCO). (2016) *Global Education Monitoring Report. Gender Review: Creating Sustainable Futures for All.* Paris: United Nations Educational, Scientific and Cultural Organization.

Unterhalter, E., North, A., Arnot, M., Lloyd, C., Moletsane, L., Murphy-Graham, E., Parkes, J. and Saito, M. (2014) *Education Rigorous Literature Review: Girls' Education and Gender Equality.* London: Department for International Development.

INDEX

access to justice *see* legislation for adolescent girls' wellbeing and empowerment

adolescence 1–11; challenging of social norms during 26; as a concept traditionally associated with sex and reproductive health 179; definitions 1; lack of concept in certain contexts of 24–25, 87

adolescent girls: impact of gender norms on life chances of 2–5, 23, 28–35, 162, 193–196

adolescent pregnancy: as a cause of school drop out 84, 94; and child marriage 9, 44; drivers of 91–93, 124–126, 170–171; health consequences of 92; outside of marriage 91–93; prevalence of 68, 84, 91–93, 125; *see also* sexual and reproductive health

African Network for the Prevention and Protection against Child Abuse and Neglect (ANPPCAN) 105–116

agency: definitions 24, 33; link between capabilities and 24, 33; normative barriers to the development of girls' 28–35; norm change and the development of girls' 31–34; *see also* decision-making power; programming for adolescent girls' wellbeing and empowerment; voice

Amhara Development Association (ADA), Ethiopia 64, 77

aspirations: of boys and men for future wives 50, 93, 133–136, 166, 171, 199; girls' own 10, 49, 77, 93, 97, 146–147, 153, 199; of parents and other family members for adolescent girls 49–50, 76–77, 93, 97; *see also* role models

assets and resources: girls' limited access to 44, 90; girls' savings groups 181–188; *see also* land

attitudes *see* changes in attitude; girls' capability development, gender norms; norms

Bangladesh: changing norms around girls' education in 28; enforcing garment workers' compliance with gender norms in 30

Because I Am a Girl (BIAAG), Viet Nam 141

behaviour *see* behaviour change; changes in discriminatory practices

behaviour change: relationship between norm change and 23, 31–32; vis-à-vis girls' willingness to counteract sexual and gender-based violence (SGBV) 22–23; *see also* changes in discriminatory practices

Bourdieu 29, 190–191

capabilities: link between agency and 24, 33; *see also* 'capabilities approach'; girls' capability development

'capabilities approach' 5, 23–24

care work *see* domestic work and care burden

changes in attitude: around child marriage 76–77; around the gendered division

of labour within households 74; around girls' education 66; *see also* norm change
changes in discriminatory practices: barriers to 94–98, 147–153, 172; around child marriage and motherhood 9, 47–49, 66–68, 131–133, 161, 164, 167–170; around contraceptive use and family planning 68–69; drivers of 31–32, 49–52, 56, 74, 94–98, 129, 164, 167, 169–170; in Ethiopia 47–52, 56, 66–69, 74; around the gendered division of labour and decision-making within households 90–91; around girl's education 67–68, 127–129, 144–147, 161, 164–166, 171; in Nepal 161, 164, 167, 167–170, 172; resistance to or backlash against 57, 95, 103–104, 115–116; in Uganda 94–98; in Viet Nam 129, 131–133, 147–153; *see also* behaviour change
child marriage: and adolescent pregnancy 9, 44; age gap between spouses in cases of 44, 164, 167, 170; age of first marriage 48, 124–125, 167; arranged 48, 86, 89, 168; becoming a daughter-in-law 135–136, 151–152, 162; boys' 48, 88–89, 98, 131–136, 147, 151–154, 168–169, 172; bride kidnapping 132, 136, 149–150; bride wealth or dowry 57, 86–87, 93–94; challenging or reporting of 50, 68; changing attitudes to 76–77; changing practice around 9, 47–49, 66–68, 131–133, 161, 164, 167–170; drivers of 9–10, 31, 48–49, 51–57, 74, 77, 87–89, 95, 124–126, 136, 151, 167; elopement, informal cohabitation or love marriage 31, 74, 87–89, 95–96, 131–132, 151, 172; in Ethiopia 43–58, 64–68, 74–77; forced 57, 74, 151; legislation on 44, 66, 83, 87–88, 95–96, 103–104, 149–150, 198; negative impacts on girls of 6–7, 172, 199; in Nepal 31, 161–164, 167–172; norms around 8, 131–133, 162–163, 165, 169, 171, 191; norm change around 8–9, 31–32, 48; patterning of 43–58, 64, 66; policy to tackle 62, 73–74, 83, 102, 147–150; prevalence of 44, 84, 86–87, 124–125, 161–163; resistance to 50, 68, 89; roles of female family members in preparing girls for 88, 91; in Uganda 84, 86–89, 93–96; 'underground' or illegal marriage 95–96; in Viet Nam 124–126, 132, 136, 149–151; *see also* nexus between girls' education and child marriage
Child Protection and Development project, Uganda 105–106

choice *see* decision-making power
Committee for Ethnic Minority Affairs (CEMA), Viet Nam 148–150
Communist Party, Viet Nam 141
community influencers *see* 'influencers'
community leaders: as enablers and opponents of changes in norms and practice 97, 145–146, 194–195; *see also* 'influencers'; religious leaders
contraception *see* sexual and reproductive health, contraceptive use

decentralised systems of governance: as a delivery mechanism for adolescent girls' wellbeing and empowerment programming 180–187
decision-making power: of girls and boys as a driver of child marriage 31, 74, 87–88, 131–132, 151, 172; of girls over choice of husband or partner 48–49, 89, 131–133, 164, 167–170; of girls over education 161; within households 90, 169
Department for International Development (DFID), UK 65
divorce: as a driver of changing norms and practices around marriage 52; girls' and women's *de facto* lack of access to 131, 134, 173, 192; as a mechanism to enable girls' mobility and school attendance 52
domestic violence 131: effect on girls of mothers' victimhood 133; girls' vulnerability to 44; increased prevalence as the perceived result of changing gender roles within households 91; suicide following 135–136; *see also* sexual and gender-based violence (SGBV)
domestic work and care burden 124, 144, 162; as a barrier to the development of girls' educational and other capabilities 44–46, 54–55, 73, 77, 84, 90, 134–136, 166; *see also* gender roles
'*doxa*' 29, 190, 194
Durkheim, Émile 192

early fertility *see* adolescent pregnancy
early marriage *see* child marriage
economic pressures *see* poverty
education: gender gap in 1–2, 44, 67, 84, 86, 124–125, 165–166, 171; informal education and behaviour change 23; opportunity costs as a driver of primary drop out 54; secondary enrolment 125; universal 124; *see also* girls' education
Education for All 8–9, 25, 47
employment opportunities: as a driver of changing norms and practices around

child marriage 32, 49; as a driver of changing norms and practices around girls' education 77, 95, 129, 145–146; as a driver of changing norms and practices around migration 77; girl' restricted access to 178; girls' restricted access to as a driver of child marriage 44–46, 56; girls' restricted access to as barrier to norm change 124–126, 152

empowerment *see* agency; decision-making power; girls' capability development; voice

ethnic minorities 123–126, 142–143; education levels amongst 125; geographic isolation of and negative stereotypes about, as a barrier to norm change 152–153; legislation for rights of 153–154; policy and programming targeting 142–143, 145; poverty amongst 124, 142; prevalence of child marriage and early fertility amongst 125, 167; vulnerability of adolescent girl 140, 147–150

family planning *see* sexual and reproductive health

female genital mutilation/cutting (FGM/C): challenging social norms around 194

'gatekeepers' *see* 'influencers'

gender-based violence *see* sexual and gender-based violence (SGBV)

Gender Inequality Index (GII) 44

gender justice: definition 5

gender norms 2–5, 22–24; conformity with 30, 73, 77, 130, 135, 153; as constraints on girls' capability development 2–5, 28–35, 162, 193–196; enforcement of 30, 77, 194; engagement of programming with 25–32, 194–196; in Ethiopia 8, 43–58, 73–77; girls' challenging of 26; around girls' education 8–9, 47, 94; around girls' obedience 53, 130, 135, 153, 162, 169, 171; around 'idleness' 54–55; around marriage and motherhood 8, 131–133, 162–163, 165, 169, 171, 191; in Nepal 8, 161–163, 165, 169, 170–171; and power inequalities 30–34; around sexual purity 44–46, 52–54, 73, 91, 161–162, 191–192; son preference 126, 152; and spiritual beliefs 29–30, 134, 192; 'sticky' 3, 43–58, 74–75, 152–153, 161, 170–171, 190–193; in Uganda 8, 29, 91, 94; in Viet Nam 8, 29–30, 126, 130–135, 152–153; *see also* gender roles; norm change

gender roles: as constraints on girls' capability development 73, 97, 133–136; in Ethiopia 73–74; gendered division of labour within households 74, 89–91; in Nepal 161–162; relating to preparation for marriage 88, 91; specific to adolescent girls 23; in Uganda 29, 88–91, 97; in Viet Nam 133–136; *see also* domestic work and care burden; girls' capability development, gender norms

Gender Roles, Equality and Transformation (GREAT) project, Uganda 106–116

Girl Hub 65

girls' capability development: barriers to 23, 26–27, 28–35, 44–46, 52–54, 63, 69–73, 83–84, 97, 133–136; enablers of 63, 65–69; gender norms and 2–5, 28–35, 162, 193–196; gender roles and 73, 97, 133–136; impacts of education and marriage on 6–7, 9–10; norm change and 31–35; *see also* agency; decision-making power; girls' education; transformational change for girls; voice

girls' education: academic success or failure 55, 72, 166; barriers to 44–46, 54–56, 70, 72–73, 94, 129–131, 152–153; boarding schools 58, 70, 128–129, 135, 166; and capability development 6–7; causes of girls' school drop out 54–56, 70, 84, 86, 94, 135, 171; changing attitudes to 66; changing practice around 67–68, 127–129, 144–147, 161, 164–166, 171; drivers of increased access to 49, 95, 164; in Ethiopia 9, 44–46, 49, 54–56, 67–68, 70, 72–73; in Nepal 9, 164, 166, 171, 178; norm change around 8–9, 28, 31–32, 77, 93–94, 126–129, 144–147, 164–166; norms around 8–9, 47, 94; out-of-school children 86; policy for 70, 93, 96, 102, 127–129; primary school completion 67, 84, 86; primary school enrolment and attendance 67, 70, 72, 164, 178; programming for 62, 67, 105–106, 127–128, 141, 144–147, 164, 167; secondary school completion 84; secondary school enrolment 46, 49, 67, 70, 84, 124, 178; tertiary education 49, 124; in Uganda 84, 85, 94–95; in Viet Nam 9–10, 124, 129–131, 135, 152–153; *see also* nexus between girls' education and child marriage

Girls not Brides 3

Girls' Opportunity Index 4

Girl Summit 3

Global Early Adolescent Study 3; in Viet Nam 141–142

harassment of girls 2; school-related 22–23,
94; *see also* sexual and gender-based
violence (SGBV)
harmful traditional practices (HTP)
see child marriage; female genital
mutilation/cutting (FGM/C)
Hiwot, Ethiopia 64, 66, 76–77
Hmong,Viet Nam *see* ethnic minorities

India: norm change around education and
child marriage in 32
'influencers' 28; programme engagement
with 108, 194–195; *see also* community
leaders; religious leaders
inheritance: girls' lack of rights as a driver
of child marriage 86–87, 90
Institute for Reproductive Health,
Georgetown University (IRH) 106
institutions: as barriers to and enablers of
girls' capability development 63, 65–73;
as barriers to and enablers of norm
change 31, 97–98, 195; engagement
of programming with 195; and power
inequalities 34
international interest in issues faced by
adolescent girls 3–5, 24–26
intimate partner violence (IPV) *see* sexual
and gender-based violence (SGBV)

The Kishori, or Adolescent Girl
Programme, Nepal 181

labour: access to girls' as a driver of child
marriage 133–136, 151; *see also* domestic
work and care burden; gender roles
land: fragmentation as a driver of changing
norms and practices around marriage
50–51; ownership as a driver of child
marriage 50–51, 199; *see also* assets and
resources
legislation for adolescent girls' wellbeing
and empowerment: on child marriage
44, 66, 83, 87–88, 95–96, 103–104,
149–150, 198; constitutional provisions
62, 65, 102; resistance to 96; to tackle
sexual and gender-based violence
(SGBV) 103, 133–134, 144; unintended
consequences of 91–92, 95–96, 103,
144; weak enforcement of 71, 75, 98,
133–134, 149–150, 198; women's rights
62, 65, 86, 95–96, 102, 133; *see also*
policy for adolescent girls' wellbeing and
empowerment
Lemoine 131
Let Girls Lead campaign 25

literacy rates 86, 125
livelihoods *see* employment opportunities

marriage *see* child marriage
MeoVac High School,Viet Nam 141, 151
migration: of adolescent girls to undertake
domestic work 56, 72, 77
mobile phone technology: as a driver
of and barrier to norm change 31,
168–170, 198
mobility: girls' restricted 90, 170
motherhood *see* adolescent pregnancy;
gender norms, around marriage and
motherhood
My Rights, My Voice (MRMV),Viet Nam 141

nexus between girls' education and child
marriage 5–11, 31–32; in Ethiopia 10,
44, 49–50; in Nepal 7, 10–11, 163–166,
169–170; in Uganda 7–8, 84, 87; inViet
Nam 129–131, 136
norm change 3, 22–23, 74–75, 190–193;
around child marriage 8–9, 31–32, 48;
barriers to 29–32, 94–98, 102–104, 142,
152–153, 170–171, 199; behavioural
science-inspired approaches to 27–34;
and the development of girls' agency
and capabilities 28–35; drivers of 31–32,
49–52, 94–98, 97–98, 129, 144–147,
197–199; in Ethiopia 48–52, 57, 74–77;
around girls' education 8–9, 28, 31–32,
77, 93–94, 126–129, 144–147, 164–166;
limitations of 165–166; in Nepal 31,
164–166, 170–171; power relations
and 30–34, 75, 103–104, 190–193;
relationship between behaviour change
and 23, 31–32; resistance to or backlash
against 31, 57, 126, 198–199; sociological
approaches to 28–32; in Uganda
93–98, 103–104; inViet Nam 126–129,
142–147, 152–153; *see also* changes in
attitude
norms: definitions 25, 27; descriptive 2, 127;
injunctive 2–3, 127; around 'social evils'
142; *see also* gender norms; norm change
Nussbaum, Martha 5, 23

Organisation for Economic Co-operation
and Development's (OECD) Social
Institutions and Gender Index (SIGI)
3–4, 44, 86, 106, 162
Oxfam 10, 141, 146–148, 151–152

Pathfinder International 106
Plan International 141, 146–148, 150–152

planning *see* policy for adolescent girls' wellbeing and empowerment

policy for adolescent girls' wellbeing and empowerment 62, 197; education 70, 93, 96, 102, 127–129; in Ethiopia 62–77; gender mainstreaming 62, 66; impact of 66, 144–147; limitations of 70, 73–74, 144, 147–150; in Nepal 178–179; political economy of 62–77; tackling harmful traditional practice (HTPs) including child marriage 62, 73–74, 83, 102, 147–150; sexual and reproductive health (SRH) 83, 96, 102–103; in Uganda 83–85, 93–98, 102–104; in Viet Nam 127–129, 142, 144–150; weak implementation of 75, 83, 85, 96, 98, 103–104, 197–198; *see also* legislation for adolescent girls' wellbeing and empowerment; programming for adolescent girls' wellbeing and empowerment

political economy: definition of gendered 63; of policy and programming for adolescent girls' wellbeing and empowerment 62–77, 190–191

polygamy 86, 171–173

poverty: as a barrier to education 54–55, 70, 84, 129, 135, 195; as a driver of changing norms and practices around child marriage 57; as a driver of changing norms and practices around early fertility 51; as a driver of changing norms and practices around girls' education 129; as a driver of child marriage and motherhood 84, 95, 124–126, 167, 199; as a driver of transactional sex amongst adolescent girls 95; urban/rural inequalities 70, 83, 123–126, 177–178, 197–198

poverty rates: in Ethiopia 43; amongst the Hmong, Viet Nam 123–124; in Nepal 177–178; in Uganda 84

power *see* power inequalities; power relations

power inequalities: as a barrier to the development of girls' capabilities 23, 62–77; gender norms and 30–34; institutions and 34; *see also* power relations

power relations: norm change and 30–34, 75, 103–104, 190–193; *see also* power inequalities

practices *see* behaviour change; changes in discriminatory practices

pregnancy *see* adolescent pregnancy

programming for adolescent girls' wellbeing and empowerment 33–34, 179–188; child protection 105–106; community

engagement and dialogue 28, 69, 74–76, 106–108, 194; education 62, 67, 105–106, 127–128, 141, 144–147, 164, 167; engagement with gender norms of 25–32, 194–196; engagement with institutional and structural constraints of 195; in Ethiopia 50–51, 62–77; girls' (or children's) clubs or groups 10, 50–51, 64, 68, 72, 74, 76, 141, 146–147, 151, 181; impact of 66–69, 72, 76–77, 108–110, 127–129, 146–147, 165, 167, 181–185; information, education and communication 28, 62–77, 104–116, 167; in Nepal 164–167, 180–187; political economy of 62–77, 190–191; preventing SGBV 105–106; savings groups 181–188; sexual and reproductive health (SRH) 51, 62, 64–66, 68–699, 104–116; shortcomings of 69–71, 73–77, 103, 110–116, 150–152, 185–187; to tackle child marriage amongst ethnic minorities 153; in Uganda 103–116; using women's cooperatives as a delivery mechanism for 180–187; in Viet Nam 127–129, 141, 144–147, 150–153; *see also* policy for adolescent girls' wellbeing and empowerment; legislation for adolescent girls' wellbeing and empowerment

qualitative research methods 12–14, 163–164

rape *see* sexual and gender-based violence (SGBV)

religious leaders: as enablers and opponents of changes in norms and practice 53–54, 77, 97; *see also* community leaders; influencers

research methods *see* qualitative research methods

resources *see* assets and resources

rights awareness: amongst adolescent girls 50

role models 9, 49, 65, 93, 97–98, 144–147, 151, 167; *see also* aspirations

Rosendorff, B. 63, 110–111

Save the Children 106

Sen, Amartya 5, 23

sexual and gender-based violence (SGBV) 164; as a cause of adolescent pregnancy 93; girls' willingness to counteract 22–23; legislation and programming to tackle 103–106, 133–134, 144; male-impunity for 22–23; prevalence of 84; risk of as barrier to girl's secondary education

55–56; school-related (SRGBV) 22–23, 199; *see also* domestic violence; harassment of girls
sexual and reproductive health (SRH): contraceptive use 51–52, 68–69; decline in informal sources of education about 88; early sexual debut 86–87; engagement in 'high-risk' behaviours 86, 95; girls' knowledge about SRH issues 51, 91; girls' reproductive burden 131–133, 165, 171; impact of legislation on service provision for 91–92, 96, 103; maternal mortality 84; policy relating to 83, 96, 102–103; programming and service provision for 51, 62, 64–66, 68–69, 83–85, 104–116; *see also* adolescent pregnancy
Sexual and Reproductive Health and Rights (SRHR) Alliance, Uganda 105
social capital *see* support networks for girls
social expectations *see* gender norms; norms
social norms *see* norms
social order: norm change and 30–34, 190–193
Straight Talk Foundation (STF), Uganda 105–115
strategy *see* policy for adolescent girls' wellbeing and empowerment
structures *see* institutions
support networks for girls 9, 26, 49–50, 69, 165, 170
Sustainable Development Goals (SDGs) 3

teenage pregnancy *see* adolescent pregnancy
'Three Is', Rosendorff's 63, 110–111
transformational change for girls 196–197; *see also* girls' capability development

unemployment *see* employment opportunities
UNFPA 150, 181
UNICEF 150
UNICEF Multiple Indicator Cluster Survey (MICS) 124, 149
Unite for Body Rights, Uganda 105
UN Women 150

violence against women and girls (VAWG) *see* sexual and gender-based violence (SGBV)
virginity *see* gender norms, around sexual purity
voice: girls' 9–10, 23; *see also* agency

wealth *see* land
Women's Development Army, Ethiopia (WDA) 66, 69, 71–72
Women's Development Programme, Nepal 178–179
women's movements 198
Women's Union, Viet Nam 142, 148

Yegna, Ethiopia 65, 77
Youth Union, Viet Nam 142, 148